Enoch's Voyage

Life on a Whaleship

Enoch's Voyage

Life on a Whaleship

1851–1854

by Enoch Carter Cloud

Edited by Elizabeth McLean

MOYER BELL
Wakefield, Rhode Island & London

Published by Moyer Bell

First Edition

LIBRARY OF CONGRESS
CATALOGING-IN-PUBLICATION DATA

Cloud, Enoch Carter
Enoch's voyage : life on a whaleship / Enoch Carter Cloud.
—1ˢᵗ ed.

p.   cm.

1. Cloud, Enoch Carter. 2. Henry Kneeland (Whaleship) 3.
Whaling—Massachusetts—New Bedford. I. Title.

G545.C52   1994
910.4′5—dc20   93-47385
                                                    CIP

ISBN 1-55921-079-6

Printed in the United States of America
Distributed in North America by Publishers Group West, P.O. Box 8843,
Emeryville, CA 94662 800-788-3123 (in California 510-658-3453) and in
Europe by Gazelle Book Services Ltd., Falcon House, Queen Square, Lancaster
LA1 1RN England 524-68765.

Introduction

This is the diary of my great, great grandfather, Enoch Carter Cloud who as a young man ran away to find adventure at sea. The log was given to me by my aunt, Ann Cloud, ten years ago, as an act of faith, perhaps, when I took my first writing class. Three years ago I moved to Provincetown, Massachusetts, a historic fishing village which forms the very tip of Cape Cod. In this setting, I decided to take the log on as a project. Having made various attempts at fictionalizing the diary, I decided that it is best left as my great, great grandfather wrote it. On August 13, the same day the diary begins, I began to transcribe his handwriting, which is beautiful to read, the tall, graceful penmanship enlivened at times by whale stamps and tiny drawings. New to Provincetown, I remember vividly the night that a huge Nor'Easter storm hit and I had a dream of words; thousands and thousands of words raced through my head. That first winter I would go out walking on the rocks of the breakwater in the freezing cold and try to imagine what life was like for this man, isolated on a whaleship the way I was isolated in the town. I went to New Bedford, Massachusetts to be in the place where his journey began. In many ways, those first months on Cape Cod, Enoch was my closest companion. A frequent diary writer myself, I felt an immediate rapport with him. The difference between our diaries is essentially that Enoch's was clearly written for his family. What he did not anticipate, I imagine, is that his log became a form of Cloud family entertainment. Nightly, after dinner, for five generations, the children were read to from this book. They were fascinated by it and loved it. Certain parts of his original diary were pasted over and I lifted those with vinegar, finding that they were mostly about his closest friends back home, and one in particular, who may have been Enoch's girlfriend. Perhaps he did not want to cause any distress to the woman who eventually became his wife. My aunt explained to me that every generation of the Cloud family, my mother's side, seems to produce someone with "wanderlust." What I did understand as my great, great grandfather's experience unfolded, is how clearly different a man he was compared to his shipmates. Enoch Carter Cloud grew up in a brick house in Columbus, Ohio at the corner of 3rd and Friend Streets, fortunate to have two loving parents and his sisters, Jules, Mandy, and Mag. Sabbaths, as well as Wednesday and Friday evenings were spent attending prayer meetings at the Quaker 2nd Church. His education was advanced and included the Quaker classics, and he pulls from memory, not only psalms from his Bible, but the poetry of Shakespeare among others. With his closest friends, Orville, Pete, Amelia and Edith, Enoch shared hopes for a bright American future. By virtue of being a young educated American who voluntarily joined as a crew hand aboard a whale ship, Enoch was immediately different from most of his shipmates. For many, such as foreigners or criminals, life on a whaleship was not the same kind of choice. As disappointment and hardships mount Enoch's discernment about life at sea focuses on a number of issues. I find it heartening to know that my ancestor found the slaughter of whales to be disturbing, among other things, and he describes the anguish of harpooned whales fighting for their lives in a sea of blood. Furthermore, Enoch's tolerance of others, in particular the island natives, is at odds with most whalemen, those of whom have had only a corrupting influence around the world. The idea of being an American under these circumstances often pains and disgusts him. On a lighter note, forward thinking finds him musing about women's fashions while in Hawaii, and he speculates that it might not be far-fetched to imagine women in bloomers one day.

It was typical from around 1820 to the time of the Civil War for newspapers to run advertisements like this one which appeared in the *New York Tribune* on July 1, 1841:

> WANTED—Immediately, 100 young men, Americans, to go on whaling voyages in first class ships. Also Carpenters, Coopers and Blacksmiths, to whom extra pay will be given. All clothing and other necessary articles furnished on the credit of the voyage. N.B.— Voyages from eight months to three years.— Advt.

This may have been just the sort of ad that Enoch came upon in 1851 and got his notion to find some joy in living a sailor's life at sea. In his late teens he left his home and traveled to Philadelphia, Pennsylvania. In the thrill of adventure, Enoch signed up with a shipping company, B. B. Howard & Son, and headed to New Bedford, Massachusetts. In August of 1851 he arrived at the center of the American whaling industry. On his first day in this port town he met a stranger on one of the wharves who advised him not to go whaling. Instead of heeding the stranger's words, he boarded the ship, The Henry Kneeland, and set out on a voyage which lasted thirty-two months and circled the globe. Enoch wrote every single day. For a young man who had never been to sea, these three years became both a physical journey as well as a spiritual journey. The ship sailed across the Atlantic to the islands of Portugal, down and around Africa, to New Zealand, up to the whaling grounds of the Japan Sea, stopping at a number of Pacific Islands, then around South America, to the West Indies and finally up the coast of the United States back to New Bedford. Perhaps Enoch, at the age of nineteen, left on this voyage to escape a mold that was too clearly set for him. His apparent good nature and earnestness would make it almost impossible for anyone to get in the way of his quest for what he desired of himself. In fact, his jounal which is being published for the first time, could have been Enoch's way of making up to his family for this time spent away. His intent was to keep a "true narrative of what he saw" and in so doing create a "familiar family companion." This commitment to his own family was so strong that it included me, over a hundred and fifty years later. The log was given by Enoch to his son, Edwin. Edwin's children spent much of their youth separated and in board-ing situations because their mother had died young and their father worked long hours away from home on the Ohio railroad. One of these children was my grandfather, Clifton, who read passages of the log to his four children among whom were my mother and aunt. The death of my mother when I was three years old lead to an unfortunate absence of the Cloud family in my life. It was not until my early twenties that I was given this log, which is roughly the same age that Enoch was when he wrote it. The experience of reading this journal brought me closer to my Aunt and more and more engaged in both Enoch's life as well as the Cloud side of my family. The only information I have about Enoch Carter Cloud is this journal, which so clearly projects to me the essense of a spirited, hard working wanderer whose thoughts remained tied to his parents and sisters. Five generations later, Enoch's observations and lessons are shared with an even larger family circle. If the goal of an adventurer is to see more of the world and return with a larger scope, I believe Enoch would rejoice in knowing how far his ideas and feelings have traveled.

My Log

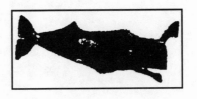

1851

August 13
WEDNESDAY

This book will contain a true narrative of all that I see during the voyage. If I intended to prepare a work for the public, a more exact conformity to the laws of rhetoric, grammar, punctuation, etc. would be observed, but as a familiar family companion, I trust it will serve to amuse each and every member of the social family circle at home. Many, I doubt not, will be the grammatical blunders, perversions of the laws of rhetoric, etc. to be found in its pages, but one consideration I think deserves notice: this first attempt to keep a regular journal demands a due share of generous criticism; and every allowance from those qualified to detect and point out errors in composition. So, relying on this version of the matter, I will go on, and endeavor to write a palpable, amusing, and instructive "log."

August 14
THURSDAY

Well, here I am, in New Bedford! And why? To go on a Whaling Voyage around the world! I met a stranger today on one of the wharves, who accosted me in a friendly manner and inquired "If I was bound a Whaling." I replied in the affirmative. "Take my advice young man," said he, "and don't go!" He then turned away and left me. I may possibly have cause to think of this when it is too late! Time will show!

August 15
FRIDAY

B.B. Howard & Son have "shipped" me, to sail in one of their ships—the "Henry Kneeland"—a strong substantial ship, "only" 47 years old and bearing the reputation of a first rate sea-boat. Thousand-tongued Rumor says—"her Captain & officers rank A. No. 1, both as gentlemen and Seamen." Glad to hear it!

August 16
SATURDAY

On board the ship! Well, let's have a peek in the little world in which I am to live, probably for years! The forecastle . . . Now, did not the particular nature of the case demand from me an answer, I would most humbly beg to be excused from publishing my opinion concerning the said Forecastle. Well, what is it, and what is it not? It is not home!! It is a hole in the forward between deck of the ship, Hy. Kneeland; about 9 feet by 16 in which 21 men are to live for 30 or 36 months. A thick dark cloud of tobacco smoke pervades this "castle" and an occasional "growl" indicates another party's presence. Ah! a low red-haired freckled-faced, uneasy sort of man, answering to "Tom," whaling from "away down East!" More Anon.

Groups of fellow-sailors are standing around deck, all engaged in animated conversation. If I were allowed to make my own thoughts & feelings a standard for others I could very easily tell the main topic of conversation. That one mighty thought, which despite excitement, adventure, novelty, and incident, will be uppermost HOME!!!

(8 AM) Pilot on board. Each quick turn of the windlass; each hearty "yeo ho," loosens the anchor from its firm bed, and now, (12 N) with both anchors at the "Cat-heads" & swelling sails in, are fast leaving our native land! Will we ever see it again? Why does each countenance of the loved home circle appear as in reality before me? Why this bitter feeling of regret: why this longing for one hour with the loved ones at home? Alas! Time has fled! It has been a voluntary launch and I must patiently abide the bitter, bitter gale!

8 Bells (4 PM) Crew called aft and listened to a brief address from Capt. Vinall—mainly consisting of a desire on his part that we perform our duty faithfully, and properly respect the Officers. He assured us that we should be treated well, care taken for our comfort, and that we should have enough to eat. (The latter, a very mighty consideration.) Time will show, how far these promises are complied with.

The crew are divided into two watches, the Starboard and Larboard. I am chosen in the Larboard.

August 17

SUNDAY

Sabbath morning at Sea! The welcome sound of the bell is not heard here this fine morning! The doors of no Sanctuary stand open here, inviting all to worship! Ah! already, (and so soon), do I remember the stranger's words—"Take my advice and don't go!"—And, how bitter does echo exclaim Too late, too late, too late!!! I dare not dwell longer on this subject! 8 Bells (4 PM) Sail ho! "Where away?" "Right off the lee beams, Sir!" Proved to be a Whaler bound home.

August 18
MONDAY

Up at 4 and hard at work; grinding harpoons, lances & spades; making foxes & nettles, etc., a general preparation for taking Whales. (7 Bells.) "There-re—she blows!!" "Where away?" "Two points on the lee bow, Sir!" Proved to be a school of "fin-backs." Truly novel & strange! Look where you would, these mighty leviathans were seen, surging, rolling & spouting, throwing the high spray high in the air, and "sounding," for another general surge and spouting. This species are not easily taken, and Whalemen give them a wide berth.

August 19
TUESDAY

5 AM Just entering the Gulf Stream! Prospect for bad weather. Last night in the mid-watch, received order to shorten sail. We clewed down the main-top-sail and I started up the main-rigging, to assist in reefing the sail. I was followed by the 3rd Mate, the Officer of the deck. The sea was running high, and very rough & the ship was pitching fearfully. Lightening, Oh! such blinding flashes I never expected to witness! In such a night, I first went aloft to "reef"!! Curses were not lacking from the 3rd Mate, and taking it altogether, I felt that I was—

> "As a weed,
> Flung from the rocks on ocean's

Foam, to sail, Where'er the surge may
Sweep, the tempest's breath prevail!"

And in this mood, after reading a chapter in my Bible and committing my soul to God, I "turned in."

August 20
WEDNESDAY

8 Bells (7 AM) Sent up to the "Crow's-nest" to look out for whales. Many "air castles" were built aloft this morning but I fear they will soon capsize! Every day brings something new! A school of porpoise, tumbling and breaching, under the bows was a scene novel & interesting. The "old Salts" predict bad weather. Saw a school of flying-fish, pursued by dolphins.

August 21
THURSDAY

The fine pleasant weather of yesterday, gave place to the approaching storm last night; this morning I first witnessed that most grand & magnificent sight in the Universe—a storm at sea!! What a field for contemplation! To attempt to describe it would be futile! My poor pen, shrinks abashed from the task! The gale is a severe one but promises a speedy close. As I stood on deck clinging to the fore rigging, I looked around and over me. The old ship now rising, up, up, up, on the crest of a huge wave, and now, plunging madly down, to the depths, walled in with mountains of pea-green water, relieved by indigo & capped with snow, formed emotions in my heart more easily imagined than described! Truly, God is merciful and slow to anger.

August 22

FRIDAY

Gale abated. The sea is still very rough, however, but will soon calm. A great spirit of petty tyranny begins to manifest itself on the part of the Officers. They certainly do not embrace Leigh Hunts' celebrated maxims.

> Power itself, hath not
> Half the might of gentleness!

but, I of all others, have a poor reason for complaining. Read the 139th Psalm, this morning with peculiar feelings of delight! The attributes of God are duly appreciated by the Psalmist. Dreamed of being home last & "eating a good breakfast," somewhat different from the fare here, which consists of something they see fit to call "Coffee," sweetened with "long-tailed sugar," salt junk & hard-bread!

8 Bells. PM Crew called aft, and the Capt. & Officers proceeded to select their boat's crews. I am chosen in the Capt's (Starboard quarter) boat and stationed at the mid-ship oar. I was then ordered to the wheel to learn the compass.

August 23

SATURDAY

The 1st Officer came forward this morning and gave us the day. Employed in washing clothes. A regular set of washer-"women"!

4 PM Crew called to scrub down the decks. A great deal of amusement on deck at the expense of the very green ones. One, in particular, who rejoices in the glorious "sobri-

quet" of "Tumbling Jack," wished to know if "the Capt. would not stop long enough at the first land we made for him to get his clothes washed!" Ask him, Jack!!

August 24
SUNDAY

Another Sabbath at sea! My thoughts turn homeward again as I review what my privilege was two weeks ago, and contrast it with my situation today! Capt. Vinall came forward this morning and distributed Bibles, Testaments & Tracts among the crew, and forbid all unnecessary work throughout the Ship. Noble example! I hope, even one man, may be benefitted through time & eternity! Oh! how different from the holy quiet of a sabbath day at home!

August 25
MONDAY

A fine morning. This morning a barn swallow flew on board. Poor little fellow! He has flown a great distance. 1700 miles is the nearest "cut" to land from this place. This afternoon, the lookout aloft "raised" some large object floating in the water. Capt. Vinall took his glass aloft & in a few moments pronounced it, a dead Sperm Whale! S. Boat ordered down to fasten to him and bring him alongside.

7 PM Whale moored alongside.

August 26
TUESDAY

Employed this morning in "cutting in" the blubber. I thought that I had a pretty good idea of the size and appearance of a Whale. But when I first saw this one (which is the largest size), I was struck dumb with astonishment! I could but look, and admire the power and glory of God! Myriads of ravenous shark surround the ship, each one seemingly very anxious to get a cut at the "King of the Deep." 4 Bells. (2 PM) blubber all cut in. Preparing for "trying-out."

August 27
WEDNESDAY

Up and at it, fittle & fat to the eyes! If this is not enough to warrant the "blues," I don't know what is! But hark to the Skipper! "Man that fish-tackle over the blubber-room!" "Aye, aye Sir!"—but what next—thought we all! "Hoist out that blubber and cast it over-board, it's worthless!" So much for inexperienced Officers, sulky on account of this disappointment.

August 28
THURSDAY

Deck's all clean again. 8 Bells AM Went below and turned in. 9 AM "All hands ahoy-oy-oy!!" "Stand by your boats!" I sprung on deck hoping to see a fine Sperm Whale close to, but I had slightly overrun the mark. The cause of excitement was a school of Black-fish, a species of Sperm Whale varying from 10 to 30 feet in length, and yielding a valuable quantity of oil. Lowered the 3 port boats & started in pursuit. Too cunning!!

August 29
FRIDAY

Quite sick today. Unable to stand my watch. Symptoms of bilious fever. Got some pills from the Medicine chest & came below. Oh! how I miss the kind attention of a Dear Mother! Truly, this is not home!!

August 30
SATURDAY

Still unwell. A storm is brewing this morning, appearances indicate a heavy one. 2 PM A severe gale is now raging. Lost the fore-top-mast stay sail. During the height of the storm my thoughts turned homeward! Oh! what would I give to be there! Say nothing, say nothing, yours was a voluntary launch!

August 31
SUNDAY

Another Sabbath morning! God, speed the time when I will be again united to my Dear Father's family; Oh! that I had heeded council & advice! But no. Ah no, my very soul was callous, and I am receiving my bitter, but just reward! A lesson has already been learned!

September 1
MONDAY

The beginning of a new month! How many doleful, dreary, long, long, months have yet to roll around e'er I see my home again! Ah! fool that I was to leave my Father's house—ungrateful, unnatural, vile man, thus to repay the best of parents for kindness of such a nature as to render me unworthy to receive it! God , in mercy forgive me ! Becalmed today. Sea as smooth as glass. Last night was one of rare splendor. The moon shone with that brilliancy peculiar alone to low latitudes—and every star seemed to rejoice in this glory with which God crowned them. "Every day brings something new—a regatta in the middle of the Atlantic!"

September 2
TUESDAY

A fine day, and still becalmed. At 9 AM, the thrilling cry of "There-re-re, she blows!" aroused all hands from the contagious lethargy into which we had fallen, and a few moments sufficed to show us a fine Sperm Whale! Lowered away the boats and pulled for him, without success.

September 3
WEDNESDAY

A bouncing, 8 knot, breeze this morning & another school of Porpoise Is lookout for a "cap full of wind!" 4 PM As much wind as we can manage. Employed in sundry deck & rigging jobs.

September 4
THURSDAY

Fine living at Sea! Potatoes "ran out" and the quality of our fare frightens dyspepsia from the ship! "Old Horse" & "Hard-bread" is the standing bill of fare! Will come to sea—eh?!!

September 5
FRIDAY

Calm again. An observation this morning informs us that we are 200 miles from the Azores. Speed, speed your way "Old Henry!" for I will soon have an opportunity of writing home! A cruise on land would certainly appear natural at the Azores, but I suppose that I will be debarred that privilege.

September 6
SATURDAY

"Wash day" again! 2 PM "Land ho!" "Where away?" "1 point on the larboard bow, Sir!" Flores, one of the Azores. 3 PM "There-re-re she blows!" Another Sperm Whale! Got the boats in readiness, leave ship & stood away for him. Too cunning—lost him!

September 7
SUNDAY

Flores, one of the Azores right ahead. The scene at sea, throughout from the time that the dim blue outline first meets the eye, 'til one is within 5 or 6 miles of the bold rock-bound shore, is truly grand! The different aspects of the land; its changing into a thousand different shapes, (as best suits the beholder) the lively appearance of the green trees & cultivated grain fields; the sight of the breakers on the rocks & above all, the lively emotions of the beholder's heart, as he looks-back and thinks of home—all tend to create new thoughts and feelings and new emotions in the mind of one who sees all for the first time. We will not go ashore today, and are accordingly, "laying off & on." 6 PM Spoke Whaling Bark "D. Franklin." Capt. of the Bark came aboard and took tea with Capt. Vinall.

September 8
MONDAY

Contrary to all expectations, received orders this morning to go ashore! At 8 in the morning cleared away & lowered the Starboard Boat & pulled for the land, distant about 3 leagues; an ugly "chop" sea was running and "pulling" was anything but easy! We finally reached the shore. Pulling around a bluff we found ourselves in a small, smooth cove at the foot of an abrupt mountain where we were met by the Custom House Officer—an old Portuguese wearing a "hat, that had been a hat," barefooted and graced with a mouthful of an old cigar—who inquired "who we were, where from, where bound & if we had any sickness on board." After receiving satisfactory answers to the above questions he permitted us to land. After hauling the boat on the beach we proceeded on our way to the "City." Numbers of women & boys met us at every step anxiously endeavoring to barter wine & fruit for knives and tobacco. These articles, (wine & fruit) can be obtained for a mere song—wine selling at 10 cents per bottle—and fruit in the same proportions. When nearly at the top of the mountain, (on which the City is built) on the side of the road we overhauled a "storehouse." One half of the house was filled with pumpkins and the other half with potatoes! Not a very well assorted stock by any means; but, "when we live in Rome, we do as Rome does," will possibly explain the reason of the curious assortment of "dry-goods." More anon.

We arrived at length at the top of the mountain. Oh! what a scene met my gaze! Right under my feet, hundreds of feet below me, rolled in sullen majesty, the mighty waves of ocean—the breakers rolling in, and bursting with an avalanche of snowy spray on the rocks—the sea gulls, screaming as they left their nests in the cliffs, and circling swiftly in the air, returned again to their young—the "old Henry," covered with a cloud of snowy canvass, rolling, pitching & wallowing in the distance—all had a strange but pleasant effect upon my mind! The scene was one of imposing grandeur! We finally arrived at the "City"(?) There is some excellent soil on this Island which the inhabitants in some measure improve. Their farms, or gardens rather, are very well cultivated. Today is a holiday day among them, but their religion (Roman Catholic) is very well stocked with indulgences; and so they have bartered potatoes, onions, pumpkins, apples, & fowl for molasses, tar, paint, etc. Was introduced to Don Jose De Costa—he invited me to his house to partake of some refreshment: consisted of wine, milk, bread & fruit— after which he took me to one side and very politely told me "that he was going on board the ship and requested me to lend him a bar of soap!" After roaming among the mountains and admiring the wonders of nature for an hour, I went to the beach again. Started the bum boats for the ship and followed them. 5 PM Again on board the Old Henry! An anxious and curious crew are crowding around me demanding a full report of all that I saw. Goats are led around from door to door—families supplied with milk in this manner was something novel at first! More anon.

September 9
TUESDAY

Standing away with a bouncing breeze for Fayal, another of the Azores, at which place I will have an opportunity to write home. The galley was discovered to be on fire this morning, but a few buckets of water served to extinguish it. A severe thunder squall raged this morning. Lightening vivid, thunder, very severe. My trust is in God!

September, 1851

September 10
WEDNESDAY

This morning at daylight, made the port of Fayal. A beautiful place, and quite a City. Immediately opposite Fayal, towering far up in the skies, with its side for some distance up dotted with houses and its top lost to view in a cloud of mist, looms the "Peak of Pico." A most beautiful scene! I did not go ashore here, owing to having gone at Flores; one of our men saw the wife & family of the late Prof. Webster. The boat's crew who went ashore this morning; "brought up" tonight with their "to'gallants, shivering in the wind, and their figure-heads handsomely battered!" So much for "agua-dient!!"

September 11
THURSDAY

Standing away for "Brava" one of the Cape De Verde's. Spoke Whale Ship—"Orizimbo." Capt Vinall lowered his boat & boarded her. An hour spent in this manner goes far to break the monotony at sea! But how unlike home!! The lack of sociability of the society of Parents, Sisters & Friends; the deprivation of all christian & religious privileges—all these deprivations are felt in the strictest sense of the word!!

September 12
FRIDAY

Tonight the regular prayer-meeting is held in the 2nd Church. Oh! how I long to be there again!! 'Tis strange that I was not contented with home! Strange! Aye! monstrous, abominable, devilish, wicked, feeling of I knew what!! My punishment is severe, but just!!

September 13
SATURDAY

A fine day. This afternoon the 1st Officer came up to me and asked me if "I knew how to 'slush' the masts!" I told him I thought I could do it! "Well, up you go—slush from royal-masts down & mind & spill none on the sail & rigging!" "Aye, aye Sir!"—and up I went! I was an interesting individual when I came down—slush from neck to heel!

September 14
SUNDAY

Oh! For one more opportunity to attend God's House at home! How I detest this fore castle, in which lewd songs for those of Zion & blasphemous wraths, for notes of prayer & praise are exchanged! How true the 5th verse of the 125th Psalm! Reading my Bible, and prayer, are two precious privileges—of which they cannot deprive me, however, and I will endeavor to improve them. Find new beauties in the 46th, 51st, 56th, & 57th Psalms.

September 15
MONDAY

Hard at work this morning "setting up" rigging, i.e. heaving it taut. "Tumbling Jack" wished to know —"if he could not get a life-preserver from the Capt. to use when he lowered with the boats!" Try him Jack! This "Jack," by the way, is something of a "fox"! When orders are given to "clew up" a to'gallant-sail, Jack is the first man at his station. But after the clew lines & buntlines are hauled up, Jack manages to fall down and slide himself into the lee-scuppers! He lays there much hurt 'til he sees a gang on their way aloft, to find the sail, and he then suddenly feels able to get up and walk for'rad! Look out for squalls Jack!!

September 16
TUESDAY

One month at sea today! It appears but yesterday that I was home, enjoying the society of Dear Parents, Sisters, & Friends! But no! I have deprived myself of all these blessings and voluntarily launched forth into the cold, unfeeling, friendless world out of the reach of council & advice and where my lot is cast there I have chosen it! God forgive my ingratitude & grant me the precious privilege of making the last days of my Parents their happiest days!! Dreamed last night of seeing my Dear Mother! Thought she told me, "that she was perfectly happy!" God grant her such a state of mind, constantly! What would I give to see her today!! 11 AM "Raised" a school of Black-fish. Lowered the Boats and pulled for them. In a few moments the Waist Boat fastened to a fine one—he drew the iron & escaped! After pulling for 5 hours after them without success, we came on board and found some cold potatoes to eat! So much for Whaling!

September 17
WEDNESDAY

Look out for a storm!

> A rainbow in the morning
> Is the Sailor's warning.

The lookout aloft "raised," "white-water" this morning. Turned out to be the breaching of a fin-back! No success yet!

Patience, my hearties. We will get enough of it, before the voyage is over yet!!!

September 18
THURSDAY

Employed in sending up royal-yards and sails. The weather is squally and unpleasant. My thoughts were directed to the Wednesday Eve' Lecture in the home church last evening & I found a longing desire to participate again in that house of God, and among his people in the worship of God! Too late, alas! too late!!

September 19
FRIDAY

A fine morning. Last night was one of surpassing loveliness! 2 of the crew thought it a fit time to settle a little difficulty, and accordingly did their best to disfigure each other's face! 9 PM "All quiet!"

September 20
SATURDAY

Wash-day again! Make a good washer "woman"—judging by the appearance of my "linen" (?) I have fairly shipped my "sea-legs" now and can "Walk a seam" without much danger of staving my figure-head!

September 21
SUNDAY

I was thinking this morning of all the dangers incident to a whaleman and curiosity led me to sum them up. 22 forms of death (and those of the worst form) constantly stare me in the face! Psalm. V.

September 22
MONDAY

A fine morning. Employed in sundry deck and rigging jobs. A chicken hawk flew on board last night and was captured by one of the crew. Got into very bad hands!!

September 23
TUESDAY

Monotony is relieved occasionally as we see the spout of a Whale or the glossy hump of the Black-fish. Raised a school of these fellows today and chased them 'til dark without success.

September 24
WEDNESDAY

Feel unusually depressed in spirits this morning. A poor place to seek consolation and no kind friend to unburden my heart to! Liberty is very sweet to the poor unfortunate whose heart is galled by the yoke of bondage!

September 25
THURSDAY

Spoke Whale Ship "Lancaster." Capt. Vinall took tea with the Commander of the L.A. staff, "Nor' Wester," bore us in sight of Brava, (one of the Cape De Verde's) this morning. Tumbling Jack felt so much elated at the prospect of securing a "monkey" at this place, as to offer the Mate a "chaw-to-backey!!" Look sharp Jack!

September 26

FRIDAY

The appearance of the heavens indicated bad weather and we put to sea again last evening. Kept on deck while raining, braiding sinnett. After finishing the sinnett, kept on deck to see it rain!

September 27

SATURDAY

Standing in again for Brava. Our object in going to this place is to procure hogs, fowls, vegetables, fruit, etc. The 185th portion of these cabin delicacies ought to belong to the greeny's—but I suppose our allowance will be "short & sweet!"

September 28

SUNDAY

Laying off Brava, becalmed. Heat almost suffocating! The crew are vainly endeavoring to find a cool place on the ship in which to refresh our parched & fevered bodies! Rendered more intolerable by the bitter remembrance of forfeited Sabbath privileges at home!!

September 29

MONDAY

Went ashore this morning. It would appear as though Nature had been trying to see how great a mass of uneven rugged rocks she could "pile up"! The view on approaching is fine and cannot fail to instruct and entertain. There are three islands in the immediate vicinity of which "Togo" (at present an active volcano) ranks 1st in point of romantic beauty. The inhabitants are blacks & speak the Portuguese language. Bartered cloth & bread for hogs, fowls & fruit. (The hogs came for'rad!!!)

September 30
TUESDAY

Standing away for New Zealand. Officers, 3rd Mate in particular, becoming tyrannical. Well, 'tis their privilege now, but "Privileges must have an end!"—thanks to "Old Hickory" for the suggestion!

October 1
WEDNESDAY

Superstition, the order of the day! A huge cat of the "Thomas" gender, who with his better half, have been discoursing "sweet sounds," much to the edification of the crew, has had his musical powers suddenly close reefed by depriving him of life! One of the crew came up to me this morning and very emphatically declared "that 'no luck' ever would follow this ship!" Lamentable, truly—a dolorous cat has "shipped his moorings" and Dame Fortune's feelings have become outraged! She accordingly refuses to smile upon the old H. K!

October 2
THURSDAY

Weather hot and squally accompanied with severe thunder & lightening. Some of the joys of a sailor's life this!!! I have already seen enough to satisfy me! But it is not over yet!!!

October 3

FRIDAY

Spoke a large East-Indiaman this evening. We ran up the far-famed "Stars & Stripes"; she flew the "cross of St. George." Bound to Madras. A large number of empty champagne bottles on the surface of the sea told a tale of luxury in her cabin!

October 4

SATURDAY

Weather still hot & squally. The ship's regulations allow 1 quart of vinegar weekly to each man. This was stopped today, and the probability is that some, if not the whole crew, will be down with the scurvy. So look-out boys!

October 5

SUNDAY

This holy day is spent by the majority of the crew in raffling with coppers, for tobacco! I have made a careful calculation, concerning the characters of Whalemen; and I find that out of every 100 men in the service, 75 are run-away-apprentices; of the remaining 25, 20 are fugitives from justice—leaving a remainder of 5 honest men!

Psalm 57, 4th verse.

October 6

MONDAY

Harsh treatment from would-be despots; "goes hard" with one that has had every advantage that an indulgent Father's home provided! Well, I would come and I am now enjoying (?) some of the delights of a "jolly" sailor's life!

October, 1851

October 7
TUESDAY

Last night was a fearful one of darkness & storms! The mighty roaring of the waves as they broke over the bows seemed calling us to their fearful embrace! Altogether, it was well calculated to bring home to mind and sharpen the pangs of the womb of repentance for a fresh gnawing at my heart!

October 8
WEDNESDAY

Storm still raging. Parted the main-royal stay this morning. Sent aloft to splice it. A very curious life this, to cause persons on land to indulge in a foolish belief that it is one of ease & happiness! Oh! ye who are now enjoying the blessings of land and all the attending privileges of Liberty—pray, pray for the poor sailor! Pray for him, who is driven aloft in the midnight hour, with a bitter curse to gather the flapping sail on the slender quivering spar; while you are peacefully surrounding the social family hearth! Never forget to pray for the Sailor!

October 9
THURSDAY

Storm abated. The meat came for'rad this morning in such a stinking condition that we could not eat it! Sent it back to the galley. This is a very fair sample of the "delights" of a Sailor's life!!

October 10

FRIDAY

Storm increasing again! Dreamed last night of being at home, conversing face to face with each loved one of the household! On awakening, I found it difficult to realize my true situation! Well, if I ever come to an anchor again in Columbus, there I'll ride, 'til the boat lover is gone! A good place to bring young rovers to their senses, is the sea!

October 11

SATURDAY

Weather still squally and unpleasant. How emblematical of life! Today; all fair & quiet—tomorrow the howling gale and tattered sails tell their own tale of the trials, troubles, and cares of life!

October 12

SUNDAY

How well does the Psalmist appreciate the blessings of gospel & Sabbath privileges when he exclaims "Psalm XXXIV. 2 V"! I frequently find myself looking forward to the time when I will see my Dear Parents and Sisters again as the happiest day of my life! And yet how slim the chance! Thousands of miles separate us and the dangers of the Sea, (and of this life in particular), loom up between us with the dimensions of a mighty mountain! I can but say with God's servant of Old, "Though He slay me, yet will I trust in Him!"

October 13

MONDAY

Last night was another of storm & terror! We are now nearing the line when we will "strike the South East Trades,"

October, 1851

and may expect fair wind & weather. Anything to vary this killing monotony!

October 14
TUESDAY

Preparations are making to receive a visit from "Father Neptune!" Not having a peculiar relish for a lathering of "tar and slush," I rid my face of a "fine pair of whiskers"! Just after sun-down we raised a large Sperm Whale. Lowered the Boats and chased him without success. Cheated "Old Nep" out of my "shave" though! Crossed the line, while out in the boats!

October 15
WEDNESDAY

We (the larboard watch) hit upon a plan a few days ago to get a better sleep while on deck at night. We post one man on the windlass to look out for the Officer of the deck and the remainder of the watch "turn in" on the for'hatch! The monitor whose turn came last night proved to have too much intimacy with Morpheus, however, the consequence of which was we were "caught napping" and sent aloft to get our eyes open!

October 16
THURSDAY

"Tumbling Jack" dressed up in his "go ashores" today and came on deck on his way aft to "see the Captain." I knew the consequences of such a step and deterred Jack from his purpose by applying a fine coat of tar to the "honorable" portion of his snowy duck breeches! He tacked ship, made all sail & anchored in his bunk!

October 17

FRIDAY

The difference in style of living between the Cabin & Forecastle causes some amusing pranks among the crew at Tumbling Jack's expense. Some of them sent poor Jack aft today to the galley, in order to "smell" the savory cabin, as they were being cooked! He expected much satisfaction when he came for'rad!

October 18

SATURDAY

I must turn prognosticator this morning and predict a change of weather! Cause,—2 "real live pigs" have been killed! Yes, killed!! And a portion of said porkes is to come for'rad!! This is truly an age of wonders!! I will just simply say that the predicted "change" will take place in from 1 to 3 days!!

October 19

SUNDAY

In a letter which I received from my Dear Mother while in Philadelphia, she cautions me in regard to joining the crew in this wickedness. I find her excellent christian advice emphatically well timed, and I do promise you Dear Mother by God's assisting grace to "walk worthily." This letter, a small knife of Sister Jule's, and Sis Mag's "tooth brush," are the only mementos I have of home! Their soiled appearance is evidence of the many times they are handled!

October 20
MONDAY

Well, the "change" has really taken place in the weather!—now, whether our "sea-pie" had any bearing on the case or not remains to be seen. I will forbear to make another prediction for the present for fear that it will not be verified! Look out though, on all extraordinary occasions!!

October 21
TUESDAY

Particular inquiries were made by the Shipping Officer in Philadelphia (when I enlisted), concerning my birthplace. This was done, they said, to prevent foreigners from enlisting in the service. Now, let's just have a look at our crew! It is composed of American, English, Irish, French, Dutch, Portuguese & Spaniards! No foreigners, sh!! We might add to the above list, goats, fowls, hogs & dogs, but at the same time, beg the pardon of the "lower race," for associating their names with a portion of the crew! We could boast the company of a pair of dulcet cats; but now, alas! one of said Cats is defunct!! "Requiescat in pace!!"

October 22
WEDNESDAY

We have everything crowded on in the shape of canvass from royal to lower-studding sails, and with a fair wind & smooth sea, are rapidly overhauling "Whaledom"! I suppose when we get up among the ice-bergs in the Arctic Ocean, we will often sigh for a little of this hot weather; but like many similar circumstances in life, our sighing will be in vain! I was standing in the waist today, "holding on to the slack of nothing," when Capt. Vinall saw me and "found me a job!" "Cloud," said he, "lay up there in the main-rigging, and "bend on" that main top-gallant-stern' sail"! "Aye, aye, Sir!" I sprang in the main-rigging, reached the main-top, slewed the boom athwart ships, cast off the gasket, and—stopped! Reason, I knew not how to proceed! Completely non-plussed, I ran-sacked my "top-locker" in every nook and corner for the desired information. It was not there: had not "shipped it"! All of the knots, gripes, hitches, bowlines & running bowlines, of which I was master, even in this case of no avail! The 1st Officer came to my relief and gave me the required information!

October 23
THURSDAY

By the time that I get back, (if I ever do) I will be a kind of "Jack of all trades"! I have to perform a part in many different branches of mechanism, and "Jack'o ditty" will explain it!

> "Weaver, blacksmith, carpenter, tailor
> Cobbler, painter, cooper & sailor!"

I frequently have "high" times; seated in a "boat-swains car"!—riding down & tarring the fore, main & mizzen to' gallant stays!!

October 24
FRIDAY

I think if the author of the ballad of "A Life on the Ocean Wave," was here today, burning under a tropical sun, swinging in mid-air by a few rope yarns, and covered with that gloppy article known to sailors by the name of tar—he would retract his sentiment! Very fine song, for landsmen!

October 25
SATURDAY

How strange it is that there exists so many just such fools as I am in the world! Place them in a happy home, surround them with friends, load them with blessings & comforts innumerable, and the effect of all this is, they become dissatisfied. I roam away to the ends of the Earth just as far from those who have treated them so kindly as they can possibly get! Well, this is a good place to cuss them!!

October 26
SUNDAY

I make it a rule to spend a portion of each day that I live in reading my Bible and in meditation. I have gained some ground I think in this way, and often, in times of danger & trouble does some passage of Scriptures that I have re-marked while reading appear peculiarly applicable. But, still, this is not home!

October 27
MONDAY

Terrific squalls of rain & wind "rage & reign supreme" in this latitude. We are now scudding "before it," under close-reefed top-sails. One hour ago we were carrying all sail, and in one more, will probably make all again. The squalls come & go in just about this way.

October 28

TUESDAY

Weather still unpleasant. Employed this morning in "breaking out" for water. Economy in the use of this, our main stay of life, must be observed! It would not answer to use it here, as we use it home!

October 29

WEDNESDAY

Another fine job of scraping the masts today! No lack of quantity, or no choice in regard to quality! Struck and took a fine "Right-Whale-Porpoise" today! In 10 minutes after he was "struck," he was scientifically dissected by the 3rd Mate, and his tender loin, heart, liver & the remainder of the "choice bits" kept aft and his "junk" sent for'rad to our parlor!

October 30

THURSDAY

Employed today in sundry "work-up" jobs. Weather begins to grow cold; flannels in good demand! I used, when at home, to love to see the approach of cold bleak Winter, but now a curious feeling of loneliness oppresses me; and I long for some familiar friend with whom to converse! Crusoe's solitary season is appreciated!!

October 31

FRIDAY

The look-out aloft caused some excitement on deck this morning by "singing out" for "white-water"! Proved to be a "jumper"—a species of Whale varying from 10 to 20 feet in length. They have a singular propensity for breaching out of the water—hence their name. Valuable to Whalemen.

November 1

SATURDAY

How time flies! It seems but yesterday that I was at home! How much does that expression, "at home," recall to my mind! I could very easily fill my book by penning all that it recalls! God, speed the time when I will be there again!!

November 2

SUNDAY

Although Capt. Vinall professes to be a religious man, yet he orders the mast-heads to be manned, as well on Sunday as any other day! This is indeed a curious kind of religion!— Looking out for Whales, on the Sabbath day! Truly, the fate of the Sailor is hard! Not even the Sabbath is his, but bending under the yoke of the petty tyrant, he must submit to all in silence!

November 3

MONDAY

Weather, cold and clear. Drawing near to the Cape of Good Hope! Hundreds of sea-fowl cover the sea and look-out where you will; all sizes from Mother Carey's chickens, to the immense Albatross surround the ship eagerly looking for any surplus meat from our pans! They get all that we can spare.

November 4

TUESDAY

Becalmed today. Sea presents the appearance of a vast polished mirror! I suppose that we will soon have plenty of work with the Boats! A good Sperm Whale "ground" is a short distance ahead! So look out for sport! That is, if "Dame Fortune" has recovered her equanimity of temper & will condescend to smile!

November 5
WEDNESDAY

Still becalmed. Wonder what each loved one at home is doing today! Well, I will tell you what I have been doing & you can report when I see you again at home! I have been employed in thinking of you all and bitterly repenting the worse than foolish step I have taken! This, by the way, generally occupies my mind every day! Well, when we meet again we will talk it over!

November 6
THURSDAY

A roaring breeze has sprung up, and the portentous scud warns us to prepare for a visit from Boreas! The doubling of Good Hope has cost many a sailor his life and many ships have been driven ashore by the force of the terrific gales which are common here! We will make the attempt, be the consequences, what they may! A strong and mighty Arm is over us to preserve our brittle cup, or dash it in pieces; and in that strong Arm, I trust!

November 7
FRIDAY

Wind increasing in violence. Handled studding and light sails. Appearances indicate coming bad weather.

November 8

SATURDAY

On deck all of last night. Wet, cold and vainly endeavoring to sustain a natural warmth in my body by means of 3 shirts & 2 coats—I thought of home! I could see my Father's family seated around a comfortable coal fire and that very moment probably speaking or thinking of the Prodigal! These seasons of the workings of memory, although in their nature productive of melancholy, yet go far toward rendering this life less intolerable!

November 9

SUNDAY

The inquiry again presents itself. "Why do Masters and Officers whale on the Sabbath?" The master says he will abandon the practice if the Officers are willing; they in turn, are willing, but the Master is not! Now, the fact is, neither are willing; they understand each other and like Ananias & Sapphira, agree together to sin against the Lord! When I subscribed my name to the Ship's articles I never dreamed that I would be compelled to violate the dictates of my conscience & trample under foot the commands of Jehovah! If sailors claim the privilege, which the Almighty granted to them in the beginning, and which is not denied to the ox and the ass on shore—it is refused them! If they plead conscience, it but exposes them to ridicule and cursing! One, mightier than they, has taken their bodies & their souls, in his own keeping—a mortal has usurped the prerogative of the Creator in this matter and the poor Sailor must submit in silence!!

November 10
MONDAY

This day set in with a light breeze & cloudless sky, but it is a day which I will long remember! At 4 PM we struck and took a large Right Whale Porpoise. Just then a rapid falling of the Barometer was observed, indicating a sudden & severe blow! All hands were called to shorten sail. While on the fore-top-sail-yard, furling the sail, a large Whale "broke water," right along-side! He saw the ship, turned short around, and with a mighty bellow started for her bows! It was a moment of intense & thrilling interest! He did not strike us, however, but rose again on our lee bow and after another mighty bellowing, "turned flukes" and left us!

November 11
TUESDAY

A severe gale is raging this morning and appearances indicate its continuance. We are now on a first rate Sperm Whale "ground" and as soon as the weather permits I suppose we will "be down!"

November 12
WEDNESDAY

Storm unabated. Sea absolutely alive with finback whales! Weather cold & severe & makes a man think of home! A very curious life, this!!

November 13
THURSDAY

Storm abated; sea is yet high & rough! 2 PM Had but "turned in" (it being my watch below) when the look-out aloft raised a large Sperm Whale! We backed the main-top-sail, got the boats ready, and stood-by to lower, when he came up again to blow. The Starboard Boat did not lower, our presence being required on board to work ship. In a few moments the Waist Boat was "fast!!" I saw her going with Rail-Road speed in tow of the "King of the Deep!" In five minutes the boats were lost to view in fog. Wove ship, and stood away in the direction we last saw them. In a few moments they hove in sight again. On looking more closely we saw the Bow Boat, containing a double crew & flying a waif of distress pulling for the ship! How eagerly I strained my eyes to see if all were there!! The fast boat was capsized by a foul line and the Whale escaped. The Starboard Boat was now ordered down to look for the whale! It was almost dark and an "ugly" sea was running "mountains high!" A bad night to go down in the boat after a Whale; but good or bad, "down I had to go!" We cruised around for 2 hours but found no whale. So much for Whaling!

November 14
FRIDAY

A fine morning. Two Right-Whales were "raised" this morning off the beam! Starboard, Larboard & Bow Boats were cleared-away & lowered. While we, the Starboard boat's crew, were "lying on our oars" one of the Whales broke water just ahead of us. We pulled up to him, the harpooner was called up & he poised his iron to dart. I was anxiously awaiting the moment where the cloud of spray, the thundering of flukes, and the smoking loggerhead, proclaimed us "fast"—but that moment did not come! The Whale was frightened, suddenly sounded, and after pulling after him till dark, we came aboard hungry, blistered & worn out!

November 15
SATURDAY

Raised Whales again today! Lowered & chased them without success. Our defunct "cat" is the main topic of conversation among a portion of the crew, but it assumes such a ridiculous form that I forbear taking any notice of it.

November 16
SUNDAY

I was revolving in my mind this morning the many dangers in which whalemen are constantly placed, and I wondered why it was that just for the sake of gold, a professeur of christianity, should deliberately desecrate God's Holy Day by lowering his boats and chasing Whales! I indulged in the hope that Capt. Vinall would never allow the boats to leave this ship on the Sabbath for whales during the voyage. 8 Bells AM had just struck, and I was about to eat my breakfast when all hands were called to shorten sail! I looked over the lee beam, and saw a school of Sperm Whales! All my cherished hope, in regard to Capt. Vinall's consistent course, was suddenly blasted by hearing him order the boats down! I thought at that moment that I would give my life to be at home! The Starboard Boat did not lower; the other boats pulled after them for 2 hours; thank God, without success!

November 17
MONDAY

Employed this morning in lashing the Boats at the Davit heads & battening the hatches. These preparations are making in order to ride safely the tremendous seas which are peculiar to the Cape, and which are now running absolutely "mountains high!" Some difficulty to keep my legs!

November 18
TUESDAY

A very ill-conditioned tumor on my left wrist gives me intolerable pain! Hand and arm much swollen. Different from a comfortable home, and loving Parents & Sisters! A bad place to be on the sick-list, this!

November 19
WEDNESDAY

Arm, completely powerless. Pain is excruciating and makes one think of home! Oh! how I long to be there! 5 PM we have doubled the Cape of Good Hope in safety and now we are "turning up the soil," of the Indian Ocean, which next to the Okhotsk Sea and Arctic Ocean, ranks 1st best, as a whaling ground. Now "Miss Fortune," just forget that unfortunate "cat," (for Bill's sake) and condescends to smile upon the Old Henry!

November 20
THURSDAY

Arm some better today. Poor Bill! That ridiculous "cat" will trouble him! He came to me this morning and, said he, "Ah! Cloud, didn't I tell you that "good luck" would show us her hind foot!" "I tell you, that this ship never will have any luck!" I endeavored to show him the inconsistency of such a foolish belief, but all to no purpose! Superstition reigns supreme in his mind and I am incapable of removing it!

November 21

FRIDAY

"Old Boreas" put a "fresh hand at the bellows" last night and in consequence, we have had to shorten sail. Appearances indicate a coming storm!

November 22

SATURDAY

Last night was a cold, dark & stormy one! I was at the wheel from 8 Bells to 9 o'clock (PM) and the groaning of the timbers, the roaring of the gale & the blinding flashes of lightening, all had a tendency to fell the mind with fear! It predominated but for a moment, however, for I was enabled to trust entire in the God of the Sea & the dry land!

November 23

SUNDAY

This day set in by allotting to me a "three hour wheel," followed by a "two hour mast-head!" The privileges of the Sabbath & the sanctuary are now duly appreciated and their loss deeply felt!

November 24

MONDAY

Potatoes run out! Now, boys, for "fine living" in our parlor between this & New Zealand! Delicacies abound in the Cabin yet, but our star has set!

November 25

TUESDAY

Bill of fare still the same! With a fine breeze we are rapidly overhauling New Zealand, the land of recent cannibalism! Tumbling Jack is determined that they shall not eat him! Look sharp Jack, you are in "good order!"

November 26
WEDNESDAY

Another storm brewing! Weather is growing cold and at home coal fires, thick coats, blankets & feather-beds are called into requisition to keep "Jack Frost" out!!

November 27
THURSDAY

Last night was another of storm & terror! A severe "Nor' Wester" set in yesterday evening & has raged with violence ever since! Everything on deck lashed down; sail furled & preventer braces bent on. The gale is very severe; a grand and terrible display of power & glory of God!

November 28
FRIDAY

Storm in some measure abated. Very uncomfortable on deck yet. Prospect for continuance good.

November 29
SATURDAY

Storm gain increasing; 2 men required at the wheel today. 7 PM Storm still increasing in violence! It has now attained a fearful heighth & things look dark & fearful! At 5 PM we were piped to supper. Just got down when all hands were called; a "white-squall" struck us right aft and the main-top-gallant-sail was torn from the yard and blown to ribbands! The sail is but on the "jack-stays" which are fastened to the yards with 3½ inch copper-spikes; just as I stepped out of the scuttle on deck a large piece of the jack-stay with a spike sticking in it, fell within three inches of my head! The force of the wind was beyond description most terrible!

November 30
SUNDAY

Employed today in cleaning up the wreck & splicing the main royal braces. All respect for the Sabbath is lost by the crew & the forecastle approaches very near to Bunyan's giant dungeons! May I make my escape as did he! What would I give for one hour at home!

December 1
MONDAY

Employed this morning in "pickling" and bending on a new main-top-gallant sail. A sail in sight to windward! Too far off to make her out. The "joys" of a sailor's life may be compared to a libertine—Both wear a suit of false-colors! They generally "run them up" when they wish to make a conquest!!

December 2
TUESDAY

The Indian Ocean is noted for being the roughest and most tempestuous body of water in the world; we have found it so thus-far & 7000 miles have yet to be navigated. E'er we take leave of it! Terrific squalls of rain now, wind & hail & violent gales accompanied with Thunder & Lightening rage from one end to the other!

December, 1851

December 3
WEDNESDAY

Weather cold & stormy. Sailing under double reefed-top-sails. What shall I add to this entry? Well, let's see! Ah! a dear little Sister is just at my elbow, (in imagination) prompting me! God bless her! I can hear her innocent prattle! I do believe that was a tear! Well, Mame, although far from you, yet your Brother's heart is warm and often throbs quickly as you are brought to mind!! God bless you!

December 4
THURSDAY

Weather is still unpleasant! Thunder & Lightening very severe! We are now on a good Right-Whale ground so look sharp aloft boys for a "blow!" These South Sea Whales are not remarkable for docility either and I expect that "old chips" (Carpenter) will have a job of mending boats!!

December 5
FRIDAY

Well, I have to log the arrival on our deck of a very important personage this morning! No other than Dame Fortune herself!! How about your "cat," Bill??! 8 AM raised Right-Whales close to. Lowered the Larboard, Waist & Bow boats & started in pursuit. In 10 minutes the Starboard Boat was "fast!" We now went down with the Starboard Boat to kill the whale! After being "struck" she "sounded" and remained down for ½ an hour. When she came up we pulled up to her but Capt. Vinall failed to get a lance at her; she again sounded. In 5 minutes she arose and bellowed. The noise made by us when we sprang to our oars arrested her attention; she quickly "slued" around, raised her enormous head out of the water, fixed her eyes on the boat, and then bellowing commenced, slowly, "sterning off!"

It was the most terrible sight I ever witnessed! We pulled up to her—Capt. Vinall darted his lance—and 3 hearty cheers burst from the 4 boats as a stream of blood shot from her spout-holes, full 30 feet in the air! I never knew before what it is to sail through a sea of blood! My feelings were now most peculiar! It is painful to witness the death of the smallest of God's created beings, much more, one in which life is so vigorously maintained as the Whale! And when I saw this, the largest & most terrible of all created animals bleeding, quivering, dying a victim to the cunning of man, my feelings were indeed peculiar! There was much danger and many narrow escapes connected with her capture, but—

> "He who sees with equal eye of God of all
> The hero perish & the sparrow fall"

—preserved us. Talking of danger, landsmen are ignorant of its meaning comparatively! A man wants to go alongside of a Whale in a small open boat in the middle of the Ocean before he can say that he has been in danger!! More anon!

December 6
SATURDAY

3 AM "Trying out." Wind fresh with a heavy sea. At 4 PM while rolling a cask of oil to windward, the ship rolled heavily, let go the cask (to avoid being crushed) which was dashed in the lee scuppers, catching the foot of one of the men & crushing it badly. Carried him below & dressed his wounds. A serious accident!

December 7

SUNDAY

Now, is the worst feature of this life in all its hateful cursed deformity—felt! If it was not that Sabbaths were spent in servile labor, the odious occupation would be less intolerable. But no, Satan would be but poorly served by these his prime ministers if they did not wantonly and premeditatedly—desecrate the Sabbath day! "Six days shalt thou labor and do all thy work, and on the seventh; do more than you are able!"—would be a very appropriate adoption for Sabbath Whalers!—More anon!

December 8

MONDAY

Oil all boiled, decks scraped & cleaned & bone stowed-down. The whale was a small one yielding but 70 bbls of oil & 500 lbs of bone. Very tired, feel as though I would like a little sleep!

December 9

TUESDAY

"Land ho!" The island of St. Pauls, a low barren uninhabited island. A brig makes regular trips between St. Pauls & the Isle of France carrying from the former to the latter cargoes of fish, which abound in great quantities in the immediate vicinity of the island. We "laid to" off the Island, lowered 3 boats and went fishing. In 5 hours we came aboard with 10 bbls of very fine fish! Caught an albatross this afternoon, "tallied" him & gave him his liberty.

December 10
WEDNESDAY

Employed today in cleaning & salting our fish. PM broke out whale-bone & scraped it. Many parcels of bone will have to be scraped e'er I see home again! I but hope, and yet it seems to belong to that peculiar species "which make the heart sick."

December 11
THURSDAY

This morning sent down fore-top sail & fore to 'gallant-sail for repairs. First lesson in sail making! Promising sail-makers, very! I think that the next ship on which I go to sea will not carry sails! We know not, however, what a day may bring forth!

December 12
FRIDAY

5 AM All hands called to shorten sail! A large cow whale with her calf were blowing off the lee quarter about ¼ of a mile from the ship. Lowered 3 port boats and started in pursuit. Chased them without success for 3 hours and came aboard. She manifested great solicitation & care for her offspring, apparently urging it to its utmost speed! More Anon!

December 13
SATURDAY

A fine day. Have been thinking of the goodness and mercy of God in sparing my life, health & limbs through all the dangers which I have passed! How much do I owe him

December, 1851

for all his mercies unto me! But how am I situated? Compelled against my will to violate His holy Day by taking Whales! and on this day so sacred to the followers of Jesus, to be engaged in servile labor! God knows that I am opposed, bitterly opposed to it; and He knows the longings of my soul for the privileges of a Christian Father's home!

December 14
SUNDAY

Did not christian principles interfere with desertion from the ship at New Zealand, I should certainly make the attempt! This life is so much at variance with my feelings that it is almost a burden! I can blame no one but—myself! God has in His All Wise providence placed me where I wished to be and here I am: worse than miserable, and here I must stay 'til He sees fit to release me! Help me, oh! God, to be resigned, submissive, meek!

December 15
MONDAY

Many a glad heart is throbbing joyfully at home in anticipation of a coming happy season, in company with friends! This privilege is now denied me but I hope yet to spend many happy seasons at home!

December 16
TUESDAY

Weather stormy & sea rough. Our meat should be well skilled in navigation! It has circumnavigated the globe three times! Fine living at sea!!

December 17
WEDNESDAY

Voyage continues the same monotonous every day drama! Nothing to interrupt it, save the occasional bellow & whistle of some mighty whale as he lazily rolls "fin-out" on the surface of the sea! The lack of something upon which to argue & exercise the mind is keenly felt!

December 18
WEDNESDAY

"All hands, ahoy-oy-oy!" "Light up men, light up and handle those sails handsomely!" "Now, clear away and lower your boats!" "Bend your backs my hearties, give away, cheerily, spring-hard, double your oars—2 solid irons in that fellow's back and $5 a piece in your bounty!" Many like expressions were addressed to the crew by Capt. Vinall this morning on seeing a large Right Whale "close to!" We pulled hard but failed to catch him. Came aboard just after we had "dined"(?) "There-re-re goes flukes!" came thundering down from aloft, the consequence of which was another "invitation" from Capt. Vinall to "attend a fishing party!" Again, no success! He "smelled the irons" and made good his escape!

December 19
FRIDAY

Feel unwell this morning. Approaching indisposition is well calculated to be accompanied with melancholy at sea. The life is in some measure tolerable, when a man is in the possession of health, but as soon as that takes leave, spirits go with it, and poor dying man gives way to dejection! PM Confined to my bunk.

December 20

SATURDAY

Still unwell. Miss the comforts of home! What would I give for a Dear Mother's company today!

December 21

SUNDAY

Weather stormy. We are now off New Holland and in a stormy latitude. Still unwell. I experience much comfort in reading my Bible, particularly the 119th Psalm.

December 22

MONDAY

A fine day & with a bounding breeze we are rapidly overhauling New Zealand. I will have another opportunity of writing home from New Z. which I am eager to improve. Would that I was the bearer of the letter!

December 23

TUESDAY

Another extraordinary occasion and another prediction! "Another pig" has been killed & we poor fellows are to have a chance of "unbending his gear!" Wonders will never cease!—At least so say the knowing ones!

December 24

WEDNESDAY

Fine horse, beans, "perfumed" "junk" & "live" bread for dinner today! So ye epicures at home, leave your scanty boards and come a whaling! Warranted to get fat, ("if you have good luck")!

December 25

THURSDAY

A "merry Christmas" to you all shipmates but never again sail so near to the island of lunacy as to be compelled to tack ship and go to sea! 2 PM We had a christmas dinner in the forecastle!!! "Duff" with r-a-i-s-o-n-s in it, rather fair "old Horse" and a half pound of butter!!! (There are 21 men in the forecastle!) At 5 PM raised a Right-Whale lowered and chased him with the usual success!

December 26

FRIDAY

Another storm breeding! Many a craft is heading for "Medicine Harbor" at home today; in consequence of damages sustained to "spars & rigging" by sailing too near the "grog tub!" A dangerous place! The best way to avoid accident is to give it a "wide berth!"

December 27

SATURDAY

Another gale is raging! Very severe. Scudding under close-reefed-main-top-sail. Think I would feel more comfortable at home! Should have thought of this before it was too late! Poor consolation!

December 28

SUNDAY

Storm somewhat abated. It appears that the sound of a church-bell would be almost as ravishing as that of an Angel's chant! Oh! how I long to hear its sacred holy melody once more!

December 29

MONDAY

Capt. Vinall is of the opinion that "some of his crew will desert at New Zealand!" Don't think you are mistaken Capt.! Several of the men have told me they intend to desert! At 4 PM "kept off" for a blow. Proved to be a Fin-back!

December 30

TUESDAY

Last night while 3 of the watch were aloft furling the fore to'gallant sail, saw a beautiful specimen of the effects of electricity! Around the arm of the yard, a small body of beautiful phosphorescent light was dancing! Down they came and reported. It was not long before the "old Henry" was doomed to sudden & certain destruction! I endeavored to give a plain philosophical reason for the appearance of the "corpse lights," but "positive, electric matter" & "friction" were words that did not occur in their dictionaries & of course I was unsuccessful! I simply predicted coming bad weather with thunder & lightning!

December 31

WEDNESDAY

The last day of the Old Year and the most stormy & tempestuous day I ever witnessed! Terrific squalls of rain, snow, hail & wind accompanied with severe thunder & lightning have raged from daylight 'til dark.

1852

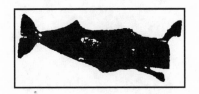

1852

January 1
THURSDAY

> "'Tis the New Year's morn! But ah! alone,
>   Shut up in this Ocean dwelling.
> There comes to my ear no cheering tone,
>   From the heart of Friendship swelling!
> And I think of the Friends I've left on land,
>   And how they, today are meeting,
> And pledging anew the friendly hand,
>   With a hearty New Year's greeting!"

Last night was another of storm & terror! Crouched under the weather bulwarks my mind averted to the last day of the year 1851! How many changes have taken place since that period! As I reviewed the sights that I had witnessed, the different places in which I had been, the persons with whom I had conversed, the sorrows & joys that I had experienced, the words that I had spoken and the actions that I had performed—the whole seemed more like a picture than reality—more like a dream than a succession of actual events! I never before realized that the past was so stern a reality—that it is indeed so grave a thing to live—that all my

January, 1852

foolish and trivial thoughts are indelibly graver on the memory of—God! To how little purpose have I lived 'til this moment! The blush of shame & confusions aptly mantle my cheek when I think of my unprofitableness! God, help me hereafter to live to some purpose! I little thought six months ago that I would be here today! God hasten my deliverance!

January 2
FRIDAY

Storm abated. Struck and took a fine porpoise today. Plenty of fin-back whales but they are not of the right kind for us! Lucky for them!

January 3
SATURDAY

Weather stormy again this morning with a strong head wind. 2 PM Raised a whale! Everything was made ready for lowering but we were doomed to disappointment again! Proved to be a "sulphur-bottom" the largest of the whole race of whales—but owing to the great depth to which they "sound" they cannot be taken. This whale was about 125 feet long & would make 300 bbls of oil! He was worth the snug sum off $14,000!!!

January 4
SUNDAY

The first Sabbath of the New Year! How lightly appreciated by thousands on land! Oh! that I had the privilege of spending this day in a land of Sabbath & christian liberty! The value of this day is now duly felt!

January 5
MONDAY

We have at length cleared the Indian Ocean & are now breasting the deep blue billows of "Old Pacific!" The reputation of which stands as high for a calm smooth sea, as does the Indian for a rough & stormy one. "We shall see, we shall see!"

January 6
TUESDAY

Weather changeable. This morning we were carrying all sail, and in the evening scudding before a gale of wind under a close-reefed-main-top-sail! A tremendous sea is running and the wind is blowing "Highland-pipes!"

January 7
WEDNESDAY

Weather still stormy. Blue sky on the lee, however, promises a fine night! Could enjoy the evening if at home. A man might as well look for enjoyment in a prison as to look here, however, where all sociability is wanting!

January 8
THURSDAY

Last night was one of rare beauty & splendor! The moon & stars seemed to rival each other in the intensity of their light; and with a fair wind and smooth sea, we peacefully glided over the bosom of Old Pacific! While pacing the deck in the mid-watch, I thought of a dear sister at home, who is very partial to such a beautiful night as that!

January 9

FRIDAY

A fine day. At 11 AM spoke Whale ship, "Florida." Went aboard and had a pleasant little "gam" of five hours. The Florida has been out 8 months and has taken 550 bbls of oil. Better "luck" than we, but I suppose they have not lost a "cat" yet! "How is that Bill?"

January 10

SATURDAY

The wind hauled a head last night and we now have a stiff to'gallant breeze. Ought to see New Zealand tomorrow. If it was the shore of America we expected to make tomorrow, I know of one heart that would beat with rather more energy than at present! Patience, patience, sad heart, "there's a good time coming."

January 11

SUNDAY

A most beautiful day. 10 AM "Land ho!" New Zealand; 2½ points on the lee bow. 2 PM Spoke whale ship "South Boston," 6 months from Fairhaven with 500 bbls of oil. Capt. Williams of the S.B. (just from Hobart Town) reports the discovery of a gold mine near Sydney, the product of which bids fair to show California "the hind foot!"

January 12

MONDAY

We are now standing along the S.E. coast of New Zealand for Doubtful Bay. Scenery on shore bold & striking. 5 PM just entering the harbor of Wanganui! On each side of the narrow passage looms up two mighty mountains, their side covered with waving trees & shrubbery & alive with the voices of innumerable birds & insects. Truly a curious spectacle for the middle of winter! As we proceeded in, the harbor widened forming an excellent protection for some 40 or 50 sail of vessels. We ran in for a short distance, let go the anchor and furled the sails. We had been in but a short time, when a canoe containing a party of "Maures & Wahinas" (men & women) came alongside and "Tenor, ae-n-goy" (how do you do) gave us a sample of New Zealand lingo! They are exceedingly fierce in the expression of the countenance and the tattooing of their face, does not lesson the almost fearful rig of their figure-heads! The males are tattooed in circles, commencing immediately around the eyes and extending to the roots of the hair on the forehead & the chin. The females tattoo the lips & sometimes the eyelids. Station in society is denoted by the style of the tattoo. As for clothing they wear either a native mat or blanket— which answers the purpose of house, bed & umbrella!

January 13
TUESDAY

I hardly knew how to walk on arising this morning after having slept all night! (The first since leaving New Bedford!) To awake and find the Old ship lying still & seeing the sun slowly crawl up the zenith from behind the hills really appeared novel! The "City" of Wanganui! Oh! dear! 5 houses & 3 pig pens is the sum total of all improvements, and unless the carpenter bears a hand, the "city" will be "minus" one of said pig pens! A British Man o' war dropped in this morning and the "bulls" are amusing themselves by gazing at Yankee

Whalemen & doubtless, thinking of the time when our fore fathers gave them the "Yankee how do!" To think of escaping here is worse than nonsense! By regulations, no seaman can travel farther than 4 miles in the interior unless he has a passport from the "Chandler Price;" among them was the steward—a negro. A party of native police, headed by the chief of Wanganui started in pursuit. On coming up with them, the negro drew a revolver and shot the chief, dangerously wounding him! They were all, however, captured and brought back. Much excitement exists among the Natives. The negro is having a hearing before the Officers of the Man o'war. Employed today in painting ship.

January 14
WEDNESDAY

"Starboard watch, for'rad there!" "Prepare yourself liberty ashore!" "Aye aye Sir!" In a short time the watch headed by "Tumbling Jack" appeared on deck rigged for a cruise in "Cannibalburgh!" Poor Jack! We get no liberty money in this port, but Jack's thirst for the "critter" compels him to barter his clothes for it and these he is, rolling along with a bundle of clothes under his arm on his way to the "Donny Brook!" This evening received orders to make one of a boat's crew to go after Capt. Vinall at the house of the Pilot, Capt. Butter. At 9 PM we pulled to the point, hauled the boat on the beach and took a short stroll; we had not proceeded far, where we stumbled upon a gang of Natives, wrapped in their mats and lying beside a few embers on the ground. They sprang to their feet, glared at us a moment and simply exclaimed "maitai" (friends, or good). After begging some tobacco they laid down again, evidently out of humor with us for disturbing their slumbers! Some of them looked as though they were "hungry!"

January 15
THURSDAY

At 8 AM, the Larboard watch was set ashore on liberty. The majority of the watch "bore up" for the "Donny Brook" but I wore ship and stood away for the mountains where I amused myself by eating calicos, peaches & plucking some beautiful flowers, listening to the thousand melodious notes of the feathered tribe, and allowing myself to be externally examined & commented upon by the Maures! I found myself much to amuse & instruct me among them: they are very "sick" when they are in possession of a suit of "civilized" clothing; and its possessor distributes it (as far as it will go) among his fellows. I saw one tall fellow with nothing whatever, but a sailor's vest to cover his nakedness! Another with a cap, another, a coat, etc. These fellows were cruising around with the fortune and importance of Stephen Girard! On one occasion I came upon a party who were engaged in preparing supper. I stepped into the midst of them to overlook their proceedings. A beef had been killed in the morning by the Pilot and this party had secured the entrails, etc. The "Wahinas" (women) dug a hole in the ground, and after heating some stones, they put their "beef" with some potatoes in the hole and covered all with the heated stones & earth. A few moments sufficed to cook their meal & it was taken out and spread on leaves. The "Maures" then seated themselves "a la Turk" in a circle & after drinking a small quantity of water, presented to each from a small calabash by the "ladies" they indiscriminately seized a "piece of sausage "in one hand & a potato in the other and proceeded to "ki-ki" (eat) in true Maure style! I was kindly invited to join in the repast but the cravings of hunger not being suffi- ciently great to warrant such a proceeding, I respectfully declined! 6 PM Came aboard, and found a good portion of the watch "3 sheets in the wind & to her fluttering!" Donny Brook's fire-water is bad for the eyes!

January 16
FRIDAY

Hard at it today "breaking out" the stowage in the fore hold, overhauling it & stowing it down again. A very fair sample of a sailor's "joys," i.e. "always at it!" Tumbling Jack "loves grog" he says, and I am of the same opinion judging by the looks of his chest, the contents of said chest are growing, "beautifully less," and unless Jack either "signs the pledge" or finds a substitute, "Donny Brook" bids fair to strip him of his outfit!

January 17
SATURDAY

After going ashore this morning I left the watch & took another cruise in the mountains. I saw some beautiful cattle grazing on the mountain's side and my mind quickly averted to domestic scenes in loved America! Cruising on a dark pass in the mountains I came upon a rush hut in and around which sat some 12 or 14 tall, robust natives. They sprang to their feet, exchanged a salute and invited me into their hut to see their chief. With some slight misgivings (being alone & some 2 or 3 miles from the ship) I cautiously entered and was presented to the chief. He was a noble looking man with his entire body fancifully tattooed; a large sharks-tooth mounted with red-sealing-wax & gold descended by a black ribbon from his right ear. He arose and greeted me after which he invited me to sit down. I spoke to him in regard to whalemen deserting and inquired how he would encourage it. He replied by producing 15 pairs of "handcuffs" crossing his wrists & bestowing sundry seven blows on the earth with his spear!!!! "I said no more to him about it!!" After presenting him with a "plug" of tobacco, I bade him adieu, got under way & came to an anchor on the beach. The botanical, geological & mineralogical productions of New Zealand are immense & form a vast field of survey for those skilled in the sciences. I would that my friend "Orville F." was here to admire them with me! Not as whalemen though! Our chance to improve would be indeed small for a man might as well "shin up" to the main royal truck & try to whistle against a gale of wind off Cape Horn as to petition for such an opportunity on a Whale Ship!!

January 18
SUNDAY

How do the privileges and blessings of home, the sanctuary & the Sabbath come home to my mind today! My soul longs for the privilege of going even once more to the house of God! No church here to which even "2 or 3" can bend their way to hear the word of life, but surrounded by wicked & hardened men, I am compelled to pass this holy day; not a single voice lifted up to the throne of Grace; not a lip moving in prayer but blasphemous oaths, lewd songs & drunken railings, are heard from ship to shore & echoed from beach to mountain! Morality is at a low ebb among the New Zealanders and they bid fair to become annihilated as our North American Indians have been by the progress of what the world sees fit to term — "civilization." Its vices, with none of its virtues have been eagerly embraced by the wretched Natives, and they have been reduced to a "Saturnalia" — the essential elements of which are idleness, theft, drunkenness and prostitution! Miserable, deluded beings! I know not whether most to pity the natives, or to blame the whites! Incidents of such a horrid, hellish & diabolical nature have been perpetrated by those hailing from a land of civilization that I dare not mention them; I blush to think I am an American citizen!! such have been the gross examples of depravity, most depraved, committed by my countrymen among a dying nation of wretched heathens that I heartily (though with much shame) adopt & pen the above senti-ment! God forgive them!!

January 19
MONDAY

This day set in with a call at daylight to man a boat & proceed 5 miles outside the harbor with 180 bbls in tow to procure fresh water. Hard work! Got a relief at 9, came onboard, got breakfast, struck the mizzens-top-mast & top-gallant-mast (for repairs), "rigged" & went ashore on liberty. The crews of the different ships in port "amuse" themselves while on liberty by drinking rum & fighting, in which I am very sorry to say a portion of our crew take an active part! Hard work & poor pay; very bad for the eyes & worse than whaling!

January 20
TUESDAY

Plenty of hard work! "Market stocked & dealers firm." Broke out stowage in the after-hold, overhauled it, and stowed down again. Four of the ship "India's" crew deserted last night, but were captured & brought back this morning by the natives. The Captain (a noted tyrant) gave them a dozen & a half apiece! Poor fellows, their heart-rendering cries entered my very soul and I thought it indeed hard that their attempt to gain sweet liberty was so cruelly rewarded!

January 21
WEDNESDAY

Not feeling well, I did not go ashore today. The crew of the ship "Albion" found a dead child (native) in the water this morning at the west end of the harbor. The native performed some curious pranks on discovering it, such as leaping high in the air, beating their breasts & howling. The ship "Huntress" arrived this morning from the Arctic Ocean, direct. Reports the loss of 18 Whale ships during the last season!

January 22
THURSDAY

Employed this morning in stowing water between decks. This afternoon the 3rd Mate & a boat's crew went "clamming." Clam soup for supper to night! "Tasted like Elkton!" Would rather be in Elkton, "boating clams in a wheelbarrow" than to be here today!

January, 1852

January 23
FRIDAY

Serious times ashore today, between the Americans & Portuguese! One of our harpooners (a large Portuguese) with some 30 others, fell upon & beat most shamefully one of his shipmates, (an American) while on shore this morning. After dinner a large number of Americans & Portuguese met on shore for the avowed intention of fighting. At 5 PM they "went at it." Resulted in the complete rout of the Portuguese. Our Portuguese harpooneer is dangerously wounded; his skull is fractured in two places. On coming on board tonight Capt. Vinall seized the harpooneer & 2 sailors (Portuguese) in the mizzens rigging & gave them 2 dozen apiece for assaulting, and beating a shipmate! One of our men was badly stabbed in the side during the melee by the 4th Mate of the ship Onzembo, (a Portuguese). Not over yet I am afraid!

January 24
SATURDAY

Employed today in tarring rigging, painting ship and sail-making. All quiet on shore.

January 25
SUNDAY

This Holy Day is spent by the majority of men in Port in fighting, drinking, & hunting! Oh! why do men, dying worms swiftly sailing to their final port, openly insult a merciful God by pursuing such a course! The time will soon come when they would give a world of gold to live another Sabbath—to get on the other tack; but then, the head-wind of death will prevent them! Fearful thought! Sailing now with (to them) a very pleasant breeze, but alas! in the voyage of life pleasant breezes with inattention to yards, sails & lookouts often drive the ship broadside on a reef and she is lost! God grant to open their eyes!

January 26
MONDAY

Weather squally with a high wind. Employed today in tarring rigging, painting ship, etc. This "city" of Wanganui is certainly without exception the worst "hole" I ever had the misfortune to be confined in! Nothing but the effect of rum-drinking is seen from morning 'til night & the sooner out of it the better for us all!

January 27
TUESDAY

Weather still stormy. Two tribes are engaged in war today some seven or eight miles from the boat. A large squad of natives "armed & equipped" passed the ship in their canoes this morning bound for the "seat of war." Their weapons consisted of a long round spear made of very hard wood, a hatchet fixed on the end of a tattooed club & a short two-edged slab of wood, bone, or stone. They are very dexterous in the use of these several implements & in their hands they are "ugly customers!" The dispute arose in regard to the abduction by the "city natives" of a young lady "the property"(!!) of a mountain swain! Peaceable measures are of no avail & "knock-down-arguments" alone will suffice to "right ship!"

January 28
WEDNESDAY

I met with quite an amusing adventure this morning with a chief of a mountain party whom I found strolling along the beach. He came up to me and in broken English asked me if "I would like to marry a fine wife"!!!!!!!!! (Oh! dear!) I told him that I should certainly have no objection to such a proceeding provided both parties were suited! "Well," said he, "if you will give me 25 lbs of tobacco & 50 dollars cash I will get you a good wife & you may live with me!" (What a predicament for a "modest youth" to be placed in!!) "Cheap" enough, thought I in all conscience but fearing lest my intended might be tempted to make an "American roast" for the benefit of her royal connection & also being vain enough to believe that some one of America's fair daughters will sail within hailing distance, I, with many thanks for his extreme kindness in offering his services to procure me a "rib" most respectfully declined his offer. After cruising along the beach for 2 or 3 miles, I tacked ship & beat homewards.

January 29
THURSDAY

Dragged both anchors today during the height of the wind. Ran a line to the beach & warped ship to her station. Hope to get out of this hole in 7 or 8 days from this time & then never to see it again.

January 30
FRIDAY

Called at daylight and ordered to man a boat to assist in towing ship "Frances Henrietta" outside. We (35 boats) indulged in a grand regatta coming back! Old Henry's boat, first best! This "pride" is a curious ingredient of a man's character! It often makes a fool of him!

January 31
SATURDAY

Through another month of wild steering & many deviations from the paths of rectitude, God has mercifully lengthened out my life & permitted me to see its close! God help me to live nearer to Thee during the coming months than I have done in the one which has just passed. I took a short cruise in the mountains this morning and overhauled an old English cooper living in a small cabin quite happy apparently with a native wife! After chatting with him on various topics for an hour I bade him adieu & bore down for the beach. He has been living here 27 years.

February 1
SUNDAY

This holy day is again wantonly desecrated by the majority of men in port by hunting & drinking. God hasten my deliverance from them all & place me once more at home! No one can appreciate the inestimable blessing of home as he does who voluntarily launches forth he knows not whether until it be too late! When he feels the difference, oh! what a valuable gem is home! Its parents, its sisters, its calm and holy fireside, its social family alter, its comfort in sickness, its sabbath & sanctuary privileges, its secret closet—all rise up as it were and audibly weep as they view the wretched prodigal in his unhappiness!

February, 1852

February 2
MONDAY

Employed today in getting off recruits—potatoes, on-ions, etc. (8 PM) ship recruited! Going to sail tomorrow! Look out now for destruction among the whales!

February 3
TUESDAY

Up at daylight, heaving anchors! (7 AM) Midst the firing of cannon & fluttering of flags (compliments from fellow whalemen) we are being towed outside! Farewell Wanganui! thou noted "city" of "3 pig pens;" I hope forever! Our acquaintance has been short but everything than sweet.

February 4
WEDNESDAY

Out of sight of land! I found that I had almost lost my "sea-legs" after having cruised so long on "Terra firma!" A short time, however, sufficed to restore them & I can now challenge the crew to "walk the seam!" After touching at some of the islands of Oceanica for fruit we will sail direct for the Arctic. It is a long time to look ahead but the anticipation of arriving at length, at home and enjoying the society of dear Parents, and Sisters lends evenings to time and it will soon pass!

February 5
THURSDAY

Ten dollars bounty for the first Sperm Whale is offered this morning! Look sharp, aloft boys, & "raise" him if you can!! Weather very hot & squally; such weather at home would make the "good folks stare!" Prospect for a storm.

February 6
FRIDAY

We will probably touch at Navigator's Island and get some fruit. Portions of this group are noted for unsurpassed beauty and I am somewhat anxious to see & judge for myself. No sign of a "blow" yet. Look sharp!

February 7
SATURDAY

A fine morning! At 10 AM raised a school of Sperm Whales! Lowered the boats and started in pursuit. In 30 minutes the Larboard Boat "went on" & struck a fine one! When the harpooneer darted his irons the boat was immediately over his flukes; as soon as he felt the irons he threw up his flukes lifting the boat entirely out of the water and throwing her some 20 feet from him! We (Starboard boat) were laying on our oars about a mile from the whale, but as soon as we discovered the Starboard B. "fast," we sprang to our oars and pulled down to kill the whale! We soon arrived on the "ground" and Capt. Vinall took his station in the head of the boat with his lance. He came up within 4 feet of us, passing, right "across our bows." Capt. Vinall gave him 5 feet of the lance but failed to reach his life. The whale now rendered furious with pain, lashed the sea with flukes & fins, snapped his terrible jaws and swimming about his own length ahead, turned with open jaws on the boat! A terrible sight! As soon as Capt. V. saw the whale turn he ordered us to stern off for our lives & then heading the boat in beaft his jaws we continued to stern off moving the boat in a continuous circle, the whale still following! The Bow & Waist Boats saw our perilous situation and came to our relief. The Waist Boat got in behind him and pulling quickly up the 2nd Mate darted his lance which reached his life; this drew the attention of the whale from the Starboard Boat and after ejecting a thick black column of blood from his spout hole, he sounded. We now laid on our oars, waiting his appearance. Capt. V. on casting his eyes down saw him coming up, immediately under us! Again, (our lives being at stake) we sprang to our oars & almost lifted the boat out of the sea! We succeeded in getting out of his way. In a few moments he "turned up"—dead! We, (the Starboard & Bow Boats) now pulled after the school which was about a mile off yet "going" at a fast rate. We pulled 'til 5 o'clock in the evening when the after oarsman of the Starboard Boat became exhausted & "threw up" his oar! Mechanically, I cast my eyes around to look for the ship; the tops of her mast were barely discernable! Here we were, 15 miles from the ship, night coming on & one of the crew exhausted! Added to this, the sky was overcast with murky threatening clouds and the wind was fast, freshening to a blow! Letting the whale go we turned and with four oars commenced pulling for the ship. Oh! how much did I suffer under that annihilating tropical sun! Feeling that life was a very burden I was tempted to throw myself out of the Boat & in this way relieve over-taxed nature of a burden which she could not much longer sustain! In a few moments the tub-oarsman became exhausted & a short time after I was unable to swing my oar! Things were now getting desperate! The wind & sea had all the time increased & we were now at their mercy! But just at this moment God interposed! The wind lulled and with renewed courage the tub-oarsman and myself grasped our oars and putting in all our strength we again got the boat under way! We arrived at the ship at length with scarcely strength enough left to climb up the side! "What can I render unto God for all His mercies unto one?" The Bow boat was yet out & was not to be seen from the masthead! Headed the ship in the direction she was last seen and stood along. We at length arrived with an exhausted crew. (11 PM) Whale moored alongside.

February 8
SUNDAY

Called at daylight to rig the cutting falls and prepare for cutting in. Another Sabbath to be spent in servile labor! I know not what to think of Capt. Vinall. He professes to be a consistent christian!! Strange consistency this! While in Wanganui the Captain of a small "potato sloop" came alongside on one sabbath morning to supply us with potatoes. Capt. Vinall ordered him away & told him "that it was not his custom to keep his crew at work on the sabbath!" Now, we might just as well suspend all operations 'til 12 o'clock tonight but to the mind of Capt. Vinall there is "risk" in waiting!! He certainly has forgotten to "walk by faith"—to trust in that "unseen hand" which fills or empties our cup of happiness & success! The "love of gain" fills his mind & not withstanding the injunction to, "keep the Sabbath-day holy, he virtually exclaims," there is risk, & if we lose him there will be a great loss! "Godliness is profitable to all things, having the promise of the life that now is and of that which is to come," and in "keeping the commandments there is great reward," but he has to settle this matter with his Maker at the judgement day! May he see his error & act accordingly!

February 9
MONDAY

"Trying out." Employed in turning the "mincing machine." I used, when at home, to think the lumber business was the hardest life in which a man could engage! A good place to "cure" all such foolish notions in the mind of young mad-caps who imagine that they have a "hard-pull" in the voyage of life, is a berth on a Whale Ship! My word for it they will soon learn to value home properly!

February 10
TUESDAY

(3 PM) Finished boiling. The whale was quite a large one (for a Sperm Whale) turning out about 70 bbls of oil. If this was only the last whale, I would feel in better spirits!

February 11
WEDNESDAY

Employed today in "stowing down" oil. Wonder what some of my "fashionable" young friends at home would think, could they see me tonight! For fear that I can not do justice to the subject I will forbear giving a description of myself now, but will do it verbally when we meet again at home! Prepare for something astounding!

February 12
THURSDAY

We have once more struck the S.E. Trades and are now booming along at a rate that would make the "sailing-master

& boatswain" of a "canal-boat" stare! Go it, old Henry, the more speed, the sooner home!

February 13
FRIDAY

Capt. Vinall has determined to proceed to the Japan Sea; if we do not fall in with whales there we will proceed to the Okhotsk; & if unsuccessful there, we will go on to the Arctic. We have altered our course & are now steering for the Japan direct!

February 14
SATURDAY

Ten dollars bounty is again offered for "head & flukes." Look sharp all! The sooner full the sooner home! Employed today in pickling & bending on a new main-top-sail.

February 15
SUNDAY

A fine day. How much better would it be if instead of a crew of 32 immortal souls occupying themselves in studying mischief, their minds taxed with anxiety to see a "blow"— their voices foul with blasphemous oaths—how much better to see this crew collected together engaged in worshipping God! There are many Whale ships that take in sail every Saturday night, "lay to" on the Sabbath and spend this holy day in Divine worship. This is as it should be! How cheering the privilege to the mind and soul of the follower of Jesus! May the time hasten when the Sabbath sun shall be joyfully hailed by every sail when the Bethel Flag shall wave aloft on

February, 1852

every ship & when every ocean river & sea shall echo the glad anthem of the sailor as his song of praise is borne on the breath of heaven to the ears of Him "who formed the sea & the dry land!"

February 16
MONDAY

Another beautiful day. An observation this morning informs us that we are 3 days sail from Navigator's Island.

February 17
TUESDAY

Employed today in making "spun-yam" with the "Wheel of Fortune!" This is decidedly a "hot" job and is warranted to bring to mind former sundry reclinings under an ample shade-tree at home!

February 18
WEDNESDAY

All hands on the lookout last night. A dangerous reef, the exact locality of which is not laid down on the chart is the cause of this. Weather continues almost insupportably hot!

February 19
THURSDAY

Land ho! Navigator's Island dimly seen in the distance! Nothing, so far, evinces any rare beauty—but I will not venture an opinion 'til I see a "little further" in to the reputed excellency of these enchanted garden spots of the South Pacific!

February 20
FRIDAY

We are now (this morning) laying off the island of Toutouilla becalmed. (8 AM) King "John Brown" (a native) his nude body lubricated with cocoa-nut oil and his muscular limbs fancifully tattooed, came along side in his canoe & requested our trade. After some preliminaries, Capt. Vinall ordered the Starboard & Waist Boat crews to stand by to lower. We took "King John" in the Starboard Boat, and after pulling 12 miles we arrived at the beach. Whether the sight of the pine-apple & cocoa-nut groves had an undue effect on my mind (being almost suffocated with heat & nearly exhausted) I am not prepared to say; but in regard to the reported beauty of this literal garden spot, if there is any fault to be found, it lies in a want of language to expose one's feelings when he beholds it! Nothing can approach so near to the "Elysium" as does this spicy grove! Oh! how I would love to describe it! How I would love to transfer to this sheet, my feelings as I gazed on this master-piece of Nature! My pen is unwilling to expose my incapability of coloring this noble picture & I must desist from a rash undertaking & await a union with Dear Parents & Sisters, then to endeavor to give them a verbal description of all that I have seen! We proceeded to the King's Palace and bartered cotton cloth for yams, cocoa-nuts, bread-fruit, taro, pine-apples, oranges & bananas. After which we loaded several canoes & the boats and pulled for the "Kneeland." The Gospel has had a good effect on the hearts of this people and the contrast between them & the wretched New Zealanders seems to increase the beauty of the one & the said deformity of the other. And now how far short is this all from home! Although a literal place of enchantment; although calling up new feelings as I look upon it—although possessing such a gorgeous stock of beauty & attraction: yet it is not home! Oh! no! The lack of the familiar face and kind word, and watchful solicitude and the sound of the voice of each loved one of the household, is as a veil thrown over the picture, depriving it of the true solid, substantial, glory of its rich colomning, and leaving it, despite its rare attractiveness, a marred & blotted picture!

February 21
SATURDAY

Becalmed again today. This afternoon, the officers and as many of the crew as could swim, "went in!" Talk of Newport or Cape May! A "dive" from the bulwarks in the deep blue water of Old Pacific, and where one can experience the delight of being tossed like a feather on the mighty waves—is decidedly "rich." Would like to "ship a good swim" and carry it home for the benefit of my friends, if such a thing were possible!

February 22
SUNDAY

This day will be long remembered by the crew!! After a calm of 3 days, which on the 3rd day became almost fearful we were visited by a typhoon! It came up about 9 o'clock this morning & its appearance was indeed appalling! The heavens were shrouded in perfect gloom in the quarter from whence it came and the perfect quiet which preceded its bursting was horrible! We had but prepared to receive it when it burst, and on it came ploughing & twisting up the sea & roaring fearfully! It struck and in an instant we were flying, "lee sail under," through the sea! But the worst was yet to come! In an instant quick as thought, the wind hauled 16 points by the compass, striking us aback & almost capsizing the ship! All that is fearfully magnificent in a storm at sea was now upon us! The deafening roar of the wind, the mountainous rolling of the sea, the creaking & groaning of the ship, the blinding flashes of lightening & the heavy rolling of the thunder,—all united to exhibit the omnipotence of God & the nothingness of man! As soon as we were "struck aback" the 1st Officer bounded into the cabin and barred the "dead-lights"—then springing on deck he ordered the main yard & mizzens top-sail, braced sharp on the larboard tack. By the time we had manned the braces, the wind hauled again to its old quarter & we were in God's mercy, safe! 107th Psalm, 23 to 32 V.

February 23
MONDAY

Weather hot & squally. Employed in making spun-yam & various ship duties. No sign of a "blow" yet! I would like a short cruise in my sister Jule's fine shady yard today! But that bitter word "too late" makes this tropical sun appear more tolerable!

February 24
TUESDAY

Employed today in overhauling & repairing brace, clew-line, buntline, halliard & sheet blocks. Will be more than glad when this has to be done for the last time! Home grows more attractive every day!

February 25
WEDNESDAY

Employed today in breaking out for water. My allowance of meat today amounted to about one quarter of a pound! Not satisfied with home, eh! Good for me!

February 26
THURSDAY

Employed today in tarring rigging. "Kid gloves" are not much needed in this department! Wonder what an "exquisite" would think could he but see the "fine gloppy" effect of tar on a fellows hands! Send to Paris, I suppose for a few!

February 27
FRIDAY

Weather hot & squally. Employed in making sinnet. No rest for "poor Jack!" Landsmen, often entertain some very foolish notions! Ranking A No. 1 among these notions is the one: "that a sailor's life is a merry & easy one!" I may be considered enthusiastic when I reply to these options, that in the first place, there is no true solid happiness apart from home! Go where you will, visit the most celebrated monuments of romantic beauty & interest, circumnavigate the globe, cross & recross every parallel of latitude, range through every clime—and the blighting reality that you are not at home, will throw a damper over the most sanguine disposition in the world!

February 28
SATURDAY

Had a famous cruise on the fore-yard last night! The 3rd Officer (officer of the deck) was asleep on the quarter deck, and I suppose, must have dreamed that some of "us" were following his example! He awoke, at any rate, came for'rad and finding some 4 or 5 of us asleep, "gently" (?) opened our eyes! "Up you go on the foreyard"—very suddenly transmogrified "us poor fellows" from the imagination society of loving friends at home, to the stern reality of unlucky sailors! Sleep with a weather eye open next time!

February 29
SUNDAY

When at home, I had the benefit of parental advice & instruction & commentaries & concordances to assist one in the study of the Bible, but now, alas! all these blessed privileges & means are forfeited & I am compelled to remain in the dark in regard to many passages of Scripture, the literal meaning of which I am ignorant. Oh! that I but listened to the best of advice & counsel!

March 1
MONDAY

The beginning of another month! Time is "ever on the wing," but when I look ahead it seems a very long time before I will be home again! Anticipation is not calculated to create a true feeling of happiness in one's breast because of the effect of that word—"uncertainty!" Patience, is the only "stand-by" in this case! At 9 AM the look-out aloft "sung out" for "black-skin!" Proved to be a school of Grampus.

March 2
TUESDAY

Employed today in making scrub-brooms. 2 PM Unbent and sent down main-sail for repairs. Tumbling Jack "stuckin" but in 5 minutes broke as many sail-needles! The consequence of Jack's clumsiness was he received a "slippery job"—slushing the masts fore & aft.

March 3
WEDNESDAY

A very hot day. Employed in various ship duties.

March 4
THURSDAY

Weather continues extremely hot. Employed today in making sinnet! When we laid enough we will unlay it and rebraid it I suppose! That is, when we braid enough.

March 5
FRIDAY

A fine cool breeze this morning. Even this slight change in Nature has the effect of killing in some measure, the cruel force of monotony! Oh for something on & about which to study! a book, a paper, a magazine, anything to set the mind at work!

March 6
SATURDAY

A rainy disagreeable morning. Cleared up at 12. At 3 PM raised a school of Sperm Whales! Lowered with no success! Pulling for 8, 10, 12 & sometimes 60 miles under a tropical sun, don't feel very pleasant! It is quite an easy matter to think of, but when the bleeding blistered hands & body, the over exerted muscles, the gnawing of hunger, the scorching of thirst & the blighting effect of the sun on the human frame, is felt it then begins to assume a serious form! "Home sweet home!" Mrs. Hemans never penned a truer sentiment!

March 7
SUNDAY

A beautiful day! My thoughts turned homeward again today, and in my mind's eye, I saw each loved member of the household gathered around the family altar of prayer! The voice of my dear Father, upraised to a Throne of Grace, appeared as though indeed audibly, as I heard him return-ing thanks to the giver of "every good & every perfect gift" for the blessings of the past and petitioning Him for a continuation of the same. I heard the voice of my honored Parent asking God to watch over the Prodigal, and then the long restrained fountain burst forth! Once more I looked. I saw the kneeling form of my Dear Mother & Sisters, and oh! how I longed to make one of that circle again! My indescrib-able loss again drew tears from my eyes! Yet again I looked, and beheld the family in the House of God! Here too, was a vacant seat and when I attempted to consider the subject of it, I was compelled to desist! My feelings were wrought up to too great a height to admit of it. Found comfort in prayer & in reading my Bible.

March 8
MONDAY

The equinoctial storm, better known to seamen by the name of "the line gale," has set in and we have as much wind accompanied with rain, thunder, and lightening as we can manage! Don't think it will last long.

March 9
TUESDAY

Gale, unabated in fury! A severe storm! A dull place is this forecastle during a storm! The wicked and blustering "heroes of good weather" find cause to lengthen the running rigging of their faces; when death & eternity are so faithfully brought to mind during the prevalence of a storm at sea! Thus it goes 'til actually comes!

March 10
WEDNESDAY

Gale abated. God has in His mercy spared our lives through another dangerous & trying season; and the strange effect of this is to cause "men" (?) to vie with each other in acts & words of blasphemy & wickedness! Truly, His loving kindness & mercy are great toward us!"

March 11
THURSDAY

Last evening I witnessed the most grand & magnificent yet terrible sight in all of Nature's works! A hurricane & water-spout! They passed about a mile astern of the ship, forming an excellent opportunity of seeing the mighty force of wind! As with other sights that I have witnessed, this also defies a description from my pen! To know is to see!

March 12
FRIDAY

Weather squally with severe Thunder & Lightning. If I was at home tonight I would doubtfully have the privilege of attending the prayer-meeting in the 2nd Church! Oh! that I had heeded "the stranger's" words! Too late, alas! too late!

March 13

SATURDAY

A fine day. At 6 AM raised a school of Sperm Whales. Lowered the boats and started in pursuit. In a short time the Bow Boat went on and struck a large one! On receiving the 2nd "2 flued" iron the whale threw up his flukes, catching the bow-oar in their ascent & knocking the bow-oarsmen out of the boat! The tub and mid-ship oarsmen, (seeing the bow-oarsman in the sea, supposed the whale had turned on the boat & he had jumped overboard), dropped their oars and sprang overboard! This left all the boat's crew (both "in & out") in a very perilous situation! The whale was fast running out the line, 3 men were overboard and the ship & the remaining boats were out of sight! The harpooneer seized the "dreg," (a square block of wood used for diminishing the speed of the whale) bent it on to the line & threw it overboard. Fortunately for all parties the iron drew leaving the boat free! One of the men was nearly exhausted when the boat got to him and must soon have perished! Came aboard at 10 PM worn out & wretched!

March 14

SUNDAY

Another fine day. Employed today in reading my Bible and thinking of home! These seasons of meditation are the nearest approach I have to home and they are duly improved! Although having a tendency to create melancholy, still I love to indulge in them, and perhaps I am in general too sanguine in my anticipations. They have gained the complete mastery and I must submit to the pleasing yoke in all patience!

March 15

MONDAY

We have crossed the Line once more, and with a fair wind & smooth sea are rapidly overhauling the "Theatre of Action"—Japan Sea! Go, Right Whales!—look sharp!

March 16

TUESDAY

Employed today in sail making. Set down and repaired Fore-top-sail. 6 PM Spoke Whale ship "Vesper." 10 months from London with 110 bbls of oil.

March 17

WEDNESDAY

Employed today in overhauling the cutting-fall blocks, cleaning the sheaves and bolts & "serving," anew the straps. Find a strong disposition to adopt the sentiments of melancholy, friendless Job in his affliction. A peculiar feeling of delight is experienced as I read and reread his expressions of friendless sorrow! How touching his remarks in regard to the quiet of the unconscious dead as they are sweetly sleeping in their nesting-places!

March 18

THURSDAY

Employed this morning in setting up the "bob-stays" and standing rigging. PM "Rattling down," i.e. repairing the "ratlines" or "Ladders," on the shrouds fore and aft. Every day brings something new!

March 19
FRIDAY

This morning the carpenter reported the splitting of the fore-top-mast. We have accordingly been hard at work today, rigging a new mast. Another sail in sight this evening off the lee quarter.

March 20
SATURDAY

"Whale-day" again! I suppose before night, "there-re-re she blow-ow-ows!" will be the signal for we poor fellows to go down and "pull ourselves to death," after these rascally whales! 10 AM A "finback" came up and "blowed" immediately alongside. He continued to swim around the ship for some time 'til at length, Capt. Vinall became vexed at his familiarity, mounted the rail and gave him a lance! It penetrated through his blubber, not hurting him much but enough to "remind him of an engagement downtown!" He left for parts unknown!

March 21
SUNDAY

A beautiful day. Have been thinking today of the mystery attending the union of qualities which appear in Jesus Christ. I see combined the Creator & the Savior; the Judge of the world, & the meek and lovely Jesus of Nazareth; the King of Kings & the bleeding form of Him "who spake as never man spoke!" Oh! what a mysterious, incomprehensible, yet heavenly thought that this second person of the Great uncreated Three is so merciful to man! So merciful to the vile wretch who breathes against him, indignity, persecution, cruel contempt & death! None so low, so vile, so wicked, but He is ready to receive, bless & save! Oh! for a heart to love Him as I ought!

March 22
MONDAY

Called all hands at 3 AM and struck fore-top-mast & fore to'gallant mast. At 10 AM had them on deck. At 3 PM the new fore top-mast was aloft, the fore sail set & the fore top-sail "sheeted home." At 4, the fore-top-gallant mast was in its place and since then have been employed in setting-up rigging. At 3 PM, spoke Whale ship "Jeannette," 17 mos. from New Bedford with 1000 bbls of oil.

March 23
TUESDAY

Employed today in sending up fore to'gallant yard, bundling the sail, setting up the rigging and breaking out for water! Hard work & plenty of it! Weather, very hot. PM Again spoke the "Jeannette."

March 24
WEDNESDAY

Employed today in overhauling our potatoes. Found many of them to be wormy & rotten. More sport in consequence, at Tumbling Jack's expense! Poor Jack! He is the target for the ship's crew!

March 25
THURSDAY

Employed today in tarring rigging. Begin to think that this job will supercede the "sinnet business!" No whales in sight yet. Alas! that "cat," that "cat"!!

March 26
FRIDAY

"Talk of the gentleman in black, and he will surely appear!" Yesterday I was congratulating a mess mate on our delivery from the task of making sinnet. Today,—"go to work at your sinnet!" proves the veracity of the proverb at the head of today's entry! So it goes!

March 27
SATURDAY

A fine day, a fine breeze & "fine stinking cod-fish for dinner!" Capt. Vinall has appeared "wolfish" enough in the past 3 days to transform himself almost into a very "critter"! A man must get used to trifles on board a whale ship! Everything in reason, however is a good maxim!

March 28
SUNDAY

This beautiful day is again fearfully desecrated by the crew! Oh! that I could but escape from this worse than Egyptian bondage! Nothing, absolutely nothing is met with which is at all congenial to my feelings! Everything is at complete variance! Well, I would come and my reward is being reaped!

March 29

MONDAY

A good many of the crew are very anxious for me to have "My Log" printed & published on returning to New Bedford! Did I claim relationship with the celebrated "Dr. Samuel Peter, Quack Humbug" of Mushroomville, Maine—this proposition would have a decided tendency to disturb my "seat of thought!" But when my extreme "youth & modesty" are considered, it will not be wondered at that I decline! I should certainly have no objection to be seized with the "cacoethes scribendi" if I was assured that the "wind would never haul ahead!" How would this look on the title page of some "popular" work to the eyes of some of my young friends at home—"By Enoch C. Cloud, author of Life in a Whaleship!!" However, I think for the present that you can sail just as well shipmates, without "bending on" to your list of favorite authors, the name of Your humble friend— Cloud!

March 30

TUESDAY

This morning fell in with a large French Merchantmen in distress! She lost her rudder in a gale and has been "beating" around, steering badly with spars for 14 days. Boarded her, but found it impossible to render any material assistance. She is named the "Jack Lafitte"—hails from San Francisco & is bound to Manila. We have furled the to'gallent sails, reefed the top-sails and hauled up the course, and intend keeping her company and tossing her (if necessary) into the Port of Guam, distant 23 leagues.

March 31
WEDNESDAY

This morning at daylight made the port of Guam. The Frenchman hauled aback his main yard, and after hoisting the "glorious Stars & Stripes" at half mast union down, we stood in to procure him a Pilot. In a half an hour the Port Captain—a man, who reminded me of Shakespeare's subject of "unbounded stomach," was aboard and we were on our way back to relieve distressed Monsieur. We "landed him" safely, on board the Frenchman, and once more headed the "old Henry" for the Japan Sea. We met with quite an amusing incident when going in for the Pilot! On our weather bow laid a large whale ship who as soon as he perceived the signal of distress at "our fore" ran up his colors at his mizzen peak, squared in his yard and bore down for us. His colors unrolled to the breeze and exhibited the Blue, White & Red (French). "There," said Capt. Vinall, "how fortunate for Capt. Gasper, here is one of his own countryman!" We immediately backed our main-top-sail & waited for the approach of the strange "Frenchman"! When just under our stern Capt. Vinall mounted the poop, and exclaimed through his trumpet, "Ship ahoy-oy-oy!" "I can't speak French–what ship's that!" "The Alabama of Ne-a-n-tucket!"— in as good English as any Yankee in New England could twang! This was followed by a roar of laughter from the crew of both ships! It proved that the Yankee had set his private signal which was exactly similar to the French National Flag!

April 1
THURSDAY

Another month has flown, carrying with it the remembrance of many unlooked for events, many joyful & many sad seasons in the experience of man! Many a bitter cup has been drained to the dregs & many a merry one quaffed by the "being of an hour!" To some, doubtless one of its many eventful moments has been the thrice-happy-period from whence they can date their deliverance from the servile yoke of sin, while to too many, alas! the golden months with all its privileges, blessings & opportunities has been allowed to whirl unheeded on, themselves one month nearer to eternity; and one more month of unimproved, misspent time for which to give account at the Bar of God! Reformation, like charity, should & must, begin at home ! In consequence, I am determined to make some improvement in the month before me! God help me!

April 2
Friday

We are once more exposed to the frowns of "Mdlle Fortune!" One of the crew of the Frenchman presented us with another fine "cat"! Now, shipmates, have a care!!! If you "make" that cat right ahead, don't fail to "ease of your head sheets" & back your main-top-sail instantly! By all means give him a wide berth! For if you but "carry-away" the "yard-arm" of his tail, Mdlle Fortune will frown! 4 PM "All hands ahoy-oy-oy!" "Halloa!" "Turn up here every one of you and stand-by to witness the curing of the cat!" "He has gone into convulsions!" It was a thrilling scene! There laid the cat, "his eyes in fine frenzy rolling" & in his violent contortions he had capsized & laid "bottom up" in the lee scuppers! Now ye trembling disciples of mad superstition, draw nigh and behold! Look on the star spirit of all goblins as his "nine lives" grapple with death; and quake & howl and perform sundry, apish acts of obeisance to your "Queen," "Miss Fortune!" and petition her that she may condescend to set her royal signet on the "lucky" side of Thomas' life and in this way secure "good luck" for the Old Henry! The carpenter approaches with a chisel!!!! Thomas' respected "tail," is "hauled taut" on the deck & with one "fell swoop" of the murderous steel, the yard arm of said tail lays a wack by his side! Alas! Old Henry your star has set!!!!!!!!

April 3
SATURDAY

A fine day. Employed in various ship duties. At 10 AM raised a whale of some kind, 4 points on the lee bow. Squared in, and stood away for him. Did not see him again.

April 4
SUNDAY

I trust that in one year from today I will be at home. Oh! who can conceive my happiness when once more united to Dear Parents, Sisters & Friends at home! When I think of home, friends & the privilege of the Sabbath, my very soul yearns to enjoy them again; but then this detestable Sabbath breaking occupation looms up and falls upon my already crushed spirit with the weight of some mighty mountain! It has, however, learned me a valuable lesson, one that I shall never, can never forget! I was filled with a foolish desire to "go to sea," to participate in the joys & excitements of a sailor's life, discontented with one of the best of homes; and well does the blood suffuse my cheeks when I say, often, really tired of attending the house of God!! But the wind soon hauled from that quarter! I have found that when the "joys" of a sailor's life come to be "close hauled," they are found to be sailing under fake colors; my dear bought experience has long ago taught me that "there is no home like my own!"—change of life, new sights at sea, roaming midst the orange groves & listening to the melodious notes of birds in the beautiful islands of the Atlantic & in enchanted Oceanica; wandering in the romantic mountains of New Zealand & constantly meeting with new & instructive sights—all fall so far short of home, that they are but as a grain of sand on the sea shore!

April 5
MONDAY

10 AM Lowered after a large school of Black and "Cow" Fish with no success. At 1 PM again went down with the like result. Several of the crew have united together and prevailed upon me to serve as "school-master!" Had to "ship" several tons of patience when I commenced, but I now find much pleasure in "learning them the ropes!" I find the most difficulty in explaining to them the rotundity of the earth; the fact of its being whirled through space, detained in its proper sphere by the laws of gravitation, etc., etc., etc. Among my "pupils" is an Irishman, rejoicing in the "cognomen" of "P. D., Esq." He came to me a few days ago with his honest countenance illuminated with a broad grin of evident satisfaction! "Well, Paddy", said I, "how do you get along with geography!"—"och, wurra, wurra, but it's as simple & aisy as 'catting the anchor,' sure!" Well Paddy, explain!—Alas! poor Paddy! He compared the earth to an egg(!!) & supposed

that the atmosphere above us was the shell or case!!! I explained his error, and endeavored by using the most simple comparisons to instill the right view of the matter in his mind. After talking to him for a half an hour I asked him if he understood then. "Now, by the powers of Mole Kelly (!!!) but I don't understand it at all, at all!!! and turning abruptly around he left me, apparently out of humor with himself for not knowing "how to get around the South Pole, without falling off on the other side!!"

April 6
TUESDAY

Tom is—dead!!!! He committed suicide!!!! All lingering doubts in regard to the actions of her royal highness, Dutchess Princess Lady Baroness fiddle-stick Fortune!! are now at an end!! Her susceptible feelings have received such a terrible shock that it has seriously affected the muscles of her eyebrows (poor old thing) causing a constant immoveable, very forbidding frown to crown her sparkling "toplights" and widening the breach between her highness & the Right Honorable Sir Henry Kneeland!! Oh! consistency, truly thou art a jewel—when found!

April 7
WEDNESDAY

This morning at 11 AM raised a large spar floating in the sea. Lowered the Waist Boat made fast & towed it alongside when we rigged a brace tackles & hoisted it on deck. By all appearances it has been swept off some Japanese junk. Weather growing cold.

April, 1852

April 8
THURSDAY

Last night a full rigged snorting "Nor' Wester" came howling down upon us & soon numbered our days of cotton shirts & thin duck breeches! "Double-sheathing" in good demand this morning.

April 9
FRIDAY

Storm still raging. Weather cold. Every preparation for the coming season in Japan Sea is being made! New boat-masts & sails, rigging & grinding harpoons, lances, coopering casks, & all the thousand & one ship jobs, upon which a landsman has never set his "toplights!"

April 10
SATURDAY

On coming on deck last night at 8 Bells, (7 PM) the anticipation of the fearful night before us was calculated to make a man feel as melancholy as a view of "the last biscuit in the bread bag & no land in sight!" Lamenting & fearing are strangers to sailors and after a short cruise aloft (taking in soil) we posted our selves in the fore rigging on the lookout for an ugly reef. Made it at 3 AM (this morning) on our weather bow. Passed it in safety and are now (8 AM) rolling, pitching & wallowing under a regular Nor' Wester! 2 PM Broke out "slop-chest" & supplied crew with thick clothes.

April 11

SUNDAY

A cold & stormy day. This evening, the sun went down in a black bank of clouds stretching themselves from East to South and looking fierce enough to "pump the salt-water in a fellow's eyes," for very fear! Blue sky on the lee, however, promises a cessation of hostilities on the part of "Squire Boreas," and a fine day tomorrow!

April 12

MONDAY

Storm abated. A beautiful though cold day. This morning at 8 AM made "Kiusui" one of the Japan Islands. It is a lovely island dotted with sugar-loaf mountains & covered with groves of Tamanna, Cedar & Pine trees. There are some 8 or 10 islands in sight forming a most beautiful scene! At 10 AM raised a school of "Hump Backs." Owing to the fact that they "understand the use of their flukes, rather too well," Capt. Vinall concluded that the boats would be somewhat safer on the cranes! When quite close to the ship, one of them made a clear breach of 15 feet out of the water! Truly a very curious sight! When he struck the water, there was a report as loud as a clap of thunder! Lucky for them that we don't feel disposed to lower! Well, a poor excuse is better than none & any port in a storm!!!!

April 13

TUESDAY

This morning a regular N. Easter set in & has been raging all day. Sea, very rough; weather, cold & wet. We have cleared the Pacific & have entered the Eastern Sea, 4 days sail from Japan Sea.

April 14

WEDNESDAY

Storm still rages, wind heavy accompanied with snow, hail & rain. Makes me think of home! We were visited last night by robins, swallows, sparrows, bitterns & canary birds in abundance! Poor little fellows! The "strong N.E." proved too much for them & they soon came back after trying to breast it this morning!

April 15

THURSDAY

"Go ho! Bill! no luck, eh!" Read this if you please! At 6 AM raised Right Whales! Lowered & pulled for them. The Waist Boat "went on" but the harpooneer, owing to misunderstanding an order from the 2nd Officer, missed the whale! (Don't laugh yet Bill!) The Starboard Boat then came up & succeeded in fastening solid! "Fact, Bill!" Now, what do you think about your "unlucky cat!" "Time enough yet, eh!" Well, I suppose we will have to wait & see! The whale was "rather ugly"—he did not make much "white-water" but enough, however, to secure to himself a plenty of sea room! In about 2 hours he was spouting thick blood & in a few moments after he "turned up!" The fears of poor Bill and some more of the crew prove to be unfounded, in regard to the consequences of the death of Monsieur Thomas! But alas! another ill omen attends us !!!! The carcass of the whale, after being cast adrift from the ship—sunk, yes, sunk— and with it sunk the ship's "luck"!! I will wait 'til I hear of a few more of these wonderful "signs!" before I overhaul some of their rotaries!!

April 16
FRIDAY

Employed in trying out today. We have entered the Straits of Corea; and are now slowly proceeding with Asia & the "Shang Hai" or Yellow Sea, on our larboard, & the Japanese Islands on our Starboard beam. View, very fine!

April 17
SATURDAY

11 AM! "There goes the last "horse-piece" in the machine!" & I know of one who is glad enough of it! I had a good opportunity to see the two most remarkable portions of a whale's body-today-the eye & ear. The eye is but a little larger than that of an ox, and the orifice of ear (with which whales have been known to hear the lowering of a boat from a ship's side for 8 miles) is about the size of a pipe stem! or one fourth of an inch in diameter! 9 PM are now running along the S.E. coast of the island of "Tsus-simma" The water is getting shoal; its color changing from the "indigo blue" of Old Pacific, to the murky pea-green of close-soundings.

April 18
SUNDAY

A beautiful day. Was thinking today of the goodness and mercy of God, to man. Man!!—What is he? A being, 'tis true, but how beset with errors, how prone to sin & how tardy to deeds of righteousness! What a selfish heart is that he locks within his breast & with what an icy indifference does he treat overtures of Divine goodness, mercy & love!! God has sent this fine weather & granted us the privilege of beholding this beautiful morning. How fitting a time for worship! But alas! the minds of Capt. Vinall, his officers & the crew are busily engaged with their moving Sea-God— the whale!! How eagerly does the look-out aloft scan the horizon for a "blow!" And with what an angry disappointed tone does Capt. Vinall answer in monosyllables the questions of the officers! But hark!! "There-re-re she blows-ows-ows!" Oh! what a change does the sight of those two whales make in the man! He is now beside himself with joy, and see how eagerly he "lays aloft" & with what a greedy exultation does he level his glass on his—Gods!!! The Larboard Boat went on & struck. The whale started immediately to windward with great swiftness, bellowing & lashing the sea with flukes & fins. He continued to run for 2 hours, when he "took the line" & escaped! A fearful account must be rendered some day for broken Sabbaths!! I can say no more now.

April 19
MONDAY

Well, here we are at last in the Japan Sea! 10 AM raised right whales. In a few moments the W. Boat was fast! Whale ran furiously to windward. In about 2 hours the L. Boat went on & gave him 2 more irons. In return for this he gave the boat a "slight-tap," with his flukes—knocking the harpooner out of the boat & "landing" him on the whale's back! He again started and ran fresh for 2 or 3 hours when the Bow Boat succeeded in giving him 2 more irons & a lance. In return for that, he threw the line out of the "chucks" with his flukes, which ran along the gunwale of the boat; caught the 3rd Mate by his legs & in a moment he was "some distance under water!!!" He miraculously cleared himself & was hauled, unhurt in the boat. The Boats had now been fast for 7 hours,—the whale still running fresh & spouting as white as snow—when the return signal was set at the mizzen peak (on board the ship) & the boat "cut line" & came aboard! So much for Right Whaling in the Japan Sea!!

April 20
TUESDAY
A calm foggy morning. Raised whales again this morning & lowered with the usual success! A Hump-back came along-side this afternoon & the 1st Officer gave him a lance, which "sought blood"—being which he lowered his boat & tried to give him the —"coup-de-grace!" No success!!

April 21
WEDNESDAY
Sea alive with right whales! Lowered 5 times without success! Old Bill's "cat" is having a decided feast of revenge! 'Tis strange that in this "cotton-spinning" age, these enlightened 19th century men (?) will so tenaciously adhere to nursery ditties and nonsensical traditions of good & bad luck! Superstition has outsailed common-sense in more than one head on this ship & the prospect now is for an increased number of votaries!

April 22
THURSDAY
Lowered again today for Right-Whales without success! Begin to have hard work now & plenty of it! Work is

nothing—but we do not get enough to eat! Capt. Vinall's soul (which would occupy but a small space in a mosquito's bladder,) is gifted with a very large stock of—selfishness! He satisfies his own palate, with the best, while the crew can not get enough—hard-bread & salt meat! Will come Whaling-eh?!!!!

April 23

FRIDAY

A fine day. Lowered after the "evil spirits," 4 times today without success! It appears that they really know what a Whale Boat is! We can get within "hailing distance" with the ship, but as soon as a Boat strikes the water they are bound off!! A storm breeding tonight!

April 24

SATURDAY

AM Now we have it! Roll & tumble, pitch & lurch, fore & aft, a regular built N. Easter! At 12 PM moderated & at 4 PM "Lay up there & shake 2 reefs out of the top-sails," was proof positive that "Old Boreas" was "bound-off!" Saw but one Right-Whale today. Sea too rough to lower.

April 25

SUNDAY

Another cold & stormy day. Read the 22nd Chapter of Genesis today, with peculiar feelings of delight. What a pattern of believing faith & genuine submission to the inscrutable ways of God, is exhibited in the conduct of Abraham when God makes the sore trial! Oh! how must his heart have throbbed with parental love when he received the command to sacrifice his only son, Isaac! And then the thrilling question put by the son to the father! Oh! for a heart like his—a holy, humble, willing submissive heart of righteousness & true holiness!

April 26
MONDAY

Lowered again today for Right Whales. A large cow (with her calf) broke water close to the Larboard Boat. The harpooneer struck the calf, but the iron drew & both made good their escape. "Old Bill" continues to "crow" about that insignificant "cat!" Go on Bill, but look sharp for a "foul line!"

April 27
TUESDAY

This morning at 6 o'clock we again overhauled the "cow & calf!" Lowered the boats & started in pursuit. In a few moments the Waist Boat was "fast solid" to the calf! (Why don't you crow Bill!!!!) The whales then commenced running with incredible velocity—the cow keeping constantly beside the calf & using her utmost endeavors to urge it to its greatest speed. In a short time, all four of the boats were fast—2 to the cow & two to the calf. As an illustration of the amazing strength of a Whale & her solicitude for her young, I will mention one incident attending their capture. The calf, in its furious struggles to escape would frequently get entirely away from the mother, but as soon as she missed it, she would turn, find it & rolling it up in her flukes, throw it away forward on her fin & then carrying her calf & dragging the 4 boats, would run with rail-road speed to underward!!

After running in this manner for 7 hours, they "brought to" (i.e. stopped running.) 2 boats pulled up & succeeded in killing the calf. Set a "waif," in his back, let him drive & turned our attention to the cow. As soon as she discovered that her calf was dead, she fought with a fury, that is utterly indescribable!! She would sometimes "stand on her head" & make a clean sweep with her flukes, from eye to eye!! To attempt to "go on" the whale now would be but sowing our hammocks for a trip to "Davy Jones' locker!"—and we gave her a wide berth! She continued to fight in this manner for an hour when she sounded. When she came up again she was close to the Bow boat, seeing which she turned and came "head-on," with great swiftness! A prick in the nose with a lance, however, caused her to turn and the boat & crew were saved! The Starboard boat then went on & Capt. Vinall gave her a lance. As soon as she felt it she threw up her flukes & bringing them down with a sweep, cut the cap off his head!! She again swept her fluke, catching the after-oar, and mashing it to atoms! At about 4 PM she turned up—dead! A very large Whale. An idea may be had of her size when her flukes measure 23 feet from tip to tip!! 6 PM Moored along-side. The calf is not in sight & I suppose we will lose him.

April 28
WEDNESDAY

11 AM Whale all cut in. At 3 PM raised the calf right ahead. Lowered the Starboard & Larboard boats (it being calm), made fast & towed him along side. 6 PM Calf cut in. A very small one; will make but 15 or 20 bbls. of oil.

April 29

THURSDAY

Boiling out. The cow whale will not make much oil, being what we call a "dry-skin." 12 N. lowered for whales, without success. Frightened by the smoke from the try-works.

April 30

FRIDAY

Still boiling. Oh! how long & dreary & monotonous is the prospect ahead! No home, no Parents, no sisters, no friends, no Sabbath & no sanctuary privileges for long, long & bitter months to come!! Why did not I think of this e'er it was too late! My punishment is almost too great to bear!!!

Home, sweet home!!!!

May 1

SATURDAY

The sun arose this morning, bright and beautiful upon as lovely a day as ever graced "Old Ocean's" bosom! We had a grand "May party" today!!! At 4 AM (rather early) the guests assembled and proceeded to clear the ground of oil, gurry & mud! After a slight repast to steady the demands of appetite the "King" made his appearance which was the signal for the commencement of "sport"—stowing down oil!! It is needless to enter into detailed account of all that transpired on the occasion; suffice it to say, that a more greasy, worn-out & sleepy crew never stowed oil before! At 12 N the guests were invited to partake of some "refreshment," got under way & bore down for "refreshment-hole," (the forecastle) when we found our tin-pans groaning under the weight of a small piece of stinking-cod-fish & our tin pots swimming with the very best brands of New Zealand ditch-water! A sumptuous repast!! (Very!!) We again repaired "to the ground," but were soon called out to shorten sail (7 PM). Scudding "before it" under bare poles. A severe gale!

May 2
SUNDAY

Storm abated. Sea fell but still very rough. Made Dago-let's Island this morning; laid "off & on" all day. Lowered for whales in the evening without success. Right!! I hope like success may attend all Sabbaths Whaling! Home grows more & more attractive!!!

May 3
MONDAY

Lowered again for whales today. Too wild—couldn't catch 'em! What will I add to this entry? Well, the same bitter reality of deprivations, the same annihilating thoughts of my loss; present themselves and ever form a theme of bitter regret; and continue to render me more miserable as I think of my ingratitude and the sad consequences of it!! Life at the very best is a burden!!

May 4
TUESDAY

A cold wet & foggy morning. Well calculated "to cure" a chap who embraced the doctrine of ease & joy at sea, in the character of a sailor!!

May 5

WEDNESDAY

A clear cold day. Saw no whales today. Cruising off Dagolet's Island. Not much prospect for "filling up" this voyage at this rate!!

May 6

THURSDAY

Lowered for whales today with the usual success! No wonder! We don't get enough to eat! About ¾ of a peck of potatoes is divided among 21 men & can anyone expect to catch whales when men are fed in this manner? All right! "Must go to sea, eh?"

May 7

FRIDAY

A beautiful day. Lowered for whales again today without success. Disaffection is being strongly manifested fore & aft. We shipped to go to the Arctic Ocean where whales are plenty & easily taken, but here we are with a pretty fair prospect to go into port as empty as when we came here! Time will soon show!!

May 8

SATURDAY

A cold wet disagreeable damp, dark very foggy morning! Fog so thick that we cannot see a ship's length ahead. Cleared up at 12 N. Raised whales & lowered without success.

May, 1852

May 9
SUNDAY

A beautiful day. Lowered for whales again today without success. All feelings of respect for the Sabbath is lost by the crew & blasphemy resounds from one end of the ship to the other! Oh! for one hour, at home!!

May 10
MONDAY

Nothing to eat & plenty of hard work . . . the order of the day! Some of the crew have openly aroused determination to refuse to do duty if we do not get more! PM Storm brewing, weather cold.

May 11
TUESDAY

A severe gale is now raging. Furled everything "laid to" & stood "quarter watches." Reminded me of "school-boy days" at home! "Stay at home & overhaul the contents of bureau drawers!"

May 12
WEDNESDAY

Storm abated. Thoughts of home & friends filled my mind today as I looked back & brought to mind this day one year ago in which I had a pleasant little romp on the banks of the Sciota, with "Orville," "Pete," "E.A." etc. etc. Alas! those happy anticipations once so fondly cherished are all blotted out! She was wrongfully thought of by many! Her father's truly nothing, but I have proved by severe trials that she was worthy of my love!! God has separated us & I pray constantly for submission to His holy will. I little thought then that I would be here today! But so it is!!!!

May 13
THURSDAY

And this is my birthday!! At the beginning of the present year I made new resolves, formed new resolutions & strengthened my determination to live nearer my God! But how far short have I already fallen! Whose but the strong arm of God has protected me when terrific storms have burst upon the ship, threatening all with speedy destruction; or when the heavens were lit up by the fierce lightenings, their bright fires reflecting back upon the bosom of the ocean, 'til all had the appearance of molten fire, or who but the Great God has protected & preserved me when taking whales? and when time & again the very breath of death has been hot in my face? But how ungratefully, viley, wickedly have I repaid all these blessings! God forgive the past & help me to live nearer to Thee in the future!!

May 14
FRIDAY

A fine day. Lowered for whales again today with the usual success! Too many "Jonah's" aboard I'm afraid!

May 15
SATURDAY

Lowered 7 times today without success! Got in sight of their "wake" each time! No nearer!

May, 1852

May 16
SUNDAY

A damp foggy morning. Hauled aback the main-top-sail & laid to. No church to attend today!! Oh! how keenly does my loss sink into my very soul!

May 17
MONDAY

A dark heavy fog continues to deck nature in a gloomy garb of melancholy & to force "Old Sol" to remain in the back-ground! Fog very thick.

May 18
TUESDAY

Fog still "hangs on!" A fine chance for "we poor fellows" to rest! No whales to be seen or heard. Employed in mending, patching, & darning!!!!!

May 19
WEDNESDAY

This morning the fog cleared away & gave us a glimpse of a clear blue horizon; the sun shone out clear & his warm rays instilled new life in the crew fore & aft! We paced the deck with comparatively light hearts & memory catered to our season of joyfulness by way of picturing green fields, murmuring brooks & happy friends at home! But with "poor Jack" "joys" are of short duration! The fog came down again and at 5 PM we were shivering under the weather bulwark, cold wet & uncomfortable.

May 20
THURSDAY

A fine morning. At 7 AM the carcass of a whale (apparently fresh) floated past the ship surrounded by hundreds of Albatross, Gulls, Carey's chickens, Nelly's, etc., etc. At 8 AM raised a strange sail on our larboard bow. Made it out to be a Japanese junk; set the to'gallants and gave chase!!! They tried hard to "show us their hind foot" but we were "taking the wind down with us," and soon overhauled them. Poor fellows! they were dreadfully frightened! We ran up the stars & stripes, which seemed to float in a true—"Columbia rules the world"—style!! Lowered the Starboard Boat and pulled along-side. They were at first unwilling to allow Capt. Vinall to board but in a few moments they consented & he went up the side. As soon as he touched the deck they ran up & proceeded to "salaam" in true oriental rig, bowing their heads to the deck & exhibiting every sign of abject fear! He asked the commander of the Junk (by means of signs) "where all the whales had gone." "Ching, sing, whang," pig-tail answered by vaulting on his hands, his feet high in the air (imitating a whale "turning flukes") "blowing" with his mouth & pointing to the Southward. After staying awhile with the polite pig-tails, Capt. Vinall took his leave & came aboard, evidently much to their relief! Cargo consisted of gold-dust, ivory, silks, indigo, etc., etc.

May 21
FRIDAY

This morning made two more junks on our lee bow. No whales to be seen. Prospect for filling up looks dark!

May, 1852

May 22
SATURDAY

This day was ushered in by a regular built "Nor' Wester"! A severe storm! Saw two junks today. Appeared to be fully qualified to weather a storm! "Lay as close" as the "Old Henry!" That is saying a good deal for the junks but the old H. must share her praise with "fellow chips"!

May 23
SUNDAY

Lowered the Larboard & Waist Boats this morning for Whales without success. Right!! It has become a subject of general conversation on the deck of the ship concerning our unsuccessful endeavors to take whales. Various absurd & nonsensical reasons are given by the crew in general, but the opinion which I have formed is that the law of God is violated and who dare ask for success!! Capt. Vinall must give an account of himself at the bar of God for all these broken Sabbaths & then how miserably empty will the name of gold sound!!

May 24
MONDAY

A fine day. Employed in sundry ship duties. Thoughts of home continue to fill my mind!

May 25
TUESDAY

A fine day. At 7 PM the lookout aloft "sung-out" for "black-skin!" Proved to be a dead whale! I was chosen (among others) to man the Larboard Boat. The whale was about 2 leagues from the ship and after putting some signal rockets, a few biscuits & a keg of water in the Boat we lowered away. It was a calm clear evening; the stars were shining brightly & a "five hour moon" was rigged out with a new and splendid robe of light. The signal lantern was set at the main-royal truck & after taking from it the bearing of a star we sprang to oars. We could not find him, however, and came aboard at 11 PM "rather tired!!"

May 26
WEDNESDAY

This morning we were scudding before it under close reefed top-sails & this afternoon we lowered for whales! Too wild! Dark, dark, prospect!!

May 27
THURSDAY

Lowered again today! One of the crew recommends painting the boats another color to secure good luck!! Chased one whale today for 9 hours! At 6 PM Capt. V. lowered the Larboard Boat and took with him a musket loaded with a brace of balls intending to "shoot a whale." Got quite near him—levelled his fusee, let fly & happened to strike the sea somewhere to windward of the whale!!!! Great shot!! Further pursuit was useless!

May 28
FRIDAY

Lowered again today with the usual success! At 12 N. a rapid falling of the barometer indicated a sudden & severe blow. Let the return signal for the boats to come aboard. 2

PM All hands took in sail. 6 PM Driving before it under a close reefed main-top-sail!

May 29
SATURDAY

Storm still rages. Some sharp lightning last night. This evening the storm abated & we shook a double reef out of the top-sails. No whales in sight.

May 30
SUNDAY

I was detailed this morning to pull the mid-ship oar in the Bow Boat. Raised whales this afternoon, lowered with the usual success! Right !!

May 31
MONDAY

Another severe gale has been raging all day. Laid to, under a close reefed main-top-sail & storm stay-sail. Would like to be at home today!

June 1
TUESDAY

Storm somewhat abated in violence. Lowered this after-noon for whales with the usual success! Such weather as this at home would call into requisition winter clothing & open the coal-yard!

June 2
WEDNESDAY

Last night was a cold & stormy one. At 1 PM a heavy thunder squall came up. Lightning vivid, thunder severe.

Lowered again for whales today with the usual success! Home continues to fill my mind constantly & no one but God knows the longings of my heart to enjoy its privileges & blessing once again!

June 3
THURSDAY

A beautiful morning & becalmed. Did no storms ever stir the bosom of the sea, it would be a pleasant place to live; but when the strong & terrible gale howls angrily over its heaving & troubled surface, and death is brought to mind a quiet fireside, on land appears doubly inviting!!

June 4
FRIDAY

Still becalmed. Last evening I witnessed I think, the most gorgeous & sublime sight in the Universe! It was a literal sun set, at sea!! Many times before I have watched the sun slowly sinking in the horizon. I have admired it, but never before was such a gorgeous display of God's glory manifested to me as that of last evening! My mind applied the scene to the last end of the christian. With Christ as his Pilot, he tranquilly approaches the "dark valley" and his face is radiant with glory as he peacefully gazes into the depths of the grave! He gradually sinks, and a happy consciousness of the presence of God serves to render his end, one of glory, tranquility, beauty & joy! "Let me die the death of the righteous & let my last end be like his!"

June 5
SATURDAY

Still becalmed. Raised whales this morning & lowered. In a few moments the Larboard Boat was fast to a fine one!! Whale sounded heavy & parted the line! Boats all gave chase. He came up in about ½ an hour, "brought to," and fought furiously. Failed to fasten again. Chased him till dark and came aboard tired, sore, hungry & blue!

June 6
SUNDAY

With the first grey streak of light the boats were down & in chase of yesterday's whale! No success, thank God no success! Oh! for a season of rest on the Sabbath!!

June 7
MONDAY

Still becalmed! 2 day's sail from "White Rock," a noted "whale ground" on the coast of Tartary. Capt. Vinall has at length consented to go to the Okhotsk if we have no success at White Rock! We will soon see!

June 8
TUESDAY

This day commenced with a light breeze which by 3 PM increased to a gale! At 4 PM made the coast of Tartary; wore around & stood out to sea again.

June 9
WEDNESDAY

A fine day. Scenery on shore magnificent, sublime!!! It really appeared strange last evening to see the sun slowly sinking behind the hills! Lowered with no success!

June 10
THURSDAY

A beautiful morning! At 9 AM raised Right Whales. Lowered the 3 port boats & started in pursuit. In 30 minutes the Larboard Boat was fast! We (Bow Boat) pulled up to get 2 more irons in. Whale "brought to" & laid still. Went on and gave him a lance. I was pulling the bow oar and as soon as the 3rd Officer darted his lance he "sung out" to stern for life, the whale having commenced to fight!! I cast my eyes over my shoulder and saw him raising his enormous eyes over my shoulder and saw him raising his enormous flukes just out of the water!! "Where you are," "if you please" thought I, "but he thought no!!" Poising them for a moment, he brought them around in one grand sweep! "If you wish for my place you can have it," I again thought as I threw myself with the 3rd Officer in the bottom of the boat! His flukes whistled as they swept the gunwale of the boat! In an hour he gave over the unequal contest, rolled over and sunk! 3 boats held on & after hard labor succeeded in raising him. 5 PM Blubber all cut in. Commenced trying out.

June 11
FRIDAY

Boiling out. At 11 AM raised whales. Lowered the Waist & Starboard boats. Waist boat went on & struck. Whale sounded heavy, came up in ¼ of an hour, perfectly frantic! Starboard boat went on & the harpooneer killed him with his iron! Looks like filling up!! I suppose Bill's "cat," has had her "spree out"! 4 PM All cut in.

June 12
SATURDAY

Boiling. Raised whales again today, lowered with no success. At 6 PM spoke Whaling Bark "Italy," 10 months from Greenport with 450 bbls of oil.

June 13
SUNDAY

At 10 AM finished boiling & "cleaned up." At 2 PM raised whales & lowered, chased them 'til 5 PM when the Larboard Boat fastened to a large one. Broke the iron and escaped! As usual, the main topic of conversation was, "our hard luck!" I thank God that the efforts of these wicked men to take a whale today were frustrated; & although I am so anxious to fill up & return home & although I know that "the more oil, the sooner home," still, I am directly & bitterly opposed to taking one drop on the Sabbath day! I feel to say with Habbakuk 3c 17-19v.

June 14
MONDAY

A fine day. Lowered for whales. Starboard Boat struck a fine one! Ran to windward & parted the iron! Lost him! The boats of the Italy also struck and lost a whale. "Lumber business, hard, eh?"!!!!!! I often sigh for the privileges of even that business! I have got in a good place to learn me a lesson!!!!

June 15
TUESDAY

Lowered this morning for whales. Larboard boat went on & struck a large cow! After 4 hours of hard labor & many narrow escapes, she gave over & turned up—dead! But two boats stove & no one hurt. She is a large fine whale of the "snorting" species!

June 16
WEDNESDAY

Boiling. At 1 PM raised a large school of Right Whales. Lowered 3 port boats & gave chase. We, (Bow boats crew) got within "one spouting" when they sounded. In 5 minutes, some 12 or 15 large ones rose immediately alongside & around us! We were literally "fenced in" and our situation was extremely perilous! The Waist & Larboard Boats dare not come down for if they had the whales would have run us down in a moment! We laid still not expecting to see the light of another day in this world! God then interposed & we were saved!!! One and another slowly settled in the sea, 'til at last there remained but one up. For him, we "pointed" the boat! At his next rising, his broad back was right under the bows of the boat!! The harpooneer buried both his irons in his back, "gave him the box line," and by that time we were "going" some! I think a "little faster" than I ever rode before! In 5 hours he spouted thick blood & sunk! Couldn't raise him! Lost him!! Try again!!!

June, 1852

June 17
THURSDAY

At 5 AM lowered for whales. Came aboard at 7 and got breakfast. At 9 AM the Larboard boat fastened to a "live Tarter!" He tried hard to escape bringing "all his forces" into requisition, flukes, fins & head—no use! He continued to fight wickedly for 4 hours when the lance reached his life & in a few moments he was floating in his own blood! Sunk! Succeeded in raising him! I found an old iron buried in his "small" an evidence that he has tired one boat's crew before!! 8 PM All cut in. At this time (11PM) the whales are making this fine night hideous with their terrific bellowings! Look out my hearties!!

June 18
FRIDAY

A severe gale has been raging all day. Saw numbers of whales. Couldn't lower. "Cooled down" the try-works. This is "prayer-meeting-night" at home!! Oh! how I long to be there again! How would I love to be at home tonight!!

June 19
SATURDAY

Storm abated. Lowered this morning for whales. Waist boat struck a large one, who very scientifically annihilated the harpooneer's oar with his flukes and barely missed the boat! Irons drew and he escaped!

June 20
SUNDAY

A beautiful day. All hands employed in boiling & stowing down oil. It is with feelings of heart felt sorrow & deep humiliating anguish that I look upon my past life!! I might have been an inmate of the best of Father's houses, surrounded by friends & enjoying the privileges of the Sabbath & sanctuary! But I have brought all upon myself! My conduct, well beings, sleepless watches & long and bitter seasons of true remorse of conscience are acknowledged severe but just lessons! At 1 PM lowered for whales. Starboard Boat struck & killed one! Sunk & lost him! Just right!!

June 21
MONDAY

A fine day. At 1 PM lowered for whales. Larboard boat went on & struck! Rather too cunning! Ran away & took a line with him! The 1st Officer came very near being killed when the harpooneer darted his irons! The 2nd iron which is "bent on" to the "short warp" was thrown but the whale was so far away that the warp did not reach him; the consequence of this was the iron came home, head first, with great violence! The 1st Officer saw it coming & stooped to avoid it. The flues of the iron ripped his shirt open along the back & went out through the rim of his hat! Narrow escape!

June 22
TUESDAY

Employed in stowing down oil. At 2 PM "chucked off" (i.e. filled up) the main hatch-ways!!! A thick fog has enshrouded us all day!

June 23
WEDNESDAY

Fog still hangs on! Came very near going ashore today! 3 Right Whales came close to the ship today when one of them made a clean breach out of the sea exhibiting an iron sticking in his "small" with a line attached! Supposed to be the same whale we struck on Monday. Did not lower. The "old 'uns" say, "his breaching" "angers" "a gale!!"

June 24
THURSDAY

A gale of wind rages! 12 N Lulled & cleared up. 3 PM Lowered for whales with no success! Went in close to land. Saw quite a city. Some of the inhabitants (Tarters) were engaged in fishing (in their junks.)

June 25
FRIDAY

Foggy again today. Lowered for whales with no success! Would like to see my friends "Orve" today! God bless him, he is my friend!! I hope yet to see the "Doctor," and chat with him about matters & things! "Pete" too, I would love to see but patience, patience is everything!

June 26
SATURDAY

This morning at 10 AM Raised whales. Lowered and struck! After being killed he sunk, but with hard labor we succeeded in raising him! 11 AM commenced raining, rained all day. Finished cutting at 8 PM (How acceptable would have been a bed !!!) Got "supper" (??) and wet, cold & worn-out, ordered on deck to "clear away the head!" So much for whaling!

June 27
SUNDAY

Started try-works at 4 AM. At 2 PM lowered for whales. No success! I often dream of being at home but when I awake & find myself still a captive my very soul groans in agony! Oh! how slowly does the hour of sweet liberty drag along! God, in mercy hasten it!

June 28
MONDAY

A fine day. At 10 AM lowered the boats and struck a whale! After being killed he sunk, but we succeeded in raising him! Prospect brightens!

June 29
TUESDAY

Boiling. Lowered for whales. Bow boat struck and killed one—sunk! Succeeded in raising him. No danger of getting the dyspepsia! Will come away from one of the best of homes, eh! Come whaling, eh! Well, ignorance of my enviable situation in life is perhaps one kind of an excuse!

June 30
WEDNESDAY

Lowered again for whales today! In a few moments the Starboard boat went on & struck a large cow! Whale sounded; when she came up close to the Waist Boat. The harpooneer darted his irons and as soon as she felt them, she turned on the boat! The 2nd Officer "pricked" her but it rendered her more furious! She came on, stove the quarter of the boat in & knocked the harpooneer overboard! In the confusion, the bow-oarsman jumped out of the boat & the tub-oarsman got 3 "turns" of the line around his legs! The line was then cut & the harpooneer & bow-oarsman picked up. The whale again attacked the boat & stove her with her head! Again she came on & struck the boat just forward of the mid-ship thwart! The Waist boat (now almost down) was then pulled away from the Whale and the Bow boat "gave her a trial!" The whale stove her in 2 places! She was now evidently bent on mischief!! And after putting out one of her eyes with a lance the boats gave her a wide berth! Her bellowings were truly terrible & the noise made by lashing the sea with her flukes & fins can only be compared to thunder! She continued to act in this manner for 5 or 6 hours when she rolled over & sunk! The line was then run to the ship, ran through the guy-block of the cutting tackles & taken to the windlass. Got her almost up when the line parted & we lost her!! Cold, wet, blue, hungry & sore!

July 1
THURSDAY

Employed in boiling & stowing down oil. Saw plenty of whales, but had but one boat fit to lower. Carpenter employed repairing them. There is one thought, (how precious!) to my mind which goes far toward lightening the otherwise intolerable burdens of this life! It is,—that my Dear Parents & Sisters remember the lone & wandering prodigal when they daily draw nigh to the Throne of God! When dangers, sufferings, privations & hardships come with all their terror, it is sweet delightfully sweet, to think that I am commended to the mercy of God by my Dear Parents &

Sisters! God bless them! Oh! how unworthy am I of such favors!

July 2
FRIDAY

A stiff breeze has been blowing all day. At 1 PM lowered for whales. Starboard boat went on & struck. He ran away with the boat immediately, defying the utmost endeavors of the loose boats to overhaul him! There was a high sea running & there was no time, given the boat to "side" them; when she met a sea she had to go through it ! I may safely say that more than 100 barrels of water were bailed out of the boat before we cut line!

July 3
SATURDAY

Lowered again this morning! Struck & killed a fine whale. 2 PM Cutting in. 3 PM Waist boat went down, struck & killed another! "Where's your abominable old 'cat,' now Bill?" Come to life, eh!!! Really something new!!! 7 PM Moored alongside! A good day's work & some prospect of getting home!

July 4
SUNDAY

All hands called at daylight to cut in. At 10 AM we were boarded by the crew of 4 Junks! (Tarters) They examined everything minutely; evidently much frightened but maintaining a tolerable degree of composure! They eagerly devoured some "scraps," (boiled blubber) and asked permission to cut away the fleshy parts of the whale's carcass. They filled their junks, and after gazing at everything a while longer they went home. 12 N finished cutting. 2 PM Lowered for whales. 2 ½ Waist boat fast to a regular "Tartar!" Larboard & Bow boats succeeded in fastening also. Bow boat slightly stove. Waist Boat's line then parted when they hauled it in, bent on 2 more irons and gave chase to another whale! Overhauled & struck him! We, (Starboard Boat) then went down, but before we got there, the line again parted & we lost him! 7 PM Dead whale in tow of the 4 boats! It was dead calm & we had to tow him about 6 miles to the ship, where we arrived, worn-out & miserable long after the sun had sunk behind the high blue mountains of Tartary! From 10 last night "til 7 this morning I was in the blubber room; from 7 'til 12, cutting in a whale; from 12 ½ 'til 1 again in the blubber room, from 1 'til 10 PM (tonight) in the boats and now I am "in for it" 'til 1 o'clock in the morning in the blubber room again! Feel "some little" tired!!!! Oh! how different from a peaceful gospel Sabbath at home!!

July 5
MONDAY

This day (with the exception of striking another whale) has been a repetition of yesterday's proceedings! Sleeping "goose fashion" (standing) is "all the go!" Employed in breaking out for water, boiling & stowing down oil. Weather warm & pleasant. Troubled without measure by the Tarters! Some 20 or 30 junks are now bearing down for us while the crews of some 8 or 10 alongside are yelling, "Sango, sango, ke-roda!"—the meaning of which I am ignorant, and truly "ignorance is bliss!!" (in this case).

July 6
TUESDAY

The 21st wonder of the world "arrived" this morning!! Capt. Vinall ordered the cook to issue "duff" 3 times per week!!!!!! 12 N The 22nd wonder!! A keg of butter!!!! I suppose, however, that we are entitled to these rare delicacies now, as we have taken just 1000 barrels of oil & 15,000 lbs of bone! Lowered for whales without success.

July 7
WEDNESDAY

A fine day. At 10 AM raised whales. Lowered, struck & killed one & brought her alongside! The Bark Italy, having no Carpenter & having had her boats all stove was "in a fix!" Capt. Rowley came aboard this evening & requested the "loan" of "Old Chips" for a few days. Capt. Vinall complied with his request!

July 8
THURSDAY

Struck & killed another whale today! Work plenty and 4 hours sleep out of 48 considered quite a luxury! Sounds, rather "worky" that!! Warranted to strengthen the muscles & give a good appetite!!! A good prescription for effeminate young chaps that imagine a life on land is "hard" & a life at sea, "easy!!"

July 9
FRIDAY

Lowered for whales. Struck, but the irons drew and we lost him! Have been thinking of home, all day! I often wonder if any dear friends think so often of me, as I do of them! Well, I hope soon to see them and oh! what a "time" there will be then!!! First comes venerable Father, then Dear Mother, next Mag, Will, & little Mary, then Jule, Albert & their sweet babe, next comes "Mandy" & last though not least, "Mame"!!!!!

Patience, patience, my soul; all in God's good time!!

July 10
SATURDAY

Struck and killed another whale today! "Blubber-logged!" (all full) No more room to stow blubber now 'til we boil some of this up! Begins to look like filling up! The sooner the better! We are now, (as ever) dependent upon God for the accomplishment of our much desired object, and if He wills it, we will succeed! May we all study submission!!

July 11
SUNDAY

A thick fog has enshrouded us all day. It really appears like a new life!! One sabbath has passed and the hateful cry of "There-re-re she blows-ows-ows" has not been heard on the ship! Oh! may the time hasten when the "abundance of the sea" will be converted to God & when the poor Sailor will have the Sabbath day in which to worship the Great God of Heaven and earth!

July 12
MONDAY

Still foggy, accompanied with a cold driving rain. What will not men endure to procure that mighty, world-governing, flattery-commanding, yet exceedingly empty thing "—gold"!!! Hardship, danger, privation, suffering, exposure, all dwindle into comparative insignificance, when pride calls upon them to reach forth & pluck the tempting fruit & their eternal salvation is forced to retire, waiting for a "more convenient season," and giving place to the things which "motte & sust can corrupt"!!!

July 13
TUESDAY

Still foggy & rainy. Cooled down the try-works. A comfortable room at home would appear "some little better" than this narrow, dark, wet & cold for'castle today!!

July 14
WEDNESDAY

Finished boiling. A fine chance to get clean!! Truly an interesting looking set of fellows! Hard to tell where some of us belong!!! All rubb-off when its "wet!"

July 15
THURSDAY

Lowered for whales. It was a dead calm and the whales were some 8 or 10 miles from the ship. The Bow boat went on & struck! Whale ran & fought. Larboard Boat succeeded in fastening also. We (Starboard boat) then lowered and pulled for the "seat of war!" Got there at length and succeeded in fastening. I had an opportunity today for the first time of striking a whale! Don't like it! When he rolled over, he was at least 12 miles from the ship; and we had the "pleasure"(?) of towing him just that far!! 11 PM Feel "somewhat" tired!!

July 16
FRIDAY

Boiling. Raised whales. Lowered, struck, and killed one. Sunk! Succeeded in raising him! I do hope that we may succeed in filling up! We cannot get home too soon for me!!

July 17
SATURDAY

Cutting in & boiling. I fear that I am too sanguine in my anticipation of soon being at home! Well, I am in the hands of a merciful God & I pray for submission to His holy will!!

July 18
SUNDAY

2 PM A thick fog has surrounded us all day and the prospect for its continuation is good. No whales in sight & very glad of it!! Experience much comfort in reading my Bible! Precious privilege!! That is, I will continue to be my undeniable privilege; let come what will!

July 19
MONDAY

Still foggy. Capt. Rowley (Bark Italy) came aboard this morning and is here yet. (11 PM) This afternoon, employed in scrubbing ship.

July 20
TUESDAY

Cleared away at 12 N Lowered for whales without success. At one time 7 boats were in pursuit of one whale! All failed to strike! On coming back, our boats & the Bark's indulged in a regatta! "Old Henry's" boats, first best!! The Starboard boat kept the lead 'til the harpooneer broke his oar & we then gave way to the Larboard Boat!

July 21
WEDNESDAY

The whales have all left this ground & we are bound after them! First, to White Rock, thence to "Woodland." If we fail at both places we will proceed to the Okhotsk! Scenery on shore, grand & imposing! Lowered for a whale, but he preferred his native element to a passage in the ship! (I suppose!)

July 22
THURSDAY

Saw no whales at White Rock and stood on for Wood-land. Employed in coopering & stowing oil. I suppose at the close of this season, we will go either to Oahu, (Sandwich Islands) or to Hong Kong (China). Prefer the latter! No choice here, however!!

July 23
FRIDAY

One year ago today, I was at home!!
How thoughtfully has Young exclaimed,
He that's ungrateful, has no fault but one,

July, 1852

All other crimes may pass for virtues in him. All my deprivations, hardships, dangers & sufferings have been brought on by my-self!! No one, but myself is to blame! Oh for the opportunity of atoning for ingratitude to the best of Parents!

July 24
SATURDAY

Raised whales. Lowered without success. Still proceeding toward Woodland. The scenery on shore is truly most sublime! I would that my friend "Orve" could see it! I then would be favored with some of his fin drawings from Nature! How I would love to see "that Orve" today!

July 25
SUNDAY

This was a beautiful morning—clear and pleasant! But oh! the aching void felt on not hearing the welcome call of the bell to the house of God! Christians on land! Oh! do improve your privileges!! Delay not, linger not, be not lukewarm, but "press toward the mark!" I would give ten-thousand worlds for the privileges of the Sabbath at home today!

At 1 PM lowered for whales. No success! "Right!!"

July 26
MONDAY

A foggy unpleasant day. This morning all hands cleaned ship. Will be glad when this job is done for the last time! Will be nearly home then!

July 27
TUESDAY

Saw some large whales today. Lowered without success. At 5 PM the lookout aloft raised some object floating in the water, supposed to be the dead body of a man. Lowered a boat and found it to be a dead deer! Spoke Bark Italy again today.

July 28
WEDNESDAY

A fine day. At 6 AM heard whales breaching & "bob-tailing" on the larboard bow. We could not see them but the thundering of their flukes was plainly heard on deck and we lowered the boats, pulled to them & chased them for 3 hours without success.

July 29
THURSDAY

Woodland in sight! Now, for it! One month more, and we will start for (I humbly trust) home! Lowered for whales, without success.

July 30
FRIDAY

Raised Whales. Lowered. Starboard boat went on & struck. The harpooneer of the Waist boat was knocked overboard, but was not hurt. 2 PM Moored alongside. 6 PM finished cutting. Suffered much today with the head-ache! No Dear Parents & Sisters to sympathize with one!!

July 31

SATURDAY

Whales are as scarce here as they were at White Rock. We will "try it," a few days longer before we leave, however! Employed in various "work-up jobs!" No rest for poor Jack! Officers motto—"No religion, no Sunday, no feelings of soundings"—is rigidly enforced!!

August 1

SUNDAY

Another month has flown & another commenced! God's mercy has preserved & protected my life, health, & limbs through many trying & dangerous seasons during the past month & it becomes me this morning to examine my heart & see if all these mercies are appreciated and if a proper consecration is made to their Giver! Do I really commence this month with a stronger determination to serve Him more acceptably by His assisting grace? God forgive the past & aid me to live nearer to Thee in the future! The brevity of life; the certainty of death & the consciousness of soon (at farthest) being summoned to the presence of the august King of Kings, all conspire to strengthen me in my determinations! I am weak & sinful! I pray for aid from on High!

August 2

MONDAY

A fine day. Employed in stowing down oil. Lowered for whales this evening without success. Our main prospect begins to look rather gloomy! But many times before a dark & gloomy morning has preceded a fine day, & it may be so, in this case!

August 3
TUESDAY

An almost impenetrable fog has enshrouded us since 8 o'clock last night. Laid to "with the main yard," "aback" all day. At 4 PM "bent" a new fore-sail. At 7 PM fog cleared away & commenced raining.

August 4
WEDNESDAY

At 8 AM, raised large numbers of whales. Lowered & gave chase! The Starboard & Larboard boats pulled for a large school on the starboard bow & the Waist & Bow boats pulled for another school on the port bow. The Starboard boat struck in the "starboard school," at the same time that the waist boat struck in the "port shoal!!" Lines parted & lost both whales!! Came aboard & repaired lines. Lowered again. Waist Boat went on & struck a fine whale! Line parted again & we lost him! 3 whales lost in one day!!! Chased them 'til dark without success!

August 5
THURSDAY

A beautiful morning! At 4 PM lowered for whales. Waist boat went on & struck! At 6 PM he was a headless carcass alongside the ship!! 12 (at night) in the blubber room cutting blubber!

August 6
FRIDAY

Boiling. Lowered again for whales! Waist boat went on & struck! Whale stove the boat; the "iron strap" parted & he escaped! No one hurt! It will be more than a joyful day, when I start for home!! It is difficult to conceive the longings of my heart, for one more opportunity to see & converse with & to enjoy the society of Dear Parents, Sisters & friends at home!! Oh! that I was there tonight!!!

August 7
SATURDAY

A foggy day. Cleared away at 12 N In the evening lowered for whales without success! How dull are these Saturday evenings on the ship! Looking forward to the Sabbath my soul turns away in sorrow & disgust as I think of forfeited privileges & desecrations! Oh! Time, hasten on thy swift careen & speedily bring the sweet hour of liberty! Speedily unite the penitent, wandering prodigal with beloved Parents & Sisters at home!!!

August 8
SUNDAY

From day break 'til 4 PM a thick fog enshrouded us. At home well calculated to make a man feel "blue," but here it brings a short season of rest, a temporary suspension of arduous labor & an opportunity to spend some time in reading my Bible. I would that a fog might enshroud us every Sabbath during the voyage! At 4 PM raised a Right Whale on the larboard bow. His actions indicated that he had been hurt with an iron. Lowered 2 boats and pulled for him without success. Right!!

August 9

MONDAY

Two boats have been chasing whales all day. The remainder of the crew employed in stowing oil & cleaning up decks. 'Tis is a happy thought and one well calculated to smooth the angry billows of this life that death is a haven of rest !! No more aching muscles no more bleeding & blistered hands, no more soul harrowings, no more bitter tears, but the unconscious particle of dust silently sleeps in its last resting place, bidding defiance to the stern changes of life's lottery, and sweetly resting beyond the reach of the ills, many ills of this fleeting life!!

August 10

TUESDAY

I was detailed this morning to pull the mid-ship oar in the Waist Boat. 9 AM raised a large school of Whales. The Bow & Waist boats pulled for 3 whales that had separated from the school & were laying "like logs" on the top of the water. On nearing them 2 of them heard us & settled, leaving the 3rd (a large cow) still up. The Bow boat went on and fastened solid! The whale ran a short distance & sounded. When she arose she was close to the Waist Boat. We pulled up to strike, when just abreast of her flukes I saw her raise them over my head, and the next thing I knew I was in the sea surrounded by fragments of floating oars and the after part of my head feeling as though I had shipped an 8 lb shot! The whale was about 20 yards from me laying still and as long as she remained so, I was comparatively safe, (excepting the danger from sharks.) The bow boat was nearest to me but I was afraid to start for her thinking the noise made by swimming would arrest the attention of the whale. I remained for some moments in my unpleasant situation & then cautiously "struck out" for the boat. The moment I started, the whale reared her enormous head out of the sea and slowly turning, started for me!! How plain did each member of the family appear to me then! I ceased to swim, tried to collect my thoughts & endeavoring to trust in God I silently prayed for deliverance from the very jaws of death!! My prayer was heard & answered! When within a few feet of me the whale suddenly "milled," seeing which I struck out with all my strength for the boat. I reached the steering oar & with the assistance of the harpooneer I got in. The Waist Boat then came alongside & took me in & we again pulled for the whale. In about an hour she "went in her flurry" (death-struggle) & is now (11 PM) snugly stowed in the blubber room. A fine large whale. Another sample of the joys of a sailor's life!

August 11
WEDNESDAY

A severe headache together with a general debility of my system & a "very sore head and neck"—the effect of "standing target" for our yesterday's whale—has confined me to my bunk. Feel bad & miss the comforts of home.

August 12
THURSDAY

Struck and killed another whale today. The prospect for "filling up", holds good! The only difficulty now will be the weather, we may expect bad weather soon.

August 13
FRIDAY

Struck & killed another whale this evening & moored him for the night. The harpooneer of the Larboard Boat was knocked overboard but unhurt. An ugly whale but the lance soon made him feel unpleasant & caused him to "strike his colors!"

August 14
SATURDAY

Employed today in stowing oil. Saw no whale and glad of it! Feel tired and would give "a fortune" to be home!! "If a man will dance he must pay the fiddler!" I think so at any rate!

August 15
SUNDAY

This has been a day of sore temptation & trial to me! God preserve my soul from all sin!

While in the blubber-room from 12 o'clock last night 'til 7 this morning my mind wandered back to my christian's Father's house! Could a Nero look into my heart & behold its workings as I drew a contrast respecting myself, and fail to drop a tear? At 7 this morning I was "relieved"—came below and anticipated a happy hour in reading my Bible. Doomed to a bitter disappointment! A whale was raised & the boats were lowered! I rejoiced in their unsuccessful attempts to strike! Capt. Vinall will not allow the crew to stow oil today—because it is the Sabbath!!!!!

August, 1852

August 16
MONDAY

One year from New Bedford today!! Truly "Time is ever on the wing!" The shipping officers in Philadelphia assured me that I would be bound home by this time!! Not much prospect of it now! We have, however, done well so far. This ship was 22 months from home on her last voyage before she took 600 bbls of oil! The superstitious ones ascribe our "good luck" to the fact that we have some 4 or 5 "fine fat rats" on board!! When will these rascally "signs" cease to affect our "luck"?!!! I suppose the next thing will be that our bad luck is occasioned by the death of the rats!!! A good place for the "rappers"!!!!

August 17
TUESDAY

Raised whales again today. Lowered the boats & pulled for them. At about 5 AM the Waist Boat fastened to a large bull. The whale ran & fought furiously for three hours when the line parted. In about one hour the Starboard boat succeeding in re-fastening. From that time 'til 4 PM he continued to run & fight, when the 2nd Officer succeeded in reaching his life. A very wicked whale! The 4th Officer was slightly hurt by his flukes; nothing serious. The 1st Officer & one of the harpooneers had an altercation while in the boats which was resumed after coming on board. (8 PM All quiet!)

August 18
WEDNESDAY

Employed today in "cutting in" blubber & stowing down oil. Feel unwell, but a whale ship is not a comfortable home, and aching limbs are but a poor security for a day's rest! Hard-labor is the remedy for all sickness! If my dear friend "Orve" was here with some of his "nice little pills" I would feel better—whether or not!!!

August 19
THURSDAY

Boiling. Saw no whales today & very glad of it! I am really tired of hearing, "There-re-re she blows-ows, there-re-re-he lays, there-re-re-goes flukes," etc., etc!! "Variety," it is said, "is the spice of life" and if we poor fellows get any at all it must come from a scarcity of whales! Spices, by the way, are somethings which we never taste in our parlor!

August 20
FRIDAY

Employed today in cleaning up decks & coopering. Saw no whales. We have taken so far, 1480 bbls of Right & 60 bbls of Sperm oil. If we succeed in taking 2200 bbls in all we will start home! But a short time is allotted us and I am afraid we will have to come another voyage yet before we see our homes!

August 21
SATURDAY

A fine day. This has been a day of comparative rest to me! This afternoon I was sized with symptoms of apoplexy—a strange dreamy dizziness with a painful fullness of the blood vessels of my head. Went aft & reported to Capt. Vinall. He bled me in both arms & administered a strong purgative. 8

August, 1852

PM feel some better—my head and temples, however, are very sore! Home, sweet home!!

August 22
SUNDAY

A beautiful day. My chief endeavor is to please God! Oh! that my heart would burn with supreme love; that firm, unwavering faith would characterize every thought, word & action! Oh! for a heart to exclaim with a Poet (whose name I much regret to be ignorant of):

> "Should pale Death, with arrow dread,
> Make the ocean-wave my bed
> Though no eye of love might see
> Where that shrouded grave might be
> Thou, who hear'st the surges roll
> Deign to save a sailor's soul!"

August 23
MONDAY

A severe gale has been raging all day. The old ship has become quite wet since she has taken in so much oil! Makes a man think of a dry "clothes locker" at home! Not the only comfort of which I am deprived!!!!

August 24
TUESDAY

A fine day. Employed in the morning in stowing oil. At 1 PM lowered for whales with success. A fine large whale! Wonder if rich ship owners at New Bedford ever think of all that men are compelled to undergo during a whaling voyage!! A good motto for the much-to-be-pitied, son's of Adam, would be—"No soul, a sailor's hard-earned wages, and a very deep pocket!!!" A good device for their coat of arms would be, "Shylock with his knife & the Merchant of Venice."

August 25

WEDNESDAY

Saw no whale today. Employed in cutting in and trying out yesterday's whale. We have the promise of "duff" every day after we take two more whales!!!! "Wonders" have not yet ceased, it appears!!! What will come next?!!!!!

August 26

THURSDAY

Raised whales again today. Starboard Boat went on & struck a large bull. He was well acquainted with a boat it seems! He allowed no chance to get a lance at him & after running 'til night we cut line & let him go! Many narrow escapes were made by the crew during the day but the Strong arm of God preserved all from danger!

August 27

FRIDAY

Struck and killed another whale today!! 7 more and we will "point her" for home!! As the voyage draws near to a close my anxiety to see my Dear Parents & Sisters daily, hourly, increases! Oh! how does my soul yearn toward them all!! For myself, I care not! Danger, hardship, privation, suffering,—are all met with a light heart; but the bare thought, that one of the loved ones at home is compelled to breast the strong tide of life's ills; racks my heart to the very core!! God forbid to cause any one of them a moment's pain!!

August 28
SATURDAY

Lowered for whales again this morning. Bow Boat went on and struck a large cow! As soon as she felt the irons she threw up her flukes and bringing them down with a cutting sweep, struck the boat just abreast of the bow thwart cutting 5 feet of the boat clean off—leaving the harpooneer standing in one part & the crew sitting in the other! A miraculous escape!! Waist boat went down & picked up the crew. Larboard Boat succeeded in re-fastening & killing the whale.

August 29
SUNDAY

A gale of wind set in last night & has been raging all day with violence. At 6 AM "cooled down" the try-works. Some rest for the majority of the crew but none for me and my "leaner," however, for we were compelled to stay in the blubber room and cut blubber! A dangerous pace in a storm! The ship would sometimes roll heavy, in consequence I would be thrown,—spade or knife in hand, clear abeam!! Not cut yet! ("Good luck")

August 30
MONDAY

A high sea running. At 6 AM raised whales. Got the boats in readiness to lower when a succession of "cat's paws" followed by a stiff top-sail breeze, set in, rendering it impossible to lower. Employed today in stowing oil, etc., etc.

August 31
TUESDAY

A fine calm day. At 2 PM the Larboard Boat fastened to a "live race horse"!! At 6 PM he was out of sight of the ship when he cut line & let him go! Came aboard at 9 PM "some little tired!!" Well! another month has passed with its varied changes, trials, joys, sorrows, hardships & dangers!!!! How fare the loved ones at home tonight I wonder!!! God grant a blessing rich & abundant to rest upon each head!! May we soon be permitted to meet again at home!

September 1
WEDNESDAY

Another beautiful day. Some time during the present month we will "close reef" our labor on the whaling ground and start for the Sandwich Islands (God grant for home!) Home!!—that word causes a thrill of joy in my heart which I would not exchange for the crown of a Napoleon!! At 9 AM raised whales. The Larboard Boat went on & harnessed "to another race horse"! He "took the line" in an instant! In the afternoon the Starboard Boat went down & struck another! He also tried hard to take the line and—succeeded!! After some hard pulling the Larboard Boat succeeded in striking. Took that line too!! The Waist Boat was the next "lucky one" succeeded in refastening & killing him! After being killed he very unceremoniously—sunk!! Couldn't raise him with the Boats, but brought the line to the ship & took it to the windlass! Three hearty cheers burst from the crew as we saw his white belly slowly raising to the surface of the sea for he had caused much hard labor in his capture. Moored him & made sail—in order to raise him permanently to the surface. Prospect for bad weather!

September 2
THURSDAY

A gale of wind has been raging all day! Succeeded with much difficulty in cutting in the whale. In the evening employed in "stowing off" the fore hold. A dangerous job in storm but we succeeded without accident.

September 3
FRIDAY

Gale still raging with fury! Notwithstanding its heighth we started the try-works! Hard times in earnest!! Working in the blubber room extremely dangerous!

September 4
SATURDAY

Storm unabated in fury! With great difficulty we succeeded in finishing our operations at 11 PM last night. The storm has increased to an awful gale with a fair prospect for its continuance!! There are 110 bbls of oil (in pipes) on deck which make it much worse for the ship! Oh! what would I not give to be at home tonight!!

September 5
SUNDAY

Storm increases!! Our situation is now critical. The pipes of oil on deck have been doubly lashed & spiked, decks cleared of every thing, hatches battened down, and every preparation made for the worst! What will become of us if the storm increases much more—God only knows! A tremendous sea is running which rolls the ship, "lee rail under" at every lurch! We can but abide the issue of the gale! God in mercy protect us!

September 6
MONDAY

After a fearful night of storm and terror, morning dawned upon a crew worn-out with watching & hard work! At about 8 AM the gale decreased in fury & we took advantage of the temporary lull & coopered the pipes of oil for stowing. As was expected, however, "the lull was but for a relief & a fresh hand at the bellows!" It came on again this evening & is now (11 PM) raging wildly!

September 7
TUESDAY

Gale still rages! Notwithstanding its heighth we succeeded with extreme difficulty & danger in stowing the pipes of oil between the decks. Well! our labors are over at last! The first voyage is closed & we are bound for the Sandwich Islands! I wandered back to my Father's house today & beheld each familiar face of that loved circle at home! As I called to mind the many happy hours spent in the society of dear friends I was happy! But the wind soon hauled from that quarter. The stern voice of the Officer of the deck (as he gave on order) quickly arrested my pleasing meditations and forcibly reminded me that I was on the deck of a whale ship!!!

September, 1852

September 8
WEDNESDAY

The storm has in some measure abated & there is a prospect for good weather. There is a flying report on deck that we are bound on a cruise in 48*North (vicinity of Fox Islands, Okhotsk Sea). The author of this report is the far famed, "Squire They-say." Accordingly, I stow it away in my locker of "if's, but's, etc." PM Employed in "breaking out" & rigging studding sails,—this certainly don't look much like cruising!

September 9
THURSDAY

A beautiful day. Employed today in overhauling bone, spreading & drying it. Things begin to look as they did on the voyage out, quiet clean decks & all sail set!

September 10
FRIDAY

The commencement of our season of rest is duly appreciated and improved accordingly! Employed in discharging our cargoes of smoke, "gurry," etc. accumulated on limb & clothes during the past voyage on the whaling ground! No whales in sight & we poor fellows are glad enough of it!

September 11
SATURDAY

Another fine day, and with a bouncing "quarter breeze," we are rapidly overhauling the Straits of Perouse. It is extremely difficult to commit to writing my thoughts & feelings when I think of home & friends!! The fact is, no one, can realize with what an anxious feeling a man thinks of home & friends, except those who have long been painfully separated from them without once hearing from them!! Their true value is never known 'til we deprive ourselves of them!

September 12
SUNDAY

A damp foggy morning. Raised whales!! Lowered with (thank God!) no success! 'Tis at least strange that Capt. Vinall will order his boats down for whales on the Sabbath-day!—The past season has been one of fortune & success. The blessing of God has rested upon him & the crew. Not a man has been killed or seriously hurt (a very common fact) yet notwithstanding these manifold mercies, he openly & premeditatedly commits a gross sin in the sight of God!—I forbear to comment!!

September 13
MONDAY

A fine day. Employed in cleaning ship, etc. Many are the for'castle yarns nightly "spun" by the crew,—many "air castles," (some of them very lofty) are "rigged," fore & aft,—much speculation,—many political arguments are entered into to pass the long watches at night! "Jack" has "slipped his sea moorings" turned "land lubber," & is at once a politician, lawyer, quack, &—humbug ! Like all the rest! Must be in fashion, even on the deck of a whale ship! Poor "Tumbling Jack" would sell his last patched shirt for a glass of the "critter"!!! Look sharp Jack!! Mind your "weather roll," or the doctors will have you yet!!!

September, 1852

September 14
TUESDAY

Another fine day. Employed in scraping the outside of the ship. Really, this season of repose is having a bad effect on the majority of the crew! It causes some of them to be affected with a very serious indisposition, denominated by the medical faculty at home, the "spring fever!" It has not yet proved fatal to any!! "Tumbling Jack" is in the most danger! His constitution is one of those peculiar kinds that can endure a great deal of "rest!!"

September 15
WEDNESDAY

Sent aloft last night from 11 'til 1 o'clock to look out for breakers. The entrance to the Straits is a very dangerous channel is the cause of this. This morning entered the Straits. View very fine!! The green waving verdure of the trees looked very inviting & went far toward relieving the wide expanse of deep blue water around us! A severe thunder squall came up at 10 AM. Lightning fierce with heavy thunder!

September 16
THURSDAY

The first morning in the Okhotsk Sea, clear keen & frosty! Great numbers of wild fowl cover the bosom of the sea & remind one of duck-shooting seasons at home! Yesterday morning I took breakfast in the Japan Sea; took dinner in the Seghalien Sea; and took supper in the Okhotsk Sea! Talk of Morse's Telegraph—eh ?!!! Go it, old Henry Kneeland!!!

September 17
FRIDAY

Prospect for a storm! It is somewhat singular that we poor fellows are not set to work making sinnet! We, however, indulge in the fond hope that we have worked hard enough during the last season to deserve a little repose; and that our exemption from "Jack's Plague" arises from the kind feelings entertained by the officers!!! (Very likely) Work on the whole is plenty & varied, however & as soon as we get in warmer weather a new stock will stand by to "keep the scurvy off"!!! And so ends the day!!!!

September 18
SATURDAY

A full rigged "Sou' Easter" is playing "Neptune's favorite" today!! Stormy weather I suppose will be "the order of the day" from this time 'til we "run our longitude out," strike the "North East trades" and get her "pointed" for the Sandwich Islands! The storm is a severe one but promises a speedy cessation.

September 19
SUNDAY

Storm abated. A high sea is still running which makes it rather unpleasant on the spar-deck, otherwise a lovely day. The first Sabbath for a long time when a cessation from labor afforded an opportunity for meditation. God, hasten my return home when each Sabbath affords this holy privilege!! What a mighty, deep, powerful word is—Mother!! I have seen hard times at sea; times well calculated to blanch my stout heart and unstring every muscle in my

frame; times, very apt to touch the fountain of my heart,—
but nothing has the effect, equal at all to that produced by
thinking of my dear Mother!! God bless her and my aged
Father too, God bless him, and my dear Sisters, God bless
you all!!!

September 20
MONDAY

A fine morning. This morning made American Island,
one of a long chain through which we are compelled to
navigate in order to reach Old Pacific! A dangerous place!
Subject to strong currents, head winds, calms & thick fogs!
"Bent on" a cable to the sheet anchor—all ready to let go in
a case of emergency!

September 21
TUESDAY

A cold foggy morning. Last night at 10 'clock a thick fog
came down rendering it impossible to see a ship's length
ahead. Tacked ship every ½ hour. At 8 Bells this morning (3
AM) called the Starboard watch & went below. They had not
been on deck 15 minutes when the 4th Officer raised land
right ahead! All hands came on deck and there right before
us loomed a great black rock!! Wove ship & made all sail. A
head wind all day.

September 22
WEDNESDAY

Last evening at 7, the wind hauled fair. Set studding sails
below and aloft & are this morning "logging 12 knots" on old
Pacific's bosom of blue! The weather, however, is unpleasant

and appearances indicate the usual "September visit" from "Boreas Neptune & Co," an established firm well known to Poor Jack!!!!! The probability is (judging from appearances) that they have a heavy account posted against us & of course we are not very anxious to have them "send in their bills" 'til the last moment!

September 23

THURSDAY

The autumnal equinoctial gale, better known to sailors by the name of the "line gale" has set in and promises to be unsparing in violence! Well a good free ship & plenty of sea-room is as safe a place as I wish to be in; blow high, or blow low!! Give me that, and then let the gale howl!!

September 24

FRIDAY

Now we have it in earnest! Everything lashed down and secured for the coming fierce encounter with the elements! The prospect this evening is for a fearful night of storm! This is the time when visions of happy, peaceful firesides and kind loving friends at home rise up & haunt the sailor; let him be below or aloft! He now doubly feels his loss, and although he may present a rough exterior, yet, a warm susceptible heart throbs quickly within his breast as he sadly thinks of absurd loved ones!

September 25

SATURDAY

Morning dawned upon a distressed ship & a weary worn-out crew!! The storm increased last night to almost a hurricane; the sea was running absolutely "mountains high" & the trembling, groaning ship as she was tossed as a feather from crest to trough, seemed like some huge monster in the agonies of death! The ship may ride it out if it does not increase, if it does not increase,—our doom is as certain, as it is fearful!!!! We are in the Hands of God and He will do right! The prospect out-board is still all dark & fearful!!

September 26
SUNDAY

Storm in some measure abated. This morning shipped a tremendous sea, which stove in the weather bulwarks, stove the Bow & Waist Boats & mashed the Starboard Boat to atoms, carrying away the davits & making the most complete wreck I ever saw! The "signal gun" (a very large & heavy one) was doubly lashed on the carriage to the weather windlass brace—parted the lashings and the gun, carriage & all capsized and brought up on the lee side of the brace against the fore life rail! What would I not give for the privileges of this day at home!

September 27
MONDAY

A comparative fine day. Employed in breaking out water and oil. The larboard water-tank (from which we use water) shipped a quantity of sea water during the gale and those alone who have been compelled to drink salt water know of the misery & suffering which it produces!! An unabated, raging thirst, which is but increased by drinking; a faint dizzy sensation in the head & stomach & a longing for one drop of pure fresh water! We are too short of water to throw this overboard; but it certainly cannot fail to produce sickness!

September 28

TUESDAY

Prospect for a continued dealing with the firm of Boreas Neptune & Co!! Employed in pumping the water-tank stowing the "infected liquid" below (to use it in case of emergency) & filling up with the only pure draught—fresh water! Seems like a new life already!!

September 29

WEDNESDAY

A severe gale is raging this morning and we are scudding before it under a close reefed-main-top-sail. The old ship is "walking" in earnest, and "wet decks & 12 knots" are hourly logged! Things begin to look "rather ugly" to windward, however & I fear that we will yet be compelled to "throw her to" before the gale breaks!

September 30

THURSDAY

Storm abated. Last night was a fearful one of storm & as I expected we were compelled to "heave to!" At about 10 o'clock the gale increased to such a fury that we dare not scud longer. "Hove her to," 'til 4 Bells this morning when we again "squared away" and drove before it! Speed, speed old Henry! I expect to hear from home at Oahu! Can't get there too soon!

October 1
FRIDAY

Opens fine & pleasant with a prospect for good weather. 9 AM Set the fore-top-sail & "shook" 1 reef out of the main. 12 N Quite calm; made all sail & now (7 PM) with a noble breeze we are rapidly overhauling our port of destination! "Tumbling Jack" continues to make a due share of sport for the crew! Many pranks are played upon him by some of the boys such as "trimming his whiskers" & tarring his face while asleep, etc.

October 2
SATURDAY

A fine day. Employed in breaking out meat, bread, molasses, sugar, etc., besides sundry other "little exercises!" The conduct of Officers improve very much as we near the port of Honolulu! There are good chances for desertion at said port—is the cause of this!! Home, sweet home! I think that I love women one degree stronger, because one of the "gentler sex" penned that most beautiful sentiment! By the way, we have a "full rigged" "woman-hater"(!!!) in the for'castle,—a pretty "smart chap" too, with whom I have some warm discussions! My Dear Mother, is a woman, and that fact, apart from all others will ever lead me to respect, love & protect them!

October 3
SUNDAY

A stiff breeze has been blowing all day. An altercation ensued today between two of the crew—an American & a Portuguese. I endeavored to separate them & after a time, succeeded. They were called aft & after being severely reprimanded were sent aloft to the to'gallant cross-trees to think it over! All respect for the day is lost by the crew & my detention in this moving ark of wickedness grows more & more intolerable! God, hasten my deliverance!!!

October 4

MONDAY

This morning the heavy rain storm of last night broke and the remainder of the day has been fine & pleasant. Employed in cleaning ship—a grand preparation for entering port!! I was advised in New Bedford to select an old ship, in preference to a new one, the reason alleged was that on a new ship the crew were kept busy cleaning her! Experience has taught me quite different! Well, it is not the first time that I have been deceived!!! Rather poor "consolation" too,—but it's the best, I've got!!

October 5

TUESDAY

Weather, squally & unpleasant. Employed in sundry deck and rigging jobs. "Tumbling Jack," thinks, he would "look-better" if he would let his mustachios grow!! My opinion was requested on the "important subject," and of course, I sanctioned it! Poor Jack is now employed in "coaxing out" the much-to-be-desired appendage to his "handsome" figure-head!!!

October 6

WEDNESDAY

Another grand cleaning up job!! We have already "scrubbed the paint off" and it will be necessary to "ply the brush" in many places to cover the naked wood! Rather more nice, than wise, I am afraid! However, the officers say that, "we did not ship to express our opinions,"—therefore— "mum"!!!!

October 7
THURSDAY

Employed in a general overhauling of every thing!!! Putting the "old Blubber-hunter," in a respectable rig for port! Much labor has been performed on the old hulk for the accomplishment of this much desired object & I sincerely hope that it is all over!

October 8
FRIDAY

Employed in making spun-yarn and "rattling-down." The cares and anxieties of the whaling ground are now over, and the crew employ our time in talking of loved ones at home! God hasten our union! Oh! how heartily sick am I of this miserable life! Monotony, killing monotony, ever stands by to lend a hand in making me more miserable!! So ends the day!!!

October 9
SATURDAY

Set in with a heavy squall of rain & wind,—succeeded by a most beautiful day! The 1st Officer came for'rad this morning and gave us the day in which to clean, wash, scrub, scour, rub, sand & dry our parlor! Employed all day in cleaning & white-washing her! (P.M.) Looks like a new hole! Must "show-off" in port!!

October 10
SUNDAY

A beautiful day. This has been a day of rest!! The hateful cry of "There-re-she blows-ows" has not been heard—no "mast-head" kept—and with the exception of necessary duty in working ship, nothing has interrupted a pleasing strain of meditation! I can almost see the members of the family today winding their way to the 2nd Church! God hasten my return home!"

October 11
MONDAY

Another fine day. Employed in rattling down & other jobs in the rigging. A sail in sight to windward. Much anxiety exists among the crew to know whether or not "she has taken as much oil as we have!"

October 12
TUESDAY

Employed in breaking out and coopering the Beef & Pork. A hard job! Found many of the barrels to be badly stoven. 11 PM Sore hands, headache, back-ache, legs-ache, & heart-ache!! Wonder if I can't boil up some "turnip tops," and produce a "celebrated lotion" for the cure of the above woeful list of my infirmities! Guess I won't be a quack!

October 13
WEDNESDAY

We have at length struck the N.E. Trades & are now "ploughing up" the Old Pacific at the rate of 8 knots an hour. No news by the morning Post!!!

October 14

THURSDAY

Spoke Whale Ship "Corea" from the Arctic direct. The Corea brings distressing intelligence from the Arctic! The Captain of Whale Ship "Vesper" was taken out of his boat by a foul line, (while fast to a whale) and seen no more! The ships, "George & Huntress" were wrecked in a gale! A ship (name not known) went down with all on board, in sight of the Huntress during the same storm! The ship "Warren" was burned—all hands saved, etc., etc.!!! The Corea reports the price of oil in San Francisco to be $90 per bbl!!(??) If this proves true we will probably sail there immediately! We shall soon see!

October 15

FRIDAY

We are still "hanging to the breeze" this morning & the "old Henry"—feels it! I had a conversation with Capt. Vinall today concerning my religious principles, etc. He presents a lamentable instance of the danger of dividing the affections of the heart between God & the world! He freely conversed with me & asked my opinion in regard to some things which are a source of unhappiness to him. How unworthy am I to point a fellow mortal of superior age, experience & knowledge to the proper version of God's dealings with him!

Oh! for 1 hour with my honored Father, tonight! How do I wish to lay before him the feelings of my young & inexperienced heart in these matters & profit by his good advice & counsel! Too late, alas! too late!!

October 16

SATURDAY

Fourteen months from New Bedford today!! At 12 N Capt. Vinall took an observation and found that we were 125 miles from Oahu. In all probability we will be lying at anchor outside Oahu-reef tomorrow! If it was only New Bedford!!!

October 17

SUNDAY

A fine day and the Sandwich Islands in sight!! Employed in bending on the cable and getting the anchor ready to let go. I trust that on next Sabbath I will have the privilege of attending the House of God! This is a privilege, which I look forward to, with joy & hail with peculiar feelings of delight! May the time hasten when I will be permitted to enjoy this blessed privilege at home!

October 18

MONDAY

8 AM Laying at anchor outside the reef. 11 AM, the Pilot is onboard and we are in the breakers over the reef in tow of—not a steam tug, but some 80 or 100 live Kannakas, who, with most diabolical yells, are taking us in gallantly! Truly a novel method of towing a ship! Beats the celebrated New Orleans steam tugs, with all ease! No danger of bursting a "boiler"!!!!!!!!!

5 PM, moored! This is said to be the most remarkable harbor in the world! Inside of the reef, (which extends for several miles, ¾ of a mile from the beach) the water is as smooth as a milk pond. It reminds me very much of our sea-port cities at home! The dense fleet of shipping with a

forest of masts might possibly "pass" for New York in miniature!

October 19

TUESDAY

Employed in cleaning ship, etc. This afternoon the Rev. S.C. Damon, (Seamen's Chaplain) came aboard and after addressing a few excellent words of advice and kind christian exhortation to the crew, presented us with some tracts and a few copies of his paper, "The Friend,"—a very neat little sheet, mainly devoted to the advancement of religion among the hardy "Sons of Ocean!"—God bless him!

It really appears strange to "read a sign" once more! "Cheap cash store; Groceries & Provisions, store, etc., etc." Convince a man, in spite of himself, that he is really, once more, in the midst of a civilized people!! Notwithstanding this, however, the fact comes home with such blighting force to the sailor that he is still a prisoner & that some time must elapse before he can nail his banner of liberty aloft, that a feeling of melancholy unfits him to enjoy it!

October 20

WEDNESDAY

Employed in "bundling" bone to be shipped home by Bark "Isabella." This evening I attended a prayer meeting in the Sailor's Bethel! I need not say that my mind wandered quickly to my Dear Father's house! I proceeded from there to the Wednesday evening lecture in the 2nd Church and such was the strength of my imagination that I almost heard Mr. Hitchcock expounding the word of life! It appears that in everything around me I am forcibly reminded of home!

This, doubtless arises from the fact that my mind is constantly employed in thinking of it! No letters for me!!! One, and another of the crew receive their letters & the kindling eye & heaving breast betoken good news from friends at home!! But for me, no information from those most dear to me comes, and I feel myself, emphatically alone!!

October 21

THURSDAY

I saw a novel "traveling vehicle" ashore today! It consisted of a small buggy, in which were seated two finely dressed ladies (Americans) engaged in an animated conversation; while they were being "shipped" about from store to store by the large Kannakas! One was forward pulling & the other astern pushing! I suppose that they were afraid to trust their fair persons in tow of a horse, consequently they patronize the "low pressure engine!" Our milkman failed to come off this morning until we had finished our breakfast, the consequence of which was—we had to drink milkless coffee! A severe lecture (of which he did not understand one word) was administered, he replied, in a lengthy appeal to our mercy (I suppose), for we understood nothing, and the matter was compromised satisfactorily to both parties! 4 PM All quiet!!! Employed in bundling bone.

October 22

FRIDAY

Had an opportunity today to see the food of the Natives and their manner of eating! It consists of "raw fish and poi,"—a kind of fermented paste of an acrid taste made from the root of "taro." "Poi," is of two qualities,—one of the consistency of cream & the other about like a thick gruel. The difference is known by the name,—"one, or two fingered poi"! Owing to the fact that it is manufactured by the "mouths" of the Natives I had not "ze confi-dance" to taste it! I am told, however, that it is quite palatable.

October 23

SATURDAY

Employed in boating the bone to Bark Isabella for shipment. A grand "militia muster" took place on shore today! A portion of the King's Royal army led the division preceded by a fine brass band. The "string-beaners" and "thundering-curb-stones" brought up the rear in fine style, gallantly assisted by a base & kettle drum! Looked fierce enough to "pump the salt water in a fellow's eyes," for very fear! I am happy to state that there were no lives lost!!

October 24

SUNDAY

A lovely Sabbath morning! The eternal Spring climate of the Islands—the green & waving trees, the ripe fruits & fragrant flowers—and paramount to all of these, the welcome call of the bell to the House of God and the consequent privilege of attending His sanctuary & joining in the voices of prayer & notes of praise—all, have caused a feeling of thankfulness in my heart which is impossible for me to describe! In a word, I was this morning transported to my native land—to my own dear home! and to any one who enjoys these blessings for the first time in 15 months my remark will be understood & appreciated! At 9 AM I went up to the U.S. Hospital to see two of our men; while there, the

Rev. S.C. Damon came in and after leading in prayer and exhorting the sick & disabled seamen to diligence in the concerns of their souls he distributed among them a few tracts. I gave him "a mite" for the relief of distressed sailors and stepped out in the yard. Right across the street, half hid amidst a labrynth of beautiful flowers stood a neat cottage. One of its occupants—a young lady—was singing a hymn to the tune of "Dundee," accompanied by a piano & as the rich tones of her full musical voice were born to my ear—I was compelled to turn away, with a bleeding heart, as I thought of a painful separation from loved ones at home! At 11 AM, I attended service in the Seamen's Bethel. Rev. S.C. Damon preached from Acts 11c 28 v. He made a beautiful application of the text and proceeded in a clear, faithful & earnest discourse to warn men, particularly seamen, of the final danger & exhorted them to a speedy change of heart. In the afternoon he invited me to his study and I availed myself of his kind offer to peruse some valuable religious works. In the evening I again attended the Bethel. I heard Mr. Damon from Zach 2c 4 v. This sermon was preached especially for the benefit of young men; and my mind quickly averted to Revd H.L. Hitchcock's "service of sermons to young men" at home! Thank God for the privileges of this day!

October 25

MONDAY

Employed today in painting ship. I am surprised to see the evidence of so much industry among the Chinese inhabitants of Honolulu! Some of the richest stores I ever saw are owned & kept by these people! I am also sorry to see the pitiful condition of the poorer classes of Chinese—the "coolies." One instance (which I observed today) I will mention. An American lady was being drawn through the streets of the City in a small buggy by one of these slaves, bare-headed & with scarcely clothes sufficient to cover his nakedness!! I felt disposed to give her a dollar to pay for the hire of a horse—but this of course, would not answer! They are much disliked by the Kannakas on account of their industrious principles; but the "pig-tails" "carry all sail" notwithstanding! The consequence is, they have "plenty of cash in their lockers" and they know how to keep it!

October 26
TUESDAY

Employed today in mooring to receive the Ship "Frances" in which we are going to ship 1000 bbls of oil home. This will be our "hardest job," I suppose, and one which I wish was over with! If any one thinks that hoisting "8 bbl casks of oil" from the hold of one ship over to the deck of another,—an easy job,—why, I say, allow him to enjoy his opinion, most certainly! I must differ with him "slightly!" If I am not thoroughly "cured" before this voyage is over, it will not be because there is a lack of enough to do it!! So ends the day!

October 27
WEDNESDAY

Breaking out oil & transferring it to the deck of the "Frances." Tonight is the regular prayer meeting at the Bethel again & I look forward to the privilege of attending it with joy! My attendance on religious services causes many a jeer from my shipmates, but I care not for this! To spend an evening with the miserable women of "pleasure" (???) is far worse than to spend one in the House of God!!! And I should be indeed foolish to suffer for ever in Hell for the sake of one evening's wandering from the known paths of rectitude! Jeer on, laugh on, mock on, deluded shipmates! God continue to keep me firm, and to open your eyes!!

October 28
THURSDAY

The prayer meeting at the Bethel was well represented by the "Sons of Ocean" last night! I invited one of our harpooneers to go with me last night & he consented. He expressed himself much pleased & promises to go again! Oh! what a blessed privilege is this! But do I appreciate it as I ought? Does my heart indeed go out & long for the enjoyment of these meetings? If I know my own heart, it does! Mingled with every source of joy there is (to me) pain & sorrow! I am not home! There is much more comprehended in that simple sentence than I am capable of describing! God grant a speedy return!

October 29
FRIDAY

Still employed at the oil. There are quite a number of tyrants in port at present! The "leading spirit" among these is the Captain of the "South America." A portion of his crew have refused duty on account of bad treatment! Poor fellows!, they report hard times! Now, only think of a "man" (???) holding a despotic sway over some 20 or 30 inexperienced helpless beings & taking the advantage of a "score of muskets" & "quarter-deck bully-ism,"—triumphantly placing his foot on their necks & proclaiming himself Supreme Ruler of the little world—a ship. I say, only think of this,—and if I had a jackass, that would refuse to lop his ears and blush for shame and pity—I would shave his head & tar & feather him!!!!! God keep me from tyranny in any form!!

October 30
SATURDAY

Still employed at the oil. The progress of the term "civilization" is doing a great deal of harm among the Hawaiians as with the New Zealanders! Vice, in all its forms seems to "reign supreme" and it is fearful, as one beholds the stamp of licentiousness imprinted on the countenances of these miserable beings to think, what a heavy account, its abettors have to render at the bar of a Just God! What a great work is yet to be accomplished before the conversion of the world!!! An evidence of its extreme wickedness is found everywhere, and the picture is truly dark & fearful!!

October 31
SUNDAY

A fine day. Rev. Damon preached in the morning from Num 32c 28 v., in the evening from Mark 13c 33 v. It is interesting to see the vast crowds of Islanders winding their way to God's house on the Sabbath! Home is again brought to mind as I hear the tolling bell and see the crowds of fellow beings coming up to the Bethel! I may be doing wickedly by allowing a feeling of melancholy to pervade my heart, but really, so keenly do I feel my loss that regret, self-reproach & sadness will have the mastery, in spite of all the privileges which I enjoy in Port! I look around me,—not one familiar face meets my anxious eye, no home, no Dear Parents or Sisters—and my heart sinks!!! I look again. The Bethel Flag is calmly floating over the "Ark of Safety," and thither I direct my steps, praying for a submissive heart in all of God's wise dealings with me! At the close of the services I come forth and go—again into that cursed for'castle!! Thus it goes! Sunshine & shade, stormy & calm and with every rose of happiness there lurks beneath the tempting flower, the sharp thorn of misery & wretchedness! I am reaping a severe & terrible reward!

November 1

MONDAY

Employed again at the oil. For one of our ladies at home to see the "fashions" in Honolulu, would be a sight worth seeing! They wear the most beautiful watered & figured silk & satin dresses but their feet & legs are (with some exceptions) both "shoeless & stocking-less." As for "bonnets," a "sailor's Sou' wester," adorned with a feather answers all purposes! Among the exceptions, which I alluded to, are the Queen, the royal family, the maids of honor & the wives of foreigners. These conform to the strict European costume! Speaking of the Queen, she is without doubt "something of a curiosity!" Like the "snuff colored lady," to whom "Uncle Jacob" "constituted" a subject,—she is "big round the waist, like a cow!" I am not prepared to say whether Her Majesty "ever lost her bustle" or not! I don't think, however, that Her Highness "has much need of a bustle!!!!!" I was smoking a cigar today while standing on the pavement in front of a Hotel, when a gentle touch on my "starboard quarter" caused me to look around! There stood a young lady who very modestly requested the loan of my cigar for a moment! I handed her the cigar & after taking a few "draws" she returned it with a captivating wave of the hand & a very polite "good-bye!" I learned afterwards that it is the custom among them to "hail" a fellow in this way & assist him to "make smoke!"

November 2

TUESDAY

The Brig "Baltimore" sailed this morning with the U. S. Mail. I sent some letters home & would prefer being their bearer myself, but that of course is impossible! I have determined to apply to Capt. Vinall for my discharge & if I succeed in getting it I will be home in 5 months from this time!! The bare possibility causes my heart to thrill with joy! Home in 5 months!! That would indeed fill my cup of earthly happiness to overflowing!! The chances are against me, however & I wait with a feeling of alternate hope & despair, which is anything but pleasant!

November 3

WEDNESDAY

Portions of the crew, "Tumbling Jack" in particular, continue to manifest a strange desire to frequent rum shops, and those other trap-doors of hell; and in connection with kindred vices, poison soul & body by drinking rum! Strange infatuation!! It is a source of the greatest wonder to me how "men" possessed of reasoning faculties can deliberately "take up a coal of fire & put it in their bosom!!" Do they not know that it will burn? Truly, the heart of man is "desperately wicked!!" Poor Jack came aboard last night, "minus" his watch-jacket!! Still employed at the oil. So ends the day!

November 4

THURSDAY

Finished at last! 800 bbls, is as much as the Frances will stow and if that gets home safe & we succeed in "filling her up," the next voyage we will be doing pretty well! I again attended the Bethel prayer meeting last night & was much refreshed! The meeting was very interesting in its nature and as usual my mind was busily employed after its close in thinking of like meetings at home!

November 5

FRIDAY

Employed in drawing water & filling pipes & casks. As ships continue to loose their sails & steer for home, my anxiety to start myself, continues to increase! I will plead hard for my discharge, but I fear that I am doomed to bitter disappointment!! The thought of going another voyage in a "Sabbath-Whaling" ship is too much! I have spoken to my friend, Rev. Damon on the subject. He very kindly laid my case before the only true christian Captain in this Port— Capt. Gellett of Ship "Arctic"—a man that never allows his boats to leave the davits for whales on the Sabbath—Capt. Gellet kindly offers to exchange one of his crew for me, but I do not wish to go another voyage in any ship! My great desire is to get home!! My case is in the hands of a "Mightier" than man & I pray for cheerful submission to His All Wise dispensations! May it please Him to grant me the great desire of my heart!

November 6

SATURDAY

Still employed in drawing water. Some of our Officers went ashore today and indulged in a grand "equestrian exercise!!!" I understand that the "Kannaka ponies" got the "weather gauge" of them while racing with some native ladies and that they were very unceremoniously "spilled" overboard! The native ladies are expert & graceful riders, and to see them coursing along the beach or along the verge of the precipices, is almost enough to make a fellow's head swim! They sit, their horses, "a la cavalier" and the long graceful folds of their riding habit renders this rather strange position for a female equestrian, becoming & allowable!! I suppose that this fashion will 'ere long be followed by the ladies in America! "Bloomerism," is but the first step of the ladder whose last rung is—coat, vest, "breeches," boots & spurs! Don't stare ladies! It will not be many years before "Mrs. B.C. & Mrs. D.E. & Miss F.G." etc., will be "holding forth," in every station in life from the Presidress of the U. States, down to "Sally Gordon," boot & shoe maker & general cobbler!! Now, is not that a compliment?!!! So ends the day!

November 7

SUNDAY

Another beautiful day. Rev. Damon preached in the morning from Isaiah & in the evening from Matthew. Excellent sermons, abounding in good solid advice & counsel! In the afternoon I was invited to attend a prayer meeting at the house of a merchant living on the "valley-road"—John Diamond, Esq. I proceeded to the house. Everything bore the mark of affluence and I hesitated to enter. I stood a few moments by the side of the door & was about to go away when a lady came out and kindly invited me to come in. I went. The meeting was held in a magnificently furnished room and as I cast my eyes around the room I did not see a single sailor beside myself there! Then came a struggle! Pride, cursed pride, was master of my heart! Most strange to me because I never experienced like feelings before! It seemed that the eyes of every one present were directed to my "sailor clothes"!! The meeting was opened by prayer, followed by singing a hymn, which was accompanied by a parlor organ. Shall I write the rest? Yes!—for I wish to see my great error and never commit its like again! Pride galled me, and charged me with being an unwelcome intruder (notwithstanding the fact that the meeting was held for sailors expressly), and finally, blushing with shame, I arose and left the room, left a holy privilege which I may never have again, left the society of christians; and wandered forth, more miserable than ever!!! God in mercy forgive that sad fall! What am I? A worm! A poor dying worm & shall "pride" ever cause me to fall again! God forbid! How applicable are the words of Job, "God hath delivered me to the ungodly and turned me over into the hands of the wicked. I was at ease but He hath broken me asunder. He hath also taken me, by my neck and shaken me to pieces & set me up for His mark!! Job 16 c 11.12 verses.

November 8

MONDAY

I went to Capt. Vinall today & requested my discharge! At first, he would not hear to it at all, but he at length gave me to understand that he will discharge me, after getting the ship ready for sea! Already, it appears like a new life! I am compelled to sacrifice my all to gain this object, but so strong is my desire to get home that I would sacrifice my right hand!!! It may well be supposed that a lighter heart fill my breast tonight! Indeed, I am almost beside myself with joy! And who would not be? Who could refrain from feeling the greatest joy in the prospect of a speedy deliverance from a life of misery and a speedy restoration to a life of happiness?!! Not I!!

November 9
TUESDAY

Employed in getting off water. Preparations are rapidly making to get to sea again! Some 14 or 15 months will elapse before the "old Henry" will "bring up" at New Bedford! Thank God. I have a prospect of being home in 5 months from this time! No one knows how I long to see my Dear Parents & Sisters again!!

November 10
WEDNESDAY

Great excitement exists on shore today between the sailors & Natives! A sailor was murdered in one of the cells of the fort last night by one of the attending officers (an Englishman) and as soon as it was known abroad, sailors of all nations collected in great numbers around the fort, determined to demolish it, then secure and lynch the murderer! A large force of soldiers (Natives) are collected inside the fort & every preparation made by the government to resist the mob & maintain order!

November 11

THURSDAY

Last evening the mob increased in numbers and formed itself into a regular battalion under the command of a chosen leader! At about 8 o'clock the firing of pistols, muskets, etc. told a tale of a deadly conflict for the ascendancy between the sailors & military! The sailors proved too much for them, and after driving the soldiers in disgrace from the place of combat they proceeded to fire the city! They began with the "Harbor Master's office," on one of the wharves. After firing the office, the intentions of the mob to burn the city were with-drawn & no more property was destroyed! The U.S. Consul delivered an address to the mob this evening, begging of them in the name of the American Republic to disperse and faithfully promising justice to the cause of the murdered seaman. This has had the effect of producing something like quiet.

November 12

FRIDAY

"The valiant company," known as the "Tin-pan, Cadets" (composed entirely of "Skippers") had a grand parade today! The object of the parade was to strike terror into the hearts of the mob! But alas, for the bravery of the immortal Cadets, the mob had all dispersed!! It was really amusing to see these "bold soldiers boy's" walking "erect" and proudly bearing arms in defence of His Majesty, "Kammeahmeah III." While marching in an open street every eye beamed forth with true bravery, but when about to turn a corner, there were evident preparations for a foot race!!!! I would pity the unfortunate carcass of a sheep that would arrest the attention of the Cadets; for while a few would be applying cold water to the temples of those who had fainted on seeing it, the rest would certainly "walk into it" with sword & bayonet & do their best to wreathe for themselves a crown of laurel! Oh! if "Old Jack, Napoleon or the Duke of Wellington" had seen the brave Cadets as they were seen today, how would they grieve to think that in their entire armies they had not such brave soldiers as them! But a truce to this eulogy, indeed the Cadets might possibly overhaul my flattering eulogy, and then my poor body might possibly be riddled with—"a rope's end!"

Quiet has been in great measure restored on shore but a bitter feeling still rankles in the hearts of the sailors! I am sorry that the affair has occurred & most sincerely wish that the whole matter may have a speedy & peaceful finale!

November 13

SATURDAY

All quiet on shore! "Jack" has ceased to cruise on "warlike tack," has "wove around" and is now "standing along" under easy sail; the same thoughtless, devil-may-care generous, tar as ever!! This is a day of joy to me!! Capt. Vinall met me in the city today & told me to get ready to be discharged on next Monday!! When he told me my heart was full! I thanked God for His mercies unto me and the prospect of soon being at home caused my heart to thrill again with true & unfeigned thankfulness & joy! Employed today in getting ready to go home!!! Really, it appears more like a dream than reality!!

November 14

SUNDAY

Rev. Damon preached in the morning from Mark owing to the late riot, seamen are compelled to go on board their ships at sun down, consequently I am debarred the privilege of attending the Bethel tonight! Well, I hope soon to be where the entire Sabbath day may be spent in the worship of God with none to molest or make afraid!

November 15

MONDAY

3 of the crew deserted last night & in consequence I am compelled to stay on board all day. Capt. Vinall told me this morning that I will have to wait 'til the ship gets outside the reef before he can discharge me! The desertion of three men is not much in my favor, but still, I dare not harbor the thought that Capt. Vinall will forfeit his word! To be disappointed now just as the glorious star of liberty is dawning, would indeed crush my heart & increase my misery ten fold! We shall soon see!

November 16

TUESDAY

Head winds prevent us from getting out today and here I am, still a prisoner and I begin to fear that there is a pretty fair prospect to remain so for one more voyage!! I may be wrong, however, (God grant that I am) in forming this opinion & allowing these fears to take hold of me! I know that "appearances are deceitful" but it is not often that I "miss my reckoning"!! Last night the officers promenaded the deck under arms!—prepared to "bring any one to" with a leaden messenger, that left the ship!

November 17

WEDNESDAY

Two more of the crew deserted last night and this morning the cooper was discharged. 1 PM Wind hauled fair; got under way & proceeded outside the reef. 2 PM Laying at anchor outside. 11 PM No discharge yet!! Can it be possible that I have been wantonly duped!! Have my feelings been trifled with? Does Capt. Vinall remember his promise!! Oh! God, if I am doomed to disappointment, if all of those bright hopes so fondly cherished, of soon being at home, are destined to be crushed, if I must go another voyage in this cursed ship, if I must be kept away from home & friends for many long & bitter months of misery yet to come,—if all these be true,—do Thou sustain me!!! Such is life! I am but the play-thing of destiny & a miserable man!

November 18

THURSDAY

Day dawned upon an anxious heart in this ship! One, whose every fibre seemed to be strung to its utmost as alternate hope & despair now caused it to throb quickly in happy anticipation and now sink dead & forsaken as uncertainty, gloomy dark uncertainty, rose up in all its terrors before me! At 4 PM I was ordered into a boat to go ashore for Capt. Vinall. This was my last hope! I thought that if I plead with him ashore he would redeem his promise! When about half way to the city we met him coming out in a shore-boat! He got in the ship's boat, and looking me coolly in the face said, "Well Cloud, I guess you must go another voyage with me"!!

My bursting heart sunk! I could say nothing, and with a crushed & bleeding soul I pulled my oar for the ship! xxxxxxxxxxxxxxxxxxxxxxxxxxxxxxxxxxxxxxxxxxxxxxxxxx*

I came aboard and went down in the for'castle. There, with my face buried in my hands, I felt myself alone! Blank despair took entire possession of my wounded spirit and I now write and sick, despairing, miserable, and alone, I close my book!!

November 19

FRIDAY

The rippling of the deep blue water of the Pacific at the bows is proof positive that I am once more afloat! But, alas! not bound home!!! 15 long months at last loom up between us with the dimensions of the mighty ocean itself and oh! how long & bitter do they appear!!

Patience, poor heart!! Dear beloved Parents & Sisters, God wills that our separation shall be widened! Oh! for a heart to feel that, "Thy holy will, howsoe'er it cross my own in all things be done!"

November 20

SATURDAY

A fine morning and out of sight of land. It appears impossible to subdue my feelings! 8 PM Unwell,—decidedly sick! My sore disappointment seems hard, but it is the will of God!!

*Enoch used these series of x's to emphasize a separate thought so as to highlight it on a page.

November 21
SUNDAY

Confined to my bunk with sickness. My pain has been great all day! Not only do I suffer physical pain but also mental agony! If ever I was miserable in my life, if ever I suffered disappointment, if ever I felt that I was but a solitary speck on the great ocean of life—that time is now!! To feel this, to be made keenly sensible of it, produces a state of mind the horrors of which are only known to those who have experienced them! The kind attention of a Dear Mother are missed and their want felt! Experience some comfort in reading my Bible.

November 22
MONDAY

Still confined to my bunk. Capt. Vinall denominates my affection,—the "Ship Fever." I can safely lay the whole at the door of the "Home Fever," and prescribe for a certain cure, a passage home in the first ship that we speak!

November 23
TUESDAY

Still very sick! As my sufferings continue to rack my body, I am led to look more steadily, I trust, up to the great "Physician of Souls," who is ever ready, able & willing to make whole the sick! The heart-rending reality of a cruel separation from loved ones at home continues to force itself upon my mind and is well calculated to add another sting to the fierce worm of disappointment!

November 24

WEDNESDAY

Still confined to my bunk, with some slight symptoms of returning health. It is absolutely necessary that I must gain the mastery of my feelings! Duty, which I owe to my employees & myself, cannot be faithfully performed as long as despair and melancholy are allowed to take entire possession of my feelings, and I am determined to endeavor to go on, just as though the great desire of my soul was accomplished! This will cost something. I am aware, for although I now see & acknowledge the "All Wise hand of God" in my disappointment, still its effect is terrible upon my mind! Some say that disappointment "in love," exceeds all grades of misery!

November 25

THURSDAY

Feel some better today! A short cruise on deck this morning had the effect of "righting ship" in some measure and a gentle fan from "Boreas's tropical billows," brought back the flush of returning health! The great "cure all" of a ship's medicine chest—"calomel"—has "taken a fancy" to me, I am afraid! Would prefer giving him a wide berth but of course I must avail myself of the only remedy on ship-board!

November 26

FRIDAY

Still improving! My "lower spars" (legs) are "all aback" today, the consequence of imprudently coming on deck yesterday! "Mr Calomel" and "contact with damp decks" don't agree well together, I see! Must "brace for'rad" pretty soon!

November 27

SATURDAY

Feel much better today! "Calomel" seems to have claimed me for a victim, sure enough for a time at least! My knee joints, hip joints, etc. are sadly out rig, and give me much pain! Don't think it will last long. I hope not at any rate!

November 28

SUNDAY

A beautiful day. Raised whales and lowered!! The same old yarn! Can't scrub decks because it is the Sabbath, but if not successful in taking whale on the Sabbath, profane & abusive language, can be used with a will!! Strange inconsistency! I "hobbled" on deck after the boats were lowered & if I ever prayed with fervor, it was then that they might not strike! Home, sweet home!!

November 29

MONDAY

Another fine day. We are once more nearing the line, bound on a cruise in the South Pacific for Sperm Whales. This time, "Old Neptune" dare not perform any of his "Jonny Raw" tricks upon us, for we have all become sailors! The ordeal has been passed, the crossed "3 times" & we are regularly appointed "true sons of Neptune"!! So, "Pass Neptune," just "keep off," "points free," and give us plenty of sea-room!

November 30
TUESDAY

Another month has whirled swiftly on, so swiftly indeed, that it seems but yesterday when October's dying groans were ringing in our ears and silently pointing to that awful word, "Eternity"! What a wise arrangement of God that man is ignorant of the future! And yet, how ridiculously feeble is his puny arm which he boastingly stretches out and pro-claims himself strong and great and wise!! Poor fool!! His excellency of wisdom, strength & greatness is but foolish in the sight of God! God looks down upon Earth's mightiest noblest men and pities the worm who is fast passing away! 'Tis strange (at last) that men will forget that they are but "as a vapor which appeareth for a little time and then vanisheth away!"

December 1
WEDNESDAY

At home, the first day of the dreary winter; here, however, the weather is extremely hot! About 4 day's sail from Navigator's Islands, whither we are bound for fruit, hogs, etc. There is a rumor afloat that we are going to come to an anchor there, for the purpose of coopering oil. I wish that we will, for I should love to explore the hidden beauties of that "fairy-land," and enjoy the delights of a day's cruise mid its beautiful, spicy groves!

December 2
THURSDAY

A hot day! Employed in "setting up" rigging. "Cruising" in the fore-yard at night, for sleeping while on watch, continues to form a portion of the endless routine of a sailor's life! By the way, the Officer of the deck who sends us up sleeps as much as any of us! "Morpheus" is a particular friend of his, and I have come to the conclusion that he is troubled with the "green-eyed-monster," "jealousy"!! If he dreams, (while holding sweet intercourse with the "drowsy god") that any of us are following his example, he is sure to wake up, come for'rad and very unceremoniously remind us that, "this ship wears a fore-yard"!! We have become accustomed to these little "head-winds," however & have only to "brace up" and beat to windward"! So ends the day!

December 4

SATURDAY

Another hot day! Employed in sundry ship's duties. "Tumbling Jack," came up to me today and with apparent earnest curiosity, wished to know "if he could not purchase a good large pair of "gold specs," for $300!!!" I referred him to one of my messmates, (an old salt) for an answer! Jack went to him, put the question & received for an answer the promise of a rope's end, for being crazy!!

December 5

SUNDAY

Another Sabbath has set in, bright & beautiful! But alas! the blessed privileges of the day are all forfeited and it is to be spent in servile labor! Oh! may the time hasten when this holy day will be given to the sailor—when even one hour will be appropriated for divine worship! To one who has enjoyed the privileges which a christian Father's house afford; their forfeiture creates an aching void which must be felt to be known!

December 6

MONDAY

Navigator's Islands right ahead! Owing to a light wind we cannot get in 'til tomorrow. The view on shore is fine & one must indeed be unnatural if he fails to enjoy it! How I would love to have my friend, "Orve" here today! Not in the capacity of a whaleman, but if it were possible to have the "Doc" standing by my side, and listening to his peculiar rich voice, remind him of a certain adventure of ours in Columbus,—the night that we "stood-by" to frustrate a certain young man in his intention of kid-napping a certain young lady! Will those days ever return Orve? Ah no! Our dreams Dear Orve, were too bright to become reality!!! I am single yet & mind you Orve if you have spliced to a "rib"—look out for squalls from a "cloudy" quarter!!!

December 7

TUESDAY

3 PM "Harry," the Pilot is on board and we are now heading in for "Pago-pago" harbor (Toutouilla). 6 PM Laying at anchor in one of the loveliest harbors in the world! I dare not attempt a description for I do not wish to mar the beauty of this Eden in doing so! 9 PM The decks have been crowded with Natives (males solely) since 6 o'clock, and the idea of eating a piece of salt junk & a biscuit is altogether preposterous!! Our friends from shore not very politely appropriated these necessaries for their own palates & gave

us in exchange pineapples, oranges, bread-fruit, yams, taro, cocoa-nuts, etc! Not an unwelcome exchange!

December 8

WEDNESDAY

Employed in rigging the "burden & purchase tackles" for hoisting out casks. A more muscular & finely formed race of people exist not on the face of the earth than the inhabitants of this island! I can safely say that I never saw "true beauty" before coming here! Being unrestrained by the "latest Paris fashions" nothing tends to deform the truly noble, symmetrical frames which with God has blessed them! How would I love to see the "wasp-waisted" coquette of America stealing an envious peep at one of the literal "venus de medici" of this island! Behold her ye slaves to "fashion," ye self murderess, as she treads her native soil, nobly proportioned, ornamented with jewels from the cabinet of her Creator, a living, walking, noble monument of God! If some of the misguided "belles" of my native land could only see these women, I venture the assertion that "stays, corsets, pads, rouge, wash-waists, flounces, diamonds, perfumed silk stockings, 40 petticoats, bustles, low-necked-dresses & fancy beau catches" would appear to them the most detestable lot of "tom foolery" that ever pride invented!! Now girls, don't put me on the "black list"! I am no woman-hater! On the contrary, I claim to be a devoted friend to the "weaker sex," one of their most faithful admirers,—but really, I have no patience with a coquette who borrows her every charm!

December 9

THURSDAY

A most beautiful day! Employed in breaking out casks and getting off water. The change from "salt-junk & hard-bread" to the most delicious tropical fruits has had the effect of brightening the glow of health on the cheeks of the crew and taking this circumstance in connection with an occasional cruise on shore, some of the crew are in danger of "forgetting to come on board again!" Had I no friends, no Dear Parents, or Sisters,—no tie to bind me to my native land, I would never leave this island! But notwithstanding the talismanic beauty of this "Eden No. 2"—the society of loved ones at home is paramount & nothing in this world can ever take its place!!

December 10

FRIDAY

Employed in rafting off water. The labors of the English Missionary at this place, (Rev. Mr. Powell) have been crowned with signal blessings & their effect is plainly observable in every one from the mere child to the grey headed adult! In the course of a cruise on shore last evening I "came to an anchor" in the house of an Islander where were collected some 15 or 20 persons (Natives), male & female. A lively conversation immediately ensued and many a ringing peal of laughter burst from the entire company as I attempted to repeat words in their native tongue, as they were dictated by a lovely young Princess at my side, whose name is "Su-soon-ga." By the way, she has taken "quite a fancy" to me, judging by appearances, but I must not allow my head to roam for it is the property of another, unknown; although, the sky seems destined to be obscured with clouds forever!! Still, I . . . Enough for the present!

I have been digressing & I must retrace my steps. The above mentioned "conversation" was kept up 'til dark. A lamp was then lighted & at a signal from one of the company all was as silent as the grave! It was a curious spectacle! I looked around the room, in the face of each one I observed a calm & holy expression of true reverential awe—not a studied, hypocritical attempt to appear so, but a simple unmistakable expression of reverence! My curiosity became excited in regard to their intentions! In a moment, however, I saw the cause! A soul-stirring melody rich, full & spirited arose like the gentle breeze of ocean and in five minutes, (after each one had joined in singing) I sat & listened to the most delicious strains of music that ever greeted my ear! It was emphatically "the music of the soul!" After the close of the hymn all kneeled and a prayer which for earnest, feeling-fervor (as far as I could judge from the manner of its delivery & from the emphasis of the leader) I never heard exceeded! It was a time of most peculiar delight to my soul! Coming so unexpected its tendency was to surprise & give me joy at one & the same time! I learn that this is the daily custom in every house on the Island! My language in regard to the occurrences of the evening, may perhaps appear "well stocked" with enthusiasm,—well, I have only to say that I have but imperfectly penned the true sentiments of my heart & if my accusers (if I have any) will but go there, see what I saw and after that, charge me with enthusiasm—why I will have to come to the disagreeable conclusion, "that they are possessed of just, no soul at all"!! So ends the day!

December 11
SATURDAY

A hot day. Employed in getting off wood & water. "This is certainly an age of wonders!" A novel proposition was made to me today, one which for a short time made me feel "quite all-over-ish," as Sam Slick has it! Well, "murder will out," and so "here goes,"—the proposition was nothing more nor less than a pressing invitation from the beautiful Princess "Su-soon-ga," to splice my heart strings to her's and become her—"better three quarters"!! There's no use "dodging" it made me feel "curious"! But principle must have its sway with me, and I informed the lovely girl that it was impossible to act in accordance with her wishes! I found no little difficulty in impressing her that I must not, dare not, accede to her proposition! Poor girl! She thinks "there is plenty of room for me to live here," and is extremely slow to believe that "America is blessed with a female who is capable of filling the endearing station of wife!" Her simple language, as she speaks to me in broken English, appears peculiarly interesting. I was much amused today to hear her say, "that I would speak to her, all the same," Mr. Powell speak "his dear wife!" Alas! Su-soon-ga, this is a life of disappointment from the cradle to the grave and it causes a feeling of sorrow to fill my heart when I think that even you, a simple, unsophisticated, artless inhabitant of Polynesia, will have many a dark cloud of life's ills to shade your sunny path, and that this side of heaven, there is no enduring happiness!

December 12
SUNDAY

This is a day which I never can forget! Rev. Mr. Powell kindly invited the ship's company to divine worship at the church on shore & at 11 AM Capt. Vinall, the Officers, & the crew went ashore & proceeded to the chapel! He preached a most feeling discourse from S. John 5 c. 39v. I believe it was the most interesting sight I ever witnessed! There, in one corner of the large bamboo edifice were seated our crew & as the man of God proceeded in his discourse, every man was drawn forward as it were, and when he had concluded his discourse, I believe that every man was sorry that it did not continue longer!! At the conclusion of the service, I stepped outside the door into a grove of Pine-apples and there I found my old friend "Powla" who was waiting to invite me to his house for dinner! To gratify him I accompanied him to his house where I found a truly excellent dinner prepared! It is proper to state that the dinner was all cooked yesterday! Not one moment of the Sabbath day is devoted to servile labor of any sort. It is a day of rest. A day devoted to the service of the Great God of heaven, the earth & the sea! A suggestion presents itself to my mind, (in the form of a question) as I meditate on these facts and it is this. "Is there not a lesson to be learned from these simple minded Islanders?" Where is the body of christians on the face of the globe that observe such a conscientious regard for the Sabbath day? And is it proper, is it christ-like, is it charitable, to call these people a heathen people? At 2 PM a sabbath-school (for the Natives) assembled at the chapel which I attended. If persons in christian lands feel disposed to become discouraged as they look out upon the mighty work to be accomplished by Missionaries—they should by all means be an eye-witness to true evidence of change of heart as they are seen among this & other people inhabiting the "Island World" of the Pacific! It may well be supposed that my mind wandered quickly to my home as I found myself once more in a Sabbath School! God hasten my return! At 4 PM a portion of the crew again repaired to the chapel and listened to another excellent address from Mr. Powell. He chose for a foundation of some truly feeling remarks, the passage in Mark (15c. 31v.). "He saved others, himself he cannot save." The privileges of this day came altogether unexpected and I sincerely hope that they will not "rise up in judgement" against any one of the crew!

December 13

MONDAY

A hot day. Employed in getting off wood & water. A beautiful figure, a well developed form & a peculiar "simple gracefulness"—are (I safely say) the least attractive features of the female inhabitants of this Island! "Firm, unyielding purity,—a total abstinence from lasciviousness in any form, & a deep-seated animosity toward "pleasure," (which gold can not remove) shine forth with a brilliancy far exceeding the costliest diamond of the first-water, and fitly adorn the dark-skinned beauty of Polynesia—as she ranks "A No. 1" in point of all that make women, "angels on earth"!!!!

December 14

TUESDAY

Still employed at the wood & water. Much speculation exists among the crew in regard to stepping on the Island! Some are for returning home, clubbing together, purchasing a small craft & coming back to the island. "Tumbling Jack" proposes to desert now! We soon frightened him out of that notion, however! I think there is a small probability that any one will "finish his castle!" There is one "draw-back," connected with a desire to live here permanently and that is the great numbers of lizards, centipedes, etc., which really seem to abound everywhere! While sitting in the chapel on Sunday I saw several huge green lizards cruising "in rather unpleasant proximity to my head!!" And while walking from one place to another the paths before one are literally covered with these ugly fellows as they lie basking in the sun! Not bit or stung yet! "Good-luck," I suppose!! So ends the day!

December 15

WEDNESDAY

Larboard watch on shore today, on liberty. I came to anchor this morning at the house of my friend "Powla," where I have been logging my adventures for the past 4 days. It is rather a "poor study," however, for I am surrounded by a score, on more of young "fifteen gas" (girls) who seem to take great delight in "pulling my whiskers," hiding my ink and a great many other childish pranks too numerous to mention! It were a sin to stop them, for their merry ringing laugh brings to mind the lovely countenance of a dear little sister at home & I love to see them happy!

December 16

THURSDAY

Employed today in "stowing off," between decks. As our liberty has been stopped, I suppose that our stay here will be short. I regret this in some measure for the reason that it is the only place that ever I have met with, in which I could discern a similarity to home! We are bound on a cruise to the

Southward & I am very sorry to learn that we will again visit Wanganui (New Zealand).

December 17
FRIDAY

Called at daylight & "hove short" for sailing. At 5 AM we "cat-headed" the anchors, "sheeted home" the top sails & to'gallant sails, "set the courses," and slowly left the far famed harbor of "Pago-pago"! On nearing the mouth of the harbor, it grew calm & we found that we were not "holding our own"! A few moments sufficed to show us that a strong current was fast drifting the ship on the rocks & the Boats were immediately lowered & we commenced towing! It was a "rub & a go" & for 5 hours we had a sample of what is denominated in whalemen's parlance, "hard work!" We succeeded at length in getting clear of the current, and after running out to a safe distance, we hauled-aback the main-top-sail, cleared away the Starboard & Waist Boats & proceeded once more to the city. At 12 N the King sent us an invitation to come to his house and take dinner! The 2nd Officer was unanimously appointed "chairman" and we followed him to the residence of the King. A dinner was prepared, which savored much of "European style," and we afterwards found that the refreshments were really prepared by Mrs. Powell!! Thanks to that christian lady for this little act of kindness to sailors! God bless her! After loading the boats with fruit we bid Toutouilla a final farewell & pulled for the ship. 7 PM The "old Henry's" swelling canvass is an evidence of the strength of the noble breeze which is wafting us swiftly toward "the other extreme"—"Wanganui"!! So ends the day!

December, 1852

December 18
SATURDAY

Out of sight of land! The wind freshened last night and in the mid-watch, we handled the to'gallants & flying-jib. This morning, a stiff "top-sail-breeze" is blowing with a pretty fair prospect of a visit from—"Boreas & Co."! Employed in "stowing the anchors" & various deck jobs! So ends!

December 19
SUNDAY

An unpleasant day! The wind freshened last night and in the first watch it was deemed necessary to "single-reef" the main & mizzen & "double-reef" the fore-top-sails! This morning, Capt. Vinall called me into the cabin and gave me some religious reading matter. My thanks are due him for this kind consideration & I also thank God for the opportunity thus offered to peruse religious books in connection with my Bible! So ends the day!

December 20
MONDAY

Weather still unpleasant. Employed in cutting wood. "Tumbling Jack" is exceedingly angry with himself,—"almost mad enough to fight" (!!!) because he did not desert while in Toutouilla! He had his "fortune made" (in imagination) with a return home over burdened with gold—but Jack's "castle" soon capsized!

December 21
TUESDAY

Weather still remains unpleasant. Watch employed in various ship's duties. After cruising in the vicinity of "French

Rock," (a noted ground) for Sperm Whales, we will again go in to Wanganui. This fact "hurts my feelings," to say the least, but I must patiently submit! "There's a good time coming" as the "Hutchinsons" have it, but it really appears to be in no "particular hurry" getting here! So ends the day!

December 22

WEDNESDAY

A fine day. Employed in cutting wood, repairing sails, etc. "always something to do on board a Yankee Whaler!" "No news by the evening chronicle!!!" So ends!!

December 23

THURSDAY

Another fine day. Employed in sail-making, etc. "Tumbling Jack" & "P. D., Esq." "ran afoul" of each other today! The vanquished party entered complaint to Capt. Vinall! He ordered them both on deck and "seizing" their left hands together gave each a piece of "rattling stuff" and compelled them to "fight it out!" "P.D." is an unusually inoffensive man & he forbore to strike Jack at all! "Jack," on the contrary, is "full of spunk," and he "swung it into" "P.D." in a manner that would make a "boatswain of a man o'war stare!" In a few moments Jack expressed himself well satisfied and Capt. Vinall ordered them to be separated. Thus far, Jack came off 1st best! But a "change came o'er his dream!" Capt. Vinall put "unfortunate Jack" in the mizzen rigging & gave him as much as he gave P.D!! 6 PM All quiet!!!!!

December, 1852

December 24
FRIDAY

Employed today in working in the rigging,—unbending the old & sending up the new fore-top-sail, etc. Spoke Whaling Bark "Columbia," 16 mos. from Sag Harbor with 1000 bbls Right Whale oil.

December 25
SATURDAY

Once more shipmates, a "merry christmas"(???) to you all! "Merry," indeed—as far as a hard days work is concerned!! Had a "roast pig" for dinner, which is the only remarkable fact connected with the day! I have been thinking in what manner said "grunter" would die, if the cook had not killed him! (11 PM Have come to no definite conclusion yet!!) Spoke Bark "Columbia" again today!

December 26
SUNDAY

A beautiful morning! "French Rock" on our lee. Some 4 or 5 ships are in sight, some of them boiling & some chasing whales. As usual, the day is to be spent in servile labor and God only knows, how I long to get freed from this worse than detestable occupation! To get home!! Often as I contrast my present, miserable life with what it was once, and what it might be now,—my very soul groans in agony! Home has attractions surpassed alone by heaven!

December 27
MONDAY

Employed in cutting wood, etc. 6 PM Spoke Whale Bark "Awashonks." Captain came on board and during the remainder of the night we sailed in company. Weather very warm & sultry. How would I love to hear from "A*xxxx*a" tonight! Affections which are fixed in youth and which "grew with our growth" are hard to be uprooted! I know not whether we will ever meet again on earth! But I do believe that we will meet & be happy together—in heaven!!

Oh! that others knew what I know!! But so it is & I must not complain!

December 28
TUESDAY

Becalmed. Still employed in cutting wood with nothing transpassing of sufficient interest to log! "Orve, Pete, Edith, Amelia,"—members of the "Mutual"!! how fare ye all to-night!! Does one single thought of the sailor ever dwell in your breasts,—or have the changes of life left no place in your memory for your— friend!! Alas! my dreams were too bright!!! I am but the wreck of what I was in those halcyon days of anticipation! God, direct me in the right channel and bring me to the safe Harbor of Heaven! God bless you all!!

December 29
WEDNESDAY

Still becalmed! The look-out aloft caused some excitement on deck this morning by reporting the breaching of a whale! Got the boats in readiness to lower, but we were doomed to disappointment! A rock, with the sea breaking over it was the cause of our delusion, and we concluded not to "fasten" to it!!

December 30

THURSDAY

Still becalmed! Several sail of vessels in sight but no chance to speak them—"want of wind!!" No Sperm Whales yet! A bounty of $10 is offered this morning for "head & flukes," so look sharp a-loft!!

December 31

FRIDAY

A fine day! Raised a school of Sperm Whales! Lowered. In a few moments, the Starboard Boat went on & struck! The irons drew & he escaped! Further pursuit was fruitless! Try again!! I suppose that he was a poor whale at any rate! (Sour grapes!!!) The last day of the Old Year!! Two years ago I was home. I was happy! But poor fool, I did not know it!! Well, I've learned it now & I've paid for my learning!!!

1853

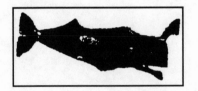

1853

The Past!!!

1853

The Future!!!

"The New Years' morn! With a voice it comes,
And it tells us, "life is fleeting"
Like a wave that a moment curls, and foams,
And anon, is seen retreating!
It tells of a world to come, where sin
Ne'er soweth the seeds of sorrow,
And it bids us hasten that world to win
Ere dawneth a hopeless morrow!"

January, 1853

January 1
SATURDAY

was ushered in bright & beautiful! As may be supposed, my mind quickly dwelt with loved-ones at home! My mind's eye dwelt long & lovingly on each dear one and such was the strength of my imagination that, at times, it really appeared that the New Year had dawned upon me at home!! But, "there is no rose without a thorn"—and stern reality left me bitterly lamenting my voluntary launch into a cold, unfeeling world and the consequent deprivation of any thing like enjoyment! If I am alive one year from today, I will be (I trust) half way home!! 2 PM Spoke Whaling Bark "Commodore Queble." She succeeded in taking a Sperm Whale yesterday & is now boiling him out. Capt Vinall boarded her & a few hours were pleasantly passed in conversation concerning home & friends! A bright "Oasis," on the great desert of Ocean! So ends the day!!

January 2
SUNDAY

A fine day. This morning Capt. Vinall called me into the cabin and gave me some tracts to distribute among the crew. The day has been spent (when I found time) in reading my Bible and in meditation. This is a daily duty and I have often felt that Christ was precious to my soul while engaging in it! Although a very weak follower of Christ, still I would not exchange my hope for 10,000 worlds like this!!

January 3
MONDAY

Another fine day. Employed in making spun-yarn & sinnet, repairing sails & various other work-up jobs on deck.

A sharp look-out aloft is kept for Sperm Whales and I suppose that "Old Henry's time," is not very far distance!

January 4
TUESDAY

10 AM Raised a school of Sperm Whales! Lowered. In a short time the Starboard Boat went on & struck! The 4th Officer was taken out of the Boat by the line but miraculously escaped unhurt! After being struck, the Whale rolled on her side and showing an ugly row of sharp teeth made for the Boat! Got out of her way & in a few moments after she was—a dead whale! Took her to the ship, made sail, and bore away for the remaining Boats—in pursuit of the remainder of the school. At about 5 Pm the Bow Boat succeeded in fastening to another fine one! He drew the irons, however, & escaped! At about 7, the Waist Boat succeeded in getting on & struck another! Just at dark he was a dead Whale! 8 PM Set signal lights on the ship & in the boats. 22 ½ PM Whales both moored! 2 AM Got something to eat & set the watch!!

January 5
WEDNESDAY

4 AM called all hands and commenced "cutting in." 22 AM finished cutting and started the works. Unfortunately, there are no ships in sight to witness our "good luck!!" After cutting in, I "took an observation," not of the Sun's lower limb, or the Planet Mars, but the "blubber-room," in the greasy latitude of which I am ordered to cruise!! After working my "apparent time," & applying the "altitude & Polar distance," I find said "blubber-room" lays somewhere

between the Fore & Main masts!! ("Straight jackets" in good demand.)

January 6
THURSDAY

Boiling. It appears "somewhat natural" to see the thick, dark columns of smoke rising over the deck of the ship, and brings to mind hard work in the coming season in Japan Sea! Well, there is one consolation at any rate! It will be the last season among those limber-tailed "coach-whips"!! My last, I mean!

January 7
FRIDAY

22 AM Finished boiling. 22 N. A gale of wind is blowing furiously, but I think it came on "in too much of a hurry" to last long! 5 PM gale moderated! Employed in cleaning up decks, etc. So ends the day.

January 8
SATURDAY

A fine day! All hands employed in tarring, rigging, etc. A general preparation for going into Port! This is "labor, thrown away," for the "Maures" (New Zealanders) are not very particular in regard to appearances!! Must be "in fashion"!!

January 9
SUNDAY

A high wind has been blowing all day. New Zealand in sight on our weather bow! Have been "beating" all day in order to make the harbor of Wanganui. At 5 PM saw a Bark. Signalized her. She flew the "Cross of St. George." So ends the day!

January 10
MONDAY

A gale of wind set in this morning accompanied with rain & fog, rendering it impossible to see a ship's length ahead! In this condition we found ourselves this morning some-where in "Doubtless Bay,"—could not see land but we knew that it was close to us! Our situation was anything than enviable, for very few persons will be found who would like to strike on the coast of New Zealand during such a gale as that which raged this morning! After barely missing an ugly rock on our larboard bow we were enabled to see (by a partial clearing of the fog) the entrance to the harbor! We "pointed her in" and away we went with a roaring gale right in our wake! Had we have made one fourth of a mile to windward of the point which we did make—the "old Henry's bones" (and perhaps some of the crew's) would have been all that was left! We ran in a short distance and let go both the anchors. Came near capsizing the ship & wrenching out the windlass when she "came to"!! I never experienced such a heavy gale before! The Whale Ship "Albiou" is the only ship in Port. Once more in Wanganui!

January 11
TUESDAY

The gale has abated and this is a fine clear day! Employed in getting off water. The "Albion" went ashore yesterday during the heighth of the gale, but with great exertion on the part of the crew, she was got off without being materially damaged!—"Wanganui!!" The same dreary, cheerful hole! Not a single improvement–oh! yes, I do remark, another grass hut ! I will be lenient on the miserable hole, however, for it affords an opportunity to write home!

January 12
WEDNESDAY

Employed in stowing oil! This is a new version of Port-duties, but, "if not at this, at something worse!" So, we will make a "virtue of necessity," and stow oil! Nothing sufficiently interesting to log! So ends the day!

January 13
THURSDAY

Finished stowing oil. Employed in cleaning up. There certainly is not much danger of Wanganui becoming the commercial mart of the South Pacific! The Natives are not celebrated for enterprise and with the exception of one or two "cute ones" among them who barter honey, apples, gooseberries, etc, for "what ever they can get," the heighth of their ambition seems to be, "to sleep all night and lie down all day!" The female portion are a most disgusting, filthy set of beings and they generally employ their time in playing cards! They owe their knowledge of this evil practice to those who hail from Christian lands! To take the two extremes of original beauty & deformity (both of the mind & body) the former is well represented by the inhabitants of Navigators Islands, the latter, by the wretched Natives of New Zealand! As for energy, they have not enough to build them comfortable houses but prefer (as I have often seen them) sleeping on the bare ground in rain & shine! The effect of this on their physical constitution is apparent and if one could fail to detect a New Zealander's nativity by his tattooed face, he could most certainly allot him his nation by the hacking cough!

January 14
FRIDAY

Employed in painting spars & yards. Capt. Vinall has determined to make the "Old Henry" the "pride of the harbor!" We received orders this morning to paint her, inside & out, from "trucks to keel!" Already, her snowy "trucks" begin to look quite proud! The "Old H" has been the "pride" of one harbor this voyage! Fact!!! She was the most beautiful modeled ship, the best sailing ship, the trimmest rigged ship, & the most successful ship in the harbor!!! To account for these wonders, it is only necessary to say, that she was the only ship in the harbor at that time!!! So ends the day!

January 15
SATURDAY

Still employed in painting. The Bark "Columbia" came in this morning. Took no oil since we last saw her! The labors of the Missionaries at this place have met with better success in this immediate vicinity since we were here before. Among the principal evidences of accomplished good is the fact that prostitution is in a great measure abolished! This is encouraging! It is really enough to make one's blood run cold, to see a father paddling a canoe containing his daughters, around the harbor, exhibiting them to the eyes of sailors, and turning them over into the hands of the highest bidder, for purposes which I dare not mention, but which are easily guessed!!! I have seen this done in Wanganui!!! Can it be wondered at that I am sick of a life in which I am compelled to witness such hellish scenes as these??!!

January 16
SUNDAY

A lovely day. All hands on liberty. I preferred remaining aboard today and have occupied my time in reading my Bible & in meditation. I am very sorry to log the disgraceful conduct of a portion of our crew on shore! They disgraced their country & themselves by getting drunk, fighting, swearing & setting an example which the Natives themselves would be slow to follow!! Oh! that men would stamp that fearful word—Eternity on their hearts! How much of suffering hereafter would be avoided if that mighty word was bore in mind!!

January 17
MONDAY

This morning the "Albion" got underway and proceeded to sea! We "gave her a gun," as she slowly passed us and after running up the "Stars & Stripes," sent 2 boats to assist in towing her out of the harbor. The Whale Ship, "John Howland" came in this morning. The "old Henry" so far "takes the lead" in point of beauty! Larboard Watch on shore, on liberty. Starboard watch employed in painting ship. So ends!

January 18
TUESDAY

A fine day. Employed in painting ship. This morning the Whale ship "Trident" arrived, direct from Mangea Island. Reports the total loss of ship "Frances" (in which we shipped 850 bbls oil). Well, so it goes! I am in debt to the ship now, and taking it altogether, I find that this is an admirable illustration of the "joys" of a sailor's life!! Work hard for 8 months, receive a little oil, have it sent home without one's consent,—it's cast away, & one finds himself to be about $80 worse than nothing!! This appears hard, but a wiser hand than man's, is ever on the helm of life!!

January 19
WEDNESDAY

Still employed in painting. A British Man o' War, the "Pandora" came to an anchor outside the harbor this morning. She endeavored to ship 25 men among the Yankees, but they preferred sailing under the "Stars & Stripes" for a short time longer! As may be supposed, the intelligence from Mangea, in regard to the loss of our oil, has thrown a damper over our feelings and made us "some little blue" as we see nothing before us, but a "very particular, dark prospect!!" (Where's the school, ma'am!)

January 20
THURSDAY

A fine day. Employed in painting. Ships, "Tamoroua & Elizabeth" arrived this morning. The former is just out from home, but can report no news. No letters for me yet!! By the way, the "old Henry" ranks, "No. 2" now in regard to beauty!

The "Tamoroua" is a "clipper"—and so "old Henry" you must "strike your colors!"

January 21
FRIDAY

Employed in getting off potatoes & onions. There is a report aft that we are to sail & whale in company with the "John Howland" during the coming season. Orders have been given to get ready for sea in 4 days.

January 22
SATURDAY

Employed in "bending on" sails, getting off recruits, cleaning up decks, wetting hold, etc. A grand "clam-chowder pic-nic" was held today on shore! It was "got up" by the Captains of ships in Port. A few of the "gentler sex" graced the occasion by their presence, and judging by appearances, (seen through the ship's glass) they had "quite a time!" It quickly brought to mind the last pic-nic which I had the pleasure of attending at home! When the members of "The Mutual," "had a time" on the Banks of the Sciota, and when Orve & Pete & Edith & Amelia all rendered me happy, as plans for the future were admirably formed and alas! they are all blotted out now ! Such is life!

January 23
SUNDAY

A rainy, disagreeable day! The majority of men in Port have been employed in drinking, fighting, etc., all day. I wrote several letters to my friends at home today, and as is usual on all such occasions, I was compelled to serve as the "amanuensis," for several shipmates.

January 24
MONDAY

"Tumbling Jack" is missing this morning and I suppose that he has taken "French Liberty"! A gang of 50 Natives have been sent in pursuit and unless Jack "keeps an eye to windward," he will be snared! Employed in getting ready for sailing.

January 25
TUESDAY

Called all hands at daylight & "hove short" for sailing. 7 AM Outside the harbor. No word of Jack! Another of the crew deserted last night but was brought back by the Natives this morning! Once more (& forever) Wanganui, farewell!!

January 26
WEDNESDAY

Out of sight of land! Employed in stowing the anchors & various deck & rigging jobs. So ends!

January 27
THURSDAY

A pleasant morning. This evening raised a school of Blackfish! All hands were at supper, (I was at the wheel) when the school were raised and had to go down in the boats without my supper! After coming on board (without success) the cook procured me some supper and I went into the for'castle. Finding no molasses there, I took my tin pot &

went aft for the purpose of getting some. On my way thither I was met by Capt. V. He inquired my errand & I told him. He ordered me for'rad and forbid me taking a drop! The reason was because we had not been successful in taking one or more Blackfish! I forbear to comment on such quintessence of meanness & small-souled-ism! So ends the day!

January 28
FRIDAY

Appearances indicate coming bad weather! Employed in braiding "5 yarn-sinnett" for the oars! At the old tricks again! The absence of "Tumbling Jack" creates quite a vacancy in the for'castle! Poor Jack! many a time he has made me laugh "til my sides ached" as he "murdered English" in his descriptions of his life on the "can-a-w-l"! I hope that he may do well!

January 29
SATURDAY

Last night the wind "hauled" N.E. and in the middle watch, we found it necessary to handle the light sails. This morning it increased in violence and this evening we are "laying to" under a close-reefed main-top-sail & fore-top-mast-stay-sail! A severe gale!

January 30
SUNDAY

Storm abated in violence; the sea is running very heavy, however! Have experienced much comfort today in reading my Bible. It really appears strange to me that I have read so much in my Bible at home and have failed to remark the more than beauties that abound from Genesis to Revelation!

January 31

MONDAY

A fine, pleasant day. Employed in making spun-yarn sinnet, etc. Thank God, the season before us is the last! At its close, we are going home, successful or not! It seems at times, impossible to wait 'til I do really see my friends again! But I am like a caged bird! I may flutter & flap my wings against the bars, but the only point gained is—sore wings! Patience, patience, is every-thing!

February 1

TUESDAY

Another month of the many that separate me from loved ones at home, has passed, and another begun! I anxiously look forward to the last one and often find myself anticipating the joy of once more seeing the loved shores of my native land! Employed in ship's duties.

February 2

WEDNESDAY

A fine day. A noble breeze has set in and the "old Henry" is hourly "logging" her "eight knots!" Employed in sail-making. "Mr Colonel" seems disposed to "stick close to me!" I am not much enamored with the old gentleman & have several times tried to insult him! No use! Something like a certain Doctor Jones, alias, "The Clown" as Aunty Callahan calls him! Sis Mag's account of the worthy Doctor often affects my mirth & I imagine I see the little Quack "cutting all kinds of fancy, bowlines & reef-tackles" in the wake of the noble figure of my "Dear Sis Mag"! So ends the day!

February 3

THURSDAY

The S. E. Trade Winds set in this morning changing a sultry atmosphere to a cool bracing standard, the effect of which has been to animate our spirits & create a feeling of thankfulness to God for health & strength! Employed in ships duties.

February 4

FRIDAY

Appearances this morning indicate coming bad weather! Employed in making spun-yarn, etc.

February 5

SATURDAY

A gale of wind set in yesterday evening & raged violently all night. Weather continues bad today. A cold, driving rain renders the spar deck an extremely unpleasant berth, which is increased by the fact that I have no dry clothes to put on! Will come whaling, eh?!!!!

February 6

SUNDAY

A fine day! I need not attempt to describe the more than joy & experience in even anticipating a deliverance from this detestable life, and a return home!! Forfeited Sabbath privileges & the society of loved ones ever fills my mind and cause a constant longing for their enjoyment! Once more at anchor, at home, and it must be something indeed extraordinary that will induce me to "heave short"—for sailing! So ends the day!

February 7

MONDAY

Raised a school of Sperm Whales this morning! Lowered 3 Boats and started in pursuit. No success! The whales were "going" and were out of sight at 4 bells (10 AM). Came aboard and employed for the remainder of the day in setting up "bob-stays."

February 8

TUESDAY

A lovely day. In the morning, employed in making spun yarn & painting the Bow Boat. At 3 PM raised a large Sperm Whale! Lowered & pulled for him. In 15 minutes a cloud of snowy spray and the tremendous thundering of his flukes, proclaimed him a "fast whale!" The Waist Boat struck him and at 6 PM he was snugly moored alongside! Quick work!

February 9

WEDNESDAY

Employed in "cutting in." The jaw-bone of our monster-whale measures 17 feet in length!! It is rendered doubly formidable by two rows of 44 teeth of prodigious size. Should dislike to get in such a place in the sea! So ends the day!

February 10

THURSDAY

Boiling. Some idea may be formed of the monstrous size of this whale when 4 bbls of oil were got from the "pans" (or hollow portion) of his jaw bone and 15 bbls of oil from his "case,"—a kind of receptacle in the middle of his head in which pure clear oil forms! It is this "head matter" (as we call it) or "spermaceti" from which "stearine candles" are manufactured at home. Those 25 bbls are worth about $750 alone!!

February 11
FRIDAY

Still boiling. The total value of the whale we are now boiling is from 5 to 6000 dollars! The sailor's share (from pulling "the stars out of his eyes") of this monster amounts to about $20! Capt. Vinall's, on the other hand, to about $350!!! So much for whaling! I often think that if persons who use lamp oil at home could but just see all that a whaleman is compelled to undergo, by way of hardship, danger, & suffering, from the time a whale is "raised" from the mast-head, 'til he is "stowed-down," in the hold—if they only knew at what a fearful risk of life & limb he launches forth upon the bosom of the mighty ocean in a small frail boat—if they could but see him "hauling up" to the thundering flukes or open jaws of a whale—then, if they could but see that boat mashed to atoms and a crew of 6 men struggling for life in a sea of blood, (as I have experienced it); if they could but see this imperfectly colored picture of a leaf in the life of a whaleman—a loud and mighty voice would go up to those in authority praying that he might be treated as a man, on his ship; and I venture the assertion that every arm in America, be its possessor the most aristocratic & wealthy male or female, would be eagerly extended to greet the hardy tar! There is no "child's-play" connected with the capture of a whale at any time!

February 12

SATURDAY

Finished boiling! Employed in cleaning up decks. Weather, squally accompanied with vivid lightning! Feel "a little tired" tonight and think I could relish a "nap" in the S.E. corner of "a certain brick house" in the City of Columbus! Well, I trust that I will yet have that privilege! Unless some of those nimble whales in Japan Sea "take a fancy to my head!" So ends the day.

February 13

SUNDAY

A fine day! Have been thinking of home & friends all day! Oh! that God would hasten my return home. Oh! that He would deal mercifully with me and speedily restore my forfeited privileges! Have been thinking of the privileges which loved ones at home have enjoyed today! A feeling of envy almost predominates, but I must patiently await my deliverance from self-imposed "misery!!" So ends the day!

February 14

MONDAY.

Stowing down oil. Navigator's Islands about 2 day's sail ahead. If we touch these many more times some of us, I think could safely venture to accept a "Pilots commission!" So ends.

February 15

TUESDAY

Employed in cleaning ship, etc. Weather continues squally & very bad! The prospect for good weather is small from this place to the line. A broad tract (through which we have to pass) is subject to typhoons, hurricanes, etc. and to look ahead it is almost enough to make a man "tack-ship!" More anon.

February 16

WEDNESDAY

Land ho! Navigator's Islands, once more! We will be debarred the privilege of going in this time on account of the weather! Appearances (4 PM) indicate a coming severe storm & made everything "snug" for the night!

February 17

THURSDAY

Last night was one of storm & terror! We hourly expected the bursting of a typhoon, but the night wore away without it, and a feeling of thankfulness, filled my heart this morning as I beheld the dawning of another day in possession of a measure of health & strength of body & mind! Weather still looks threatening! To look "out-board" last night, there was certainly nothing very fascinating to be seen! Unless any one "has a fancy" to see terrible lightning and mad columns of black & furious clouds gyrating in vast circles and threatening to let loose their mighty power of wind upon a ship on a lee shore! I must confess that I was glad to see daylight!

February 18

FRIDAY

Terrific squalls of rain & wind accompanied with severe lightning rage constantly! The main "drift" of employment consists in "clewing up & down" top-sails, shortening now, and now "making" sail as a terrific blast of wind bursts from angry clouds and raging for a quarter of an hour passes away & gives place for another more powerful! Very bad weather! These are the times when home appears doubly attractive!! So ends the day!

February 19

SATURDAY

This has been a comparatively pleasant day, unmarked by the severe squalls of the past week, the contrast appears greater than it really is, but "all's well that ends well" (so says the "Immortal Bard of Avon") and we will make a virtue of necessity & call it—a fine day!

February 20

SUNDAY

Becalmed! My thoughts have been with loved ones at home all day!! In imagination, I again knelt at the family altar!! I went with my Dear Father's family to the House of God! Such was the strength of my imagination that the quiet holy day,—the hush of the hum of life,—the glad tolling of the bell,—the assembled congregation,—the loud anthem of praise & the earnest exhortation of Mr. Hitchcock were all—being enjoyed!! Oh! Time! thrice thy speed would not too swiftly restore me to these forfeited privileges!! Oh! why was I such a fool!! Why did I launch madly forth into a wide friendless world? Why did I sacrifice true happiness and sentence myself to a life of worse than misery!

February 21
MONDAY

Still becalmed! Weather almost insupportably hot! Employed in making spun yarn. Think I could relish a cruise in "Sis Jule" fine shady yard today! By the way, those tasteful little circles, squares, etc., in her front yard will be all abloom I suppose when I get there! Look out Jule! I am fond of flowers! That "one little flower" of yours, I suppose is capable of saying "Uncle Dick" now Jule!! God bless you & yours, my sister!

February 22
TUESDAY

Still becalmed! The extreme heat of the weather exceeds anything that I ever experienced before! Employed in making spun yarn. A decidedly hot job! This is "Washington's birthday," but I doubt whether the "Father of his country" ever felt it so warm as this! He, no doubt, experienced "warm times" during the struggle for independence, but he possessed a peculiar "cooling" ingredient which had a strange effect on "Johnny Bull" sometimes!! So ends!

February 23
WEDNESDAY

Still becalmed! Weather continues extremely hot with heavy thunder showers. Employed in making . . .

[Page ripped]

add "Noah Murray" but the last time the old gentleman "fainted" on seeing me, he had "a rib"! So ends!

February 24

THURSDAY

We managed, last night, by dint of much bracing, squaring, etc to log 5 knots! The light breeze was truly very refreshing, but with the remainder of "Jack's" comforts it was "short & sweet!" Employed in ship's duties.

February 25

FRIDAY

A rainy disagreeable morning! A light breeze sprung up this morning and we are now (8 PM) slowly progressing toward the line!

> "Give to me, the roaring breeze
> With the white waves heaving high!"

The author of that song is acquainted with the horrors of a calm, I think!! I heartily concur with the above sentiment! So ends the day!

February 26

SATURDAY

A fine day! Employed in washing, mending, etc. What would some of my "fashionable" friends, or rather acquaintances, think if they could but see me "evading into the wash-tub!" Thank God I am not ashamed to work! If any one thinks less of me because I "wear" a pair of tar-stained-horny-hands, a weather beaten face, "home made" clothes & shoes & a well patched shirt, they would oblige me by giving me a "wide berth!" There is no room in my heart for either a "cock-or-hen-sparrow," whose factory nerves are so amazingly acute as to enable them to "smell" a "working-man" through a 3 feet brick-wall.

February 27
SUNDAY
[Page ripped]

February 28
MONDAY
A noble breeze has set in and with "square yards" we are rapidly overhauling the Japan Sea! Once more there will complete my "whaling" in this ship and I hope that I will never be such an ass as to come in another! Not while sane, at any rate! Employed in various ship's duties. So ends the month.

March 1
TUESDAY
Another month, — "blustering stormy March" has set in! What it will bring forth we know not! As I enter upon it my thoughts are away to my native land to my home! Looking in upon my Dear Father's family; how anxiously do I seek each loved member! Are they all there? Has the icy hand of Death (God forbid) been lain upon one of them? Is one afflicted with ill health? These, as my mind wanders far over the wide waste of waters which separate us and dwell among them! God preserve us all & hasten our meeting around the family altar! So ends the day!

March 2
WEDNESDAY

The fine breeze still hangs on! Employed in making spun yarn & various ship's duties too uninteresting to mention! A "booby" perched himself on the mizzen to'gallant-yard-arm this afternoon and continued to maintain a very quiet "look-out" 'til 9 o'clock PM. The cabin boy "got his eye on him" at that time, went up & made him a prisoner! After an hour's combat with the pigs & dogs his liberty was given him and the speed of his flight evinced the joy with which he bade adieu to a Yankee Whaler!

March 3
THURSDAY

Our noble breeze still hangs on and is swiftly waltzing us to the theatre of another season's action! Employed in sundry ship's duties. So ends!

March 4
FRIDAY

A beautiful day! Have finished the "spun-yarn" at last!! Having used up all the "old Junk" in the fore-hold, we have no "stock" (at present) upon which to operate! Glad of it! Find some other job next I suppose worse than the spun yarn!! So it goes!

March 5
SATURDAY

We are in about 2°15′ S. today, with as hot a sun beaming down upon us as "ever fried tar from out a ship's decks!" This breeze will, however, (if it continues) soon waft us into a cooler clime! Sharp look-out, kept for reefs, lagoons, etc. We have entered the limits of the "Dangerous Archipelago," is the reason for this!

March 6
SUNDAY

A lovely day! "Forenoon-watch" on deck! Employed in reading my bible and in meditation. How does my soul long for the privilege of this day at home! And yet, how careless & indifferent have I become in regard to the interests of my soul! Oh! how vile, weak, empty, sinful & hell-deserving has become my heart!! Deal not with me, Oh! God in anger or justice, but deal mercifully with me a sinner!!!

March 7
MONDAY

This day set in dark & gloomy; rendered less melancholy, however, by being accompanied with "Jack's particular friend,"—a fine breeze! One day's sail from "King's Mill Group" of islands! I suppose that we will touch at one of the islands for fruit, etc.! Employed in various deck & rigging jobs. So ends!

March 8
TUESDAY

(8 AM) Land ho! "Woodle" Island, (one of the King's Mill Group). Several Whale ships have been "cut off" & their crews murdered in this vicinity by the Natives, an exceed-ingly fierce & savage race of beings, who make war & bloodshed a pastime! These are near (4 Bells) (10 AM) some 50 or 60 canoes bearing down for us; and the savage yells of

their naked, ferocious looking crews are not calculated to make a man feel an undue account of security! We are well prepared to resist them, however, in a case of treachery. We "backed" our main-top sail, to admit some of them to the deck. A canoe containing the King came first. When within a ship's length of us a native seized the "warp" in his teeth and taking an emblem of peace & good-will in one hand, sprang over board and swam to the ship!! We "laid to" some time & bartered tobacco for mats, cocoa, nuts, fowls, turtles, etc. While the Natives were on board, the crew was divided into guards. I had the larboard for'castle-deck for my station and many a fine mat was offered me by some Natives alongside, if I would allow them to make fast their canoes & come onboard. A limited number was allowed on board at one time & I was compelled to refuse. Once I had to cut away the canoe of a Native who notwithstanding orders to the contrary, had made fast to the fore chains! He did not look very pleasantly at me! 6 PM Out of sight of land! Quite an excitement was caused on deck in the "dog-watch" by seeing a young Kannaka rise "Phoenix, like" out of the fore hold and after taking a turn or two on the for'castle deck—slowly stalk aft!! It appears that he wished to go in the ship and communicating his desire (by means of signs) to some of the crew, they "stowed him away!!" Capt. Vinall rigged him in a suit of clothes and the poor fellow is now much richer than the King of his native Island—possessing a shirt & pair of breeches!! So ends the day!

March 9
WEDNESDAY
Weather hot & squally. Employed in rattling down & various deck & rigging jobs. Wonder if any of the "old

Mutual" are married yet! "Orve" if you have spliced to a "rib," just look out for your "running rigging"! I will not spare you, Orve, but just make up your mind to "stand" a box of Charley Klei regalias! "Pete" if you have committed matrimony, make up your mind for something terrible! Yes, rest assured that I will—endeavor to follow your example! "Edith," I should not wonder much to hear that you had become some lucky chap's better 5/6th! "Amelia," I don't think that you are married!!

What a curious life is this! I sometimes think, but enough now!

March 10
THURSDAY

Employed in walking the deck and "seeing it rain!" Nothing else can be done, so for fear that our blood will become stagnated, we are kept on deck to see how handsomely the pattering drops strike and roll down in the lee scuppers!! So much for whaling! Go it!!!!

March 11
FRIDAY

A fine day. Employed in various deck & rigging jobs. A noble breeze has set in and the "Old Henry" "feels it"! Japan Sea, with its host of "limber tails" grows nearer every hour and it will not be long before the Old Henry's try-works will evince the value of the lance, spade & harpoon!

March 12
SATURDAY

Wash day! "Jack" overhauls his clothes locker and rolling up his sleeves, "wades into" the wash-tub! Would like to have a "dandy" here today, "just to show him how to wash his shirt!" Could learn him how to soil his hands with tar also, if he desired it!! A fine chance for "exquisites" in a Whale ship! And so ends the day & week!

March 13
SUNDAY

Another beautiful day! As usual, I have been thinking of home & friends! My bright thoughts soon fled before the dull reality of a Whaleman's life, and I was left in a state of mind which no one could desire to experience! Well, deliverance will certainly come at some future day whither in the form of death, or a happy reunion with those who are dear to me! I sometimes feel that either form would be eagerly embraced! So ends the day!

March 14
MONDAY

Employed today in repairing try-works and sail making. A noble breeze still continues to urge the "Old H." to her utmost! If it continues, we will make Guam (Ladrone Islands) about next Monday. The absence of "Tumbling Jack" created a vacancy in the "mirth department;" said vacancy has been filled to satisfaction by "Old Blossom!" "Bloss," by the way is something of a "singer" and "Old Dan Tucker," "Dandy Jim," & "Yankee Doodle" are nightly cruelly murdered by him! A peculiar aversion to the 3rd Officer causes "Bloss" to be continually employed in inventing mischief! The 3rd Officer in turn keeps an eye on him and if caught asleep, a cruise aloft on the top-sail-yard is sure to follow! Once perched aloft he keeps the rest of us awake as he loudly sings the good qualities of "Lieutenant Cow," "The Tough Hoss " & "The Buzzard"!! Look out for squalls "Bloss," if he manages to "get run" of your meaning!! So ends the day!!

March 15

TUESDAY

Fine weather still continues! Employed in preparing for the coming season in Japan Sea. Some are making bread-bags for the boats; the harpooners are cleaning, grinding, & "setting up" irons, lances & spades, the Carpenter is planing up boat-boards & the Officers are painting their boats! The whales will "suffer"!!!!!

March 16

WEDNESDAY

A fine day. Employed in overhauling & cleaning, cutting spades, etc. Wonder if the Baltimore & Ohio Railroad is completed to Wheeling yet? I don't know, but I think I would be tempted to take passage in an "air car" (if Yankeedom possesses any) for Columbus! My desire to get there is so strong that I fear prudence would be compelled to stand in the back-ground if an air car was really to start from New Bedford!! Patience!!

March 17

THURSDAY

Employed in various ship's duties. "Old Bloss" gives great satisfaction in the performance of his "duties"!! A "new song" is nightly added to his already extensive list & the prospect for more is good! I learn from "Bloss," that he has "blown" the base-drum for a Militia company in New Jersey! Must rig him a tin-pan for practicing! Go it Bloss!

March 18

FRIDAY

Employed in "breaking out," and cleaning our last Whale's teeth! Not a "pleasant job" by any means, I think, but "sailor's" did not ship in the Whaling Service "to think"! At least, so says one of our Officers! (Nor to eat, I suppose, either!!) So ends!

March 19

SATURDAY

One day's sail from Guam. I have written a letter to my Father's family, which I am going to send from Guam, if an opportunity offers. Would that I was its bearer! So ends the week!

March 20

SUNDAY

Land ho! Guam on the lee bow! 2 PM Capt. Vinall ordered his boat cleared away and in a few moments we backed the Main-top-sail, "luffed to the wind," lowered & commenced pulling for the City. A coral reef surrounds the Island upon which the sea breaks, forming a scene at once terrible and magnificent! There is but one passage through the surf which is barely wide enough to admit a boat with the oars "shipped out." This passage is designated by two high stakes on either side and an occasional "slick" in the channel. We pulled up to the spot where the rollers "broke their caps" and laid on our oars, consulting the propriety of venturing through. The least mismanagement on our part & our mangled bodies would in a very few moments strew the beach!! In order to go through safely, the boat must be kept exactly before the sea! The 2nd Officer took the steering oar and after a word of firmness and caution from Capt. Vinall, we sprang to our oars and pulled in! The noise of the breakers was equal only to thunder, and as we were "flung " with the velocity of thought on the crest of a magnificent roller, with the sharp ledges of coral right under us, I can assure any one that my feelings were "somewhat peculiar!!" It was not "fear," but the awful grandeur of the scene had such an effect on my mind that, allowing I was disposed to fear, "I would not have had 'time' to do so!" Almost everyone knows that the sea breaks in 3 successive rollers on a shore of which the first is less powerful than the second & the second, less powerful than the third! We entered the surf on the first of the three and looking behind, or rather over us and seeing an awful "snow-cap't-avalanche of Ocean" thundering after us with the speed of thought, we were led to "calculate our course in case it caught us!!" We, however, got through safely and approached the City. After hauling the boat on the beach, etc. I took a short cruise in the City. I was attracted by a chime of bells in the dome of a Cathedral about a mile from the beach, and "getting under way," I "bore down" for it. In front of the Cathedral was a large wooden cross erected on a circular platform of stone. On the head of the cross was a scroll with the word "Inri" inscribed on each arm, and about half way down the upright portion of it were large spikes driven into the wood and immediately under the spike, drops of blood were painted! I remarked several others erected in various portions of the city. Leaving the vicinity of the Cathedral, I started on another cruise. I had not proceeded 50 yards before I came to a large plaza in which were some 3 or 400 people engaged in cock-fighting! So much for the church of Rome! A little farther and I overhauled a venerable "Padre." Around his black robe he wore a leather belt, the end of which was thrown over his right hand and hung to his feet. On the spot which covered his hand, an image of our Saviour was fastened, and everyone whom he met in his walk was compelled to remove his hat & kneel to the ground—the image was then presented to his lips for the purpose of kissing it! Being an unbeliever (in such a religion) I could not do it myself, and accordingly I "kept off—about 4 points," and gave the "old Padre" a wide berth! 6 PM Capt. Vinall collected the crew and gave us passports from the Governor and money enough to procure a boarding house, intends remaining on shore all night. One of our harpooneers and myself took a cruise to the Northward and soon overhauled one "Don Pedro" with whom we engaged supper & lodging. I seated myself in front of the house after tea and—thought of home! When will I be there? At about 4 Bells (10 o'clock) I went in and feeling fatigued threw myself on a couch and set sail for the "Land of Nod !" A "fair wind" soon "brought me in sight," and I continued to cruise "off and on" for about half an hour. A curious feeling (as though I was surrounded by legions of "singing Angels") continued to oppress me and although anxious to divine the cause of it, still I found it impossible to thoroughly arouse myself! I made a desperate effort & succeeded in awakening. What a strange sight met my eyes! Some 8 or 10 ladies were kneeling on a mat beside me and while they were chanting a vesper, their eyes were fixed earnestly & reverentially on some object, apparently on the wall! I cast my eyes in the direction of their's and saw a large wax figure of our Saviour dressed in robes of costly silks, gold, etc. standing in a kind of niche in the wall! A feeling of sorrow filled my heart as I thought of those deluded souls who were so zealously engaged in violating the Commandment! After the close of their worship, the wife of Don Pedro took a cup of "holy water" and sprinkled the faces of all who were in the house! I did not let her know that I was awake when she "sprinkled" me and after muttering an "Ave Maria" over me, she proceeded to the next sleeper,—my messmate! He knew nothing of it 'til I informed of it this (Monday) morning!

March 21
MONDAY

At length dawned and I arose and walking through a grove of Cocoa nut trees, came to the beach. I stooped down and wrote with my finger in the sand the names of absent loved ones!! I stood gazing at the names which I had traced in the sand when a small feathery wavelet rolled over them & they were gone!! How emblematical of life! Filled with new & instructive thoughts, I turned away and directed my steps toward my boarding house where I found my ship-mate anxiously awaiting my coming. We strolled once more through the City and many times detected some bright black eyes peering upon us from balconies, casements, etc! My companion began to "dislike whaling" in a few moments and remarking a lovely Spanish girl sitting at her window, he directed my attention thither & inquired of the "state of my mind!" I immediately informed him that America's fair daughters were the only ones who commanded a place in my heart's locker! After cruising a little farther we visited the Fort. I went to the top of its gray stone tower and with my knife, carved my name & those of dear friends at home! At 12 N we launched the boat and after bidding adieu to Guam, proceeded for the "Old Henry," via "the breakers"! We had gone but 3 ship's lengths when we struck a rock, stove & the boat badly! It was next to fool-hardiness to venture into the breakers in this condition; but, sailors must not heed trifles, and we dashed into them! When we got through, the boat was nearly filled with water & we peaked our oars and "bailed" to keep her afloat ! 2 PM Once more on board the Kneeland! As curious a crew as ever reefed top-sails have besieged me ever since, and I am compelled to relate all that transpired while ashore! 6 PM out of sight of land! Spoke whale ships, "Alabama" (of "Blue, White & Red notoriety"), "General Scott," and "Enterprise." So ends!

March 22

TUESDAY

A fine day. Employed in breaking out for water, etc. "Jack Grasshopper," our King's Mill Native, received his cold-weather outfit today and the poor fellow is proud enough! Alas! poor Jack, you have exchanged happiness for misery!

March 23

WEDNESDAY

Prospect for bad weather! Employed today in "setting up" casks & pipes & overhauling potatoes. One year from today, I hope to be almost home! I would give ten-thousand-worlds if they were at my disposal, to be there tonight! God alone, knows how I long to see my Dear Parents & Sisters again!

March 24

THURSDAY

A gale of wind set in last night and has raged all day! Scudding before it, under close-reefed top-sails! Wonder who is President? I think the Whigs "missed it" in nominating Genl. Scott! That he is capable of filling the chair, there can be no doubt, but I think that Daniel Webster was right when he said, "that, unless the Whig Party ceased to nominate Military chieftains, they would only be known as a name!" However, politics will never "drive me mad,"—at least, not 'til I am nominated for President myself! So ends the day!

March 25

FRIDAY

AM Gale still rages! 4 PM Moderating. 6 PM Made sail. We have "run our longitude out" and have yet some 15 degrees of latitude to run before we "bring up" in Japan Sea! At 5 PM raised a school of Blackfish! Notwithstanding the roughness of the sea, Capt. Vinall ordered down the boats! Stove the Starboard & Waist Boats in lowering. Had we succeeded in striking, we could not have saved the fish, and it appears that Capt. Vinall's only motive in ordering down the boats was a desire to see others suffer! So much for whaling!

March 26
SATURDAY

A fine day. Employed in washing, mending, and "splic-ing, running rigging!" "Splicing rigging" has become a part of our daily duty! They must be a sorry "set of halliards" or a sorry piece of rigging that is unbent and stowed away in the "rag bag"! We "part" something everyday! Lay up & splice it!!

March 27
SUNDAY

Becalmed! It is a custom of mine to earnestly desire God to make every Sabbath a day of quiet, holy meditation & prayer! My prayer is often answered, and when unanswered, I can easily trace an unfaithful feeling in my heart, or see the All Wise dealings of God with the children of men! God, hasten my return to the land of Sabbath rest!

March 28
MONDAY

A breeze sprung up last night, which brought us in sight of "Crown Island" one of the Loo Choo group! 6 PM raised a "Hump-back" whale! Gave him a wide berth! Employed in various ship's duties. Weather is growing cold and flannel shirts begin to feel comfortable. So ends!

March 29
TUESDAY

A gale of wind set in last night and has been raging ever since. We may not expect to have much good weather 'til the middle or last part of April! Japan Sea is not celebrated for fine weather either early or late in the season!

April, 1853

March 30
WEDNESDAY

Last night (in the mid-watch) as we were standing along under close-reefed-top-sails & courses, we were struck by a typhoon! Called all hands and although carrying short sail, we found it impossible to "take it in," before losing the fore-top-sail! It burst with the report of thunder & it was no sport to gather the remains of it & confine them to the yard! The force of the wind was powerful beyond description & at one time things looked rather doubtful in regard to the ability of the ship to weather it! 6 PM heading for the Straits of Corea under close-reefed-top-sails. So ends the day!

March 31
THURSDAY

A fine day. Made "Judo, Wukido & Sulpher Islands." Employed in splicing the "Starboard main-top-mast-swifter," having "parted it" during the typhoon. One at a time, now a "brace," now a "stay," now a "buntline," & now a "clewline" the old rigging "goes"!! Splice them, my hearties, splice them!! Can't afford new ones! Not until we lose a man or two!!

April 1
FRIDAY

One more month has passed & I am one month nearer Eternity!—"Eternity"!! A short word & easily, quickly spoken! But oh! how vast its import !! "Will this eternity be spent in Heaven or in Hell" is a question which I find forcing itself upon my mind, and demanding a full, clear & explicit answer! By God's assisting grace it will be spent by me in

Heaven! A great help to me is in the thought that I am daily presented to God and His mercy by my Dear Parents & Sisters! I cannot describe the happiness which I experience when thinking of this fact! God bless you, loved ones, God bless you! 4 PM raised a school of Black-fish! Lowered Bow Boat, struck, but the iron drew & he escaped! We will soon be among the "limber tails" of Japan Sea! I cannot look forward with that peculiar anxiety to see a whale spouting blood which some of the crew cherish! I would rather be excused from assisting in their capture at all, but I am "in the scrape" now & must await my deliverance! So ends the day!

April 2
SATURDAY

A fine morning. Employed in unbending, sending down & repairing main-top-sail. This (by rights) is "wash-day," but we are employed in ship's duties and consequently will be compelled to postpone the "sanitary" movement for another week! So ends.

April 3
SUNDAY

A rain storm set in this morning, rendering it very unpleasant. 1 PM reefed top-sails and furled the main-sail. The storm continued to increase in violence from that time till 9 PM when we were compelled to "heave her to" under a close-reefed main-top-sail, fore-sail & storm-stay-sail! A heavy gale, but I don't think it will last long. Have experienced much comfort today in reading my Bible and in meditation. God hasten my return home! So ends!

April, 1853

April 4

MONDAY

A fine day. Employed in bending on "reserve," main-sail & "close-mizzen,"—preparations for the whaling ground! Saw "Fin & Hump-back" whales. Not the right kind! Mr. Horsley, (2nd Officer) brought me his log-book this morning and requested me to write the title page and draught a ship "laying aback." Complied with his request. So ends the day!

April 5

TUESDAY

Another fine day! Employed in sundry work-up jobs. Weather, cold & unpleasant. Thick clothes in good demand! "I may be mistaken" (???) but I "think" that I would prefer being at home tonight! Well, I am "enjoying"(???) some of the "delights" of a sailor's life now!

April 6

WEDNESDAY

Employed in repairing Boat's sails. We have entered the Straits of Corea, once more! A head wind and thick heavy weather renders our situation in some measure dangerous; we have, accordingly bent on the cable to the "best bower" and are all ready to "let her go" in a case of emergency and either "ride" or go-ashore! Land is in rather unpleasant proximity and "I should not fancy a berth on its barren plains!" So ends!

April 7

THURSDAY

Becalmed! Have a fine view of the coasts of Asia and Japan! Just at sundown, raised a sail on the Starboard Quarter. Couldn't make her out. 9 PM prospect for bad weather! And so ends!

April 8

FRIDAY

Spoke Whaling Bark, "Belle," a beautiful clipper craft hailing from Warren. Seven months from home & clean. Reports the probable election of Pearce to the Presidency! At 2 PM a heavy gale set in and we are now (8 PM) "laying to" under a close-reefed main-top-sail & fore-topmast-stay-sail! A heavy gale!

April 9

SATURDAY

Gale still rages! Last night was one of storm & terror! Cold, wet & "blue." I crouched under the lee of the bulwarks and thought of home! It is enough to say that my loss was felt! Oh! ye, who nightly surround the cheerful fire on the social family hearth,—do you ever pray for the sailor! Have you the most remote idea of his privations, sufferings, hardships & dangers? Do you ever picture his situation on such a fearful night as the one which has just passed? Do you think, while enjoying the society of Dear Parents, Sisters, Brothers & Friends, of his hard lot ? Shut out from the world, all social intercourse cut off & deprived of everything like enjoyment or happiness, he is indeed deserving of your prayers! God grant that the time will soon come when the sailor will feel that all christians make him a special subject of prayer!

April 10
SUNDAY

A fine day. In a late paper (procured from the crew of the "Belle") I see it stated that the Cholera is raging in Columbus! It is impossible to describe the uneasiness which this report gives me!——Can it be that a Beloved Parent, or Dear Sister has fallen a victim to this terrible disease! Has the voice of anyone of them been hushed in—Death ? Oh! God! Their lives are in Thy Hand!! Protect & preserve us all & unite us yet together on Earth!!

April 11
MONDAY.

A clear, cold morning! Employed in "serving" "tacks & sheets!" 12 N set in to rain & blow! 2 PM double-reefed the top-sails-furled the main-sail and "got wet"!! So ends the day!

April 12
TUESDAY

Saw large numbers of the "wrong kind" of whale. This evening made the coast of Tartary. "Wore round" and "stood off." Weather, threatening! So ends!

April 13
WEDNESDAY

"Standing along" the coast of Tartary! Prospect this morning for another gale! Persons often speak of the severity of the American Coast but if it exceeds this, "it is more than severe!" Weather extremely cold! Once more, in Japan Sea!

April 14
THURSDAY

A gale of wind & rain is raging this morning and we are slowly "beating off" land under close reefed-top-sails! Every drop of water "feels wet" and "weighs" "something less than a pound!" If this is not enough to thoroughly cure a "rambler," I don't know what is! So ends the day!

April 15
FRIDAY

Storm still rages! Saw a sail to windward. Suppose her to be the "Belle." This day one year ago we took a Right Whale! The scene out-board is somewhat different, however, today and there is not much danger of lowering! "So blow," whales while Jack laughs! (Don't laugh too loud!) Employed in shivering under wet clothes! So ends!

April 16
SATURDAY

Storm, in some measure abated. The wind has been playing "Neptune's favorite" for several days and the "tune" is becoming "stale"! Would prefer hearing a more gentle melody, just for change! This is "wash-day" but Jack has "too much respect for his fingers," to plunge them in a tub of cold water! Must send my washing to the accomplished Mrs. Cook, or rather "Mrs. Street"!! by the way, wonder if poor "Ned Street" & "Mrs. Cook" came to terms with "old John" in regard to that affair of Cupid! Alas! "Ned," "the course of 'true love' never did run smooth!" Poor Mrs. Cook! Her troubles were great when I last saw her!

April 17
SUNDAY

Gale continues to decrease. Weather very cold! It will be more than happiness when this detestable occupation "brings up" at New Bedford! This Holy Day now looked forward to with regret and sorrow, will then be hailed with joy, and the present deprivation of its holy privileges will then serve to increase the pleasure of its christian enjoyment! Speed, speed, good ship!

April 18
MONDAY

A clear cold morning. Made "Dagolet" & "Seal" Islands. "Came to" off the latter, lowered the Starboard Boat and went ashore to procure some seals, the skins of which we used for "line buoys." The sight on shore was truly most remarkable! Thousands of seals & sea lions covered the rocks and when aroused from their slumbers by the boat's crew, they would make a supremely ridiculous appearance as they "paddled," barking into the water! Killed 7 seals & 1 sea lion! A slight blow on the nose with a club was sufficient to "slip their moorings" and in 30 minutes we had them on the ship's deck, skinned & ready for use! So ends!

April 19
TUESDAY

A fine day! Spoke Bark "Belle." Reports having chased Right Whales since we last saw her! (Probably a "fish story.")

5 PM (So much for charging fellow man with "fibbing.")
Raised Right Whales! Lowered with no success! Be careful
how I charge persons with "spinning fish yarns" in future!!

April 20
WEDNESDAY

A particularly cold day!! 9 AM Raised Whales! Lowered.
In a few moments the Larboard Boat went on & struck! The
whale "did not like" that, however, and very unceremoniously—mashed the boat to atoms!! No one hurt. The Waist
Boat picked up the crew and in a few moments succeeded in
picking up the line also! We (Starboard Boat) then went
down & brought the wreck of the 1st Officers's boat to the
ship after which we started for the scene of action! On
arriving, we found the Waist Boat to be "split in the chucks"
rendering it impossible to "haul on," the whale! Took the
line & the Larboard Boat's crew in the Starboard Boat and
then with a boat's gunwale on a water line "took a ride!!"
Many times in the course of this fearful day it came near
proving our last ride!! The wind was blowing fresh and a very
heavy sea was running; the whale maintained a steady run to
windward, the consequence of which was the boat was about
half the time literally under water! Two men were compelled
to bail constantly, yet notwithstanding this fact, we were up to
our knees in water the whole time that we were fast!! Many
times a "beam sea" would break clear over the boat and
to describe the feeling which the excessive cold water
produced—it was as though we were being torn limb from
limb by some infernal machine for torture!! I will never
forget this fearful day of suffering! Why , Capt. Vinall, "held
on line" I cannot conceive!! There was no prospect, however

distant, of saving the whale & why he punished himself & the crew I cannot conceive! We held on line 'til we threw 12 harpoons, 4 lances, & 2 spades into the whale and then, night coming on and being several miles from the ship & boats, we "hauled up" as close to the whale as our little remaining life would allow & cut line! To pull the oars—we could not & as for setting the sail & "trimming aft the sheet"—there was not enough energy among the entire boat's crew to do it! We sat like dead men for several minutes before we started for the ship. We arrived at length and I safely say, that to get up the ship's side was the hardest work that I ever performed!! Such was the extreme suffering which this day's work caused me, that I would not turn my hand to live!! This may sound "rather curious" to some, but it is fact!! And so ends the day!

April 21
THURSDAY

A fine morning "& aching bones"! Lowered for whales without success! Last voyage's "unlucky times" are being re-enacted I suppose! Well, "they say" that "a bad beginning makes a good ending!" and seeing that this is the only consolation we have, we will stick to that!

April 22
FRIDAY

Weather still continues fine. Lowered several times for whales without success! 5 PM Saw a large ship on the horizon, supposed the "John Howland." "White Rock" (2 days sail) is our next stopping place and we are now slowly proceeding in that direction!

April 23

SATURDAY

8 AM Raised Whales! Lowered 3 Boats and started in pursuit. The whale was close to the ship and I was standing on the Quarter-deck looking at the Waist Boat which was about "going on"! In 5 minutes after the deafening bellow & the thundering flukes, proclaimed her, fast and looking over the rail I saw the boat (in the midst of a cloud of snowy spray) in rather "uncomfortable proximity" to a very "limber" & wicked looking pair of flukes! Feeling alarmed for the safety of my shipmates I eagerly strained my eyes to see if any one was missing! Suddenly—as quick as thought—boat, crew & whale vanished!! A sickening feeling of horror oppressed me as I saw that the whale had taken the boat down with him (a frequent occurrence) and my heart almost sunk as I thought of 6 brave messmates being so quickly hurried into eternity! Thank God—the lines parted—the boat (after going down some 15 or 20 feet) arose with her crew and all were safe! The parting of the line is all that saved their lives and unless God had mercifully interposed that would not have been done! Really, this voyage promises a good amount of adventure & hair-breadth escapes! So ends!

April 24

SUNDAY

A fine morning. Lowered for whales with no success. Right!! I hope that like success may attend all Sabbath Whaling , during the voyage! 'Tis most strange & unaccountable to me that men professing to be possessed of "reasoning faculties," men too, whose education plainly teaches them the import of the 4th Commandment—will, after pulling all day for whales on the Sabbath, come on board and complain of ill success! Dare they wish to succeed? Would not a desire to succeed be nothing more or less than an expressed wish that God would revoke His unalterable Word and connive at sin?!!! It can be nothing else! Fearful thought!! God, hasten my return home!! So ends the desecrated Sabbath!

April 25
MONDAY

Another fine day! Lowered twice for whales today without success! 'Tis said that "the darkest hour is just before daylight" and if that holds good, our daylight will e'er long dawn! I hope so, for I am more than sick of this life and a sight of my Native Land would appear most acceptable at any time!

"Home, sweet home!!"

April 26
TUESDAY

A cold, wet day. Saw no whales and glad of it! A sail in sight to windward. Employed in "feeling miserable and shivering under wet clothes." So ends!

April 27
WEDNESDAY

"Very like a whale!" ("Shakespeare") 6 AM Raised a poor, little, mean, ugly, rascally, villainous, "scrag-head" whale! At 7 AM he was snugly moored alongside, a victim to the Waist Boat's harpoons! The rascal's actions denoted a desire "to make work for the Carpenter" and he would doubtless have succeeded had not a peculiar instrument which whalemen see fit to call a lance, found its way to his vitals! So ends!

April 28
THURSDAY

Boiling! A commencement has been made & I hope that it will continue & soon "tell" on our cargo! If this was only the last whale now, but then I suppose I would say, "if we were only in sight of New Bedford now!" So it goes! Patience! A time for all things!

April 29
FRIDAY

Finished boiling. Spoke whale ship "Thomas Nye." No success this voyage! Reports having seen a number of ships with like success! 6 PM Prospect for bad weather. And so ends the day!

April 30
SATURDAY

Lowered for whales without success! "Hard work" will be plenty for some 3 or 4 months now, and I suppose that some of us will long, many times, for a little sleep before the voyage is over! Well, our consolation (???) at such times is, we can "take it out" in wishing and make up our minds to be disappointed! Another sample of sailor's "many joys." So ends!

May 1
SUNDAY

A beautiful day! At 11 AM raised whales and chased them 'til 4 PM when the Larboard Boat went on & struck! The ways of God are mysterious, but, at the same time, they are all right! Oh! for 1 hour with my Dear Father tonight! How do I feel my loss now! I would give life itself could I but lay before him the feelings of my heart tonight! Could I but receive advice & counsel from him in regard to the strange conflict which is now worrying in my soul! God, direct me!!

May 2
MONDAY

Another fine day. Boiling. 9 AM Raised Whales. Starboard Boat went on & struck a fine one! Depressed in spirits today & longing for home!! So ends the day!

May 3
TUESDAY

Boiling. Lowered for whales without success! "Old Bloss" thinks that "he would rather 'hoe corn' than whale!" Well, "Blossom" I know of another that would prefer the use of the "hoe" to that of the "harpoon"! "Blossom" is very anxious for me to go home with him, and "teach school!" (Wonders will never cease!) He guarantees a full school (including himself) and promises to be a "good boy"! (Don't know about that, Bloss!)

May 4
WEDNESDAY

Employed in stowing oil. This thing of "keeping a log" is attended with many advantages to me; I intend to keep a daily journal as long as I live; and if one is faithfully kept—a true entry of all backslidings, shortcomings, errors in life, etc. made, it certainly will prove of great benefit to the keeper! I am sorry that I neglected keeping one so long as I did! And so ends the day!

May 5
THURSDAY

A damp, foggy morning. Employed in stowing oil! At 12N raised a large Cow & calf! Lowered Larboard Boat, succeeded in fastening to the calf and from that time 'til 4 PM, they maintained an obstinate running fight! The lance finally "brought their colors down" and at 7 PM the calf was snugly stowed in the Blubber Room and the cow safely moored along-side!

May 6
FRIDAY

An unpleasant foggy day! In the morning, "cutting in;" in the afternoon, stowing oil. A bad strain in my breast (received in the Blubber Room) threatens to be troublesome! I have been spitting blood today and a feeling, by no means comfortable, warns me to apply a remedy of some sort forthwith! Try & weather it without going to the Medicine Chest, for Calomel would surely be prescribed if one of these ugly fighting whales would knock a fellow's head, adrift!

March 7
SATURDAY

Boiling. Spoke Whale Ship, "Benjamin Morgan" of New London. Three whales this voyage. The "old Henry" "has the lead" so far! I care not, however, who "has the lead" if we only "fill up" and get home safely! I suppose if some persons could read my log they would be led to charge me with being a kind of "home-sick-chap" who was never satisfied unless in sight of his own family! Thank God for a heart to boldly plead, Guilty!! I would rather "slip my moorings" tonight than to be informed that the time will come when I will be dead to the holy influence of Dear Parents & Sisters at home!!! They do exert a powerful influence over me and I pray God, that though I live to be as old as Methuselah it will never cease!! So ends the week!

May 8
SUNDAY

Another fine day. Lowered several times for whale without success. A man is thrown into some strange company in the Whaling Service! It exceeds in point of danger all other branches of sea service; and I often think that this fact should influence those who are engaged in it & act as a check to the proverbial wickedness of the Sailor! But it really appears to me that the Devil sends the "flower of his ranks" on board Whale Ships, and specially commissions them to faithfully caricature their illustrious master and to show to the world a faithful representation of the character of the prime-minister of his dominions! More anon!

May 9
MONDAY

Employed in stowing oil, chasing whales, and thinking of home! If I have not learned a lesson (and paid for my learning too) I certainly will never learn one in this world! But nonsense! The case will admit of no "ifs"!! I have learned a lesson! One that will last too! Well, it's my own fault & I should not complain! So ends!

May 10
TUESDAY

Raised Whales, a cow & calf. Lowered. In a short time the Larboard Boat went on & struck the Cow! She immediately "brought to" and commenced to fight! The calf was not idle during the contest and his flukes, fins & head were brought into constant requisition against the deadly assault of man against his Parent! While the Waist Boat was engaged in combatting with the cow, the calf suddenly turned upon it with great fury! He came under and with his head mashed her to pieces! Just as he was about to strike the 2nd Officer darted a lance at him, this but increased his fury and he came the 2nd & 3rd time for the remains of the boat! Both were finally killed and no one was seriously hurt!

May 11
WEDNESDAY

Boiling. Lowered for whales without success! My breast continues to "growl" occasionally & I have found it necessary to apply a strengthening plaster & I don't know but that something serious may yet grow out of it! Well it has a powerful constitution (thank God) to contend with and I must say that I am not much afraid of it!

May 12
THURSDAY

Still boiling! Raised whales and lowered with no success. In my dreams of home (which occur every time that I sleep) the countenances of loved ones appear strikingly plain & often I find it extremely difficult to realize my present situation after awaking from a pleasant chat with my dear friends in dream-land! "There's a good time coming!"

May 13
FRIDAY

My birth-day!! What a curious lottery is life! If any one had told me two years ago today that I would be in the Japan Sea at this time chasing whales, I should have been tempted to inquire if there was a vacant room in the Lunatic Asylum which was strong enough to confine my informer! Well, I am here at any rate . . . and as Capt. Maryatt makes "Jacob Faithful," exclaim, "There's no use crying!" If alive I will spend my next birth-day at home (God willing). Employed today in stowing oil, and so ends the day!

May 14
SATURDAY

A gale of wind set in last night and has been raging all day violently. It promises a speedy cessation now. (9 PM) So ends!

May 15
SUNDAY

A fine morning. Saw no whales today & very glad of it! There is not a man in the ship so anxious to get home as I am and I know that the sooner full, the sooner home, yet I would rather come another voyage than to fill the ship, this, by Sabbath whaling! I have determined to write a series of articles on Sabbath-Whaling for publication if I live to get

home. They will be intended principally for Captains of
Whale ships, and I think that the advantage of personal
experience will materially assist me in my contemplated
duty! So ends the day!

May 16
MONDAY

Employed in stowing oil. At 4 PM a gale of wind set in
and it promises to be rather severe! Saw a Japanese Junk
today, the first this voyage! Wonder if loved ones at home
ever think of me? If they think of me as often as I think of
them, their minds must be busy indeed! It must be more
than ordinary transactions if I fail to devote a portion of
each day in thinking of those who are dear to me! God speed
our union!!

May 17
TUESDAY

Gale still rages! A very severe storm! Have been explaining the rare attractive properties of the Western-Country to
the Officers today! The 3rd & 4th Officers, one of the
harpooneers, and several of my mess-mates are all bound
out! (I rather guess not!) So ends!

May 18
WEDNESDAY

Gale abated in violence. Sea still very rough. Employed
in feeling "peculiarly blue" and longing for a reunion with
Dear Friends at home! It appears that notwithstanding my
determination to "make the best of it"—my unwilling determination on board the ship causes a feeling of melancholy to

pervade my heart, despite my most strenuous exertions to the contrary! I begin to think that I may as well allow it full sway, for it is determined to have the mastery!

May 19
THURSDAY

A fine day. Employed in sundry ship's duties. Wonder how my friend Dr. Skinner "comes on" these days! I sometimes wish that I had studied medicine with the Doctor—if by any means he would have been successful in "learning me the bones"! Let me see—"zygomatic process of the temporal bone" is somewhere between the crown of the head & the sole of the foot—the "intercostal muscles" "hold forth" somewhere in the region of the ribs,—the "right femoral artery," the "tibia," & "fibula" belong to the thigh & leg,— the "lachrymal gland" & "lachrymal duct" belong to the eye—the "dura-mater" & "pia-mater" are peculiar to the brain, etc., etc.! There Doctor, what do you think of that! "E. C. Cloud, M.D." (Not , "mule-driver!")

May 20
FRIDAY

Another fine day. Spoke "Belle." One whale (50 bbls) since we last saw her. It is pretty near time that the "Old Henry" had taken another start! Look sharp aloft boys, and let's get through with this horrible mockery, which those who love it see fit to call a life!

May 21
SATURDAY

Raised several large whales! Lowered. After a great deal of pulling, paddling & sailing, the Larboard Boat succeeded in striking—a regular monster! The largest whale I ever saw! 6 PM moored alongside. And so ends the week!

May 22
SUNDAY

Cutting & boiling! Lowered several times for whales without success! It really causes a feeling of true sorrow to pen the first line & a half of this day's log! What does it say? "Employed in willfully, coolly & premeditatedly transgressing the holy law of God, and bidding defiance to His most holy and just commandments!" Whose ears will not tingle as this truthful statement is made?!! Whose soul will not wither as this fearful declaration exhibits the mad sinner in his true light! Can it be thought strange that I am a miserable man, shut up in this "floating hell," compelled to participate in such a fearful occupation without a chance of escape for long & bitter months to come?

May 23
MONDAY

Still boiling. Lowered several times in the morning for whales without success. In the evening a gale of wind set in and is now (11 PM) raging violently. So ends!

May 24
TUESDAY

Gale abated. Finished boiling. Our monster whale has "turned up" 175 bbls of oil ! This is certainly a large quantity of oil to boil from one animal! It gives a faint idea of the monstrous size of the terrible animals with which we have to deal! But to know all—to be an eyewitness of their amazing strength & agility—to see them in all their monstrous dimensions—to be seated in a frail boat, in the middle of the ocean, exposed to their fury—when one experiences all—my word for it—there is no sport connected with any part of it!!

May 25

WEDNESDAY

Employed in stowing oil. Saw whales today but it was too rough to lower. My breast is somewhat troublesome today! Look out for "calomel"!! So ends!!!!

May 26

THURSDAY

Becalmed. At 9 AM raised whales. Lowered. The whales separated after we lowered and each boat selecting a whale, they continued to follow them up vainly endeavoring to "go on" 'til 4 PM. At that time, the boats were separated some 8 or 10 miles from each other and the Starboard Boat was getting quite "handy" to a large cow & bull that had been together all day. The whales had, to all appearances, "kept run" of the boat and had safely eluded the cunning of Capt. Vinall up to that time. The bull (a large & wicked one) by some means or other "lost run" of the boat at about 4 PM, the consequence of which was he had two solid harpoons in his broad back "before he knew it!" A "cut" with his flukes,—which for strength, fury, & malice I never saw equaled, followed this rather "striking" act of "friendship" on our part, and fortunately for us it fell short of the mark! When his flukes struck the sea there was a report as loud as thunder! The only damage sustained was a hair breadth escape from death and a broken boat mast! Rather close "cutting"!! 7 PM moored.

May 27
FRIDAY

A fine morning! Cutting in. 12 N finished. 1 PM Started works. 2 PM Lowered for whales. 3 PM Waist Boat fast to a Tarter! 4 ½ PM Dead! 5 PM Moored! 8 PM Took "tea" (?) 11 ½ PM Feel sleepy! 12 (mid-night) "Blue." 1 AM 8 Bells and a chance to get a little sleep!! So ends!

May 28
SATURDAY

A foggy morning. Employed in cutting in, and boiling! 7 more whales (like the last) will fill the "Old Henry" nicely! I hope that we may take them!

May 29
SUNDAY

Boiling. Saw no whales today and very glad of it! Well, this cannot last forever! God grant a speedy deliverance!

May 30
MONDAY

Employed in boiling & stowing oil. The "lower hold" is full and the "between-decks" alone remain to be filled! Well, 6 good whales will do that handsomely! Spoke the "Belle." Has struck 5 whales since we last saw her, without success! The Captain of the "Belle" is an old fidgety sort of a chap, and I should think that he is not over stocked with that very valuable article, generally styled—"common sense." Capt.

Vinall wished to purchase a few casks from the old gentleman today and he replied by "offering Bark & all!" He is quite angry because we have been successful and he has not! Patience, old gentleman, patience!

May 31
TUESDAY

Finished boiling. Employed in stowing oil between decks! "Duff" is to be issued 3 times per week from today and I really think that this wonderful phenomena will have the effect of filling us up! And so ends the month!

June 1
WEDNESDAY

Employed in stowing oil! Where was I two years ago, and where will I be one year from today? I humbly trust that the magic word Home, will answer both questions! God grant it!

June 2
THURSDAY

A fine day. Employed in "setting up" pipes, and thinking of home! What a "raft" of objects for love "loom up" before me, when I sit down and think of home!! First on the list are my Beloved Parents and my mind wanders back to infancy and I trace the holy love with which they have watched over me, notwithstanding my many acts of ingratitude towards them! Next come my Dear Sisters and I long to meet them again at home and prove to them that I am worthy of a Sister's love! And then, thoughts of Amelia fill my mind & I wonder if we are destined to be happy together in this world!

June 3
Friday

A fine day. Employed in stowing bone & sundry ship's duties. The whales have all left this latitude it appears and where they have gone remains to be found out! Thinking that they are paying a visit to their friends at "White Rock" we are bound after them to make one of the "party." So ends the day!

June 4
Saturday

One month from today and I hope to be bound home! If my legs were only long enough, I would like to step across and see my friends tonight! (Where is "Jack" and his "7 league boots I wonder!") Employed in feeling as though I would have no particular objections in being at home!! So ends!

June 5
Sunday

A most beautiful day! Undisturbed by the hateful cry of "There-re-she blows-ows-ows!" It really appears like a new life to have one Sabbath dawn and die, without being desecrated by lowering for whales! God grant many such!

June 6
Monday

Employed in sundry ship's duties. Saw no whales and holding our course for White Rock. Prospect for filling up this month begins to look dark!

June, 1853

June 7
TUESDAY

Employed in setting a new "try-pot" in the works. Look sharp aloft boys! Only 6 more! So ends!

June 8
WEDNESDAY

A foggy disagreeable day. Employed in sundry ship's duties. It is a matter of much curiosity to me, how persons who come whaling once will be such "thick-headed asses" as to come again! I cannot for the life of me see one single attractive feature in any part of the life; but, all that is disgusting, hateful, filthy, demoralizing, & vile mark each page of its miserable journal and tend to increase my utter disgust of its most "allowable" transactions! So ends!

June 9
THURSDAY

"Woodland" on the weather bow! No whales in sight. We took some fine whales on this ground last voyage and I hope that our "lucky-star" will rise above us, this! There is no reason to believe that we will even see a single whale here now, because we saw them last voyage. They are constantly changing their "ground" and where ever "brett" (their food) abounds there we will see whales! So ends!

June 10
FRIDAY

A fine day. Saw no whales. One of the crew (a French-man) is confined to his bunk with a very bad side! He got into a row in Maui (Sandwich Islands) before he joined our ship and had several of his ribs broken. It appears that while leaning across the top-sail yards (reefing) he has refractured them! Poor fellow! he is suffering great pain! I have voluntarily appointed myself the "for'castle doctor" and my "professional skill" is brought into "active service" almost every day! I went to poor Harry today and asked him how he felt. He replied by pointing to his side and groaning deeply. I looked at the injured part and applied some wormwood & whiskey. After this, I tore a wide strip from my blanket and wound it tightly around him and then advised him to try and get some sleep. I was in the for'castle at 20 PM and Harry was awake. He immediately arose and seizing my hand, continued to thank me and express his sincere gratitude for several minutes. My feelings were touched when I heard this strong-man; vowing eternal friendship with a quivering voice & a moistened eye; for a simple act of duty which I performed to a suffering fellow being! More anon.

June 11
SATURDAY

Ran in, close to land; saw whales & lowered. No success! How glad will I be when I log for the last time that simple sentence—"Lowered for Whales!" It is my own fault that I have had occasion to log it at all; and when (after this voyage) I log it again, something will happen a little out of the way of ordinary transactions!! Employed in spelling h-o-m-e!

June 12
SUNDAY

A fine morning. Spoke Bark "Neva" of Greenport and ship "Benjamin Morgan." At 22 N a heavy fog came down and for the remainder of the day we were enshrouded in its gloomy drapery, and employed our time in shivering under wet clothes! Home, sweet home!!

June 13
MONDAY

A foggy disagreeable day. We will have to "work smart" if we fill up this month! Time is flying and there is yet room for 600 bbls of oil! A very small quantity but it is extremely slow in making its appearance! "Wait a little longer!" So sing the Hutchinsons!!

June 14
TUESDAY

A fine day. Lowered 3 times for whales today without success. The Bark Neva succeeded in striking 3 whales, but saved one! Our turn next! So ends.

June 15
WEDNESDAY

In the morning lowered for Right Whales, but with no success. In the afternoon, lowered for "Siberian" Whales! To take one of these monsters would be to take a prize! They average 300 bbls of oil apiece, and the quality of their oil is more valuable than Right Whale oil! It is useless to attempt their capture, however, for they will "take a line" in a "jiffy"! And so ends.

June 16
THURSDAY

A thick fog has completely hid "Old Sol" from our wet shirts all day! Employed in ringing the water out of our clothes & thinking of a "good fire" at home! So ends!

June 17
FRIDAY

Still foggy with an occasional clearing away. At such times we saw whales and chased them without success. Employed in writing "enigmas" (during my watch below) and giving them to the Captain & Officers to work. They have said that I cannot compose one which they cannot solve! I affirm that I can! We'll see!

June 18
SATURDAY

Still foggy! Our prospects for filling up are about as dark & dismal as the day which has just passed! Don't growl! All right! The Main-top-sail-"tie" parted today and let the yard down on the "cap" "by the run"! Some one will be killed yet with that same yard! The "runner-block" fell within 3 inches of a man's head today and grazed the arm of another! Look out boys! "One hand for the owners & the other for—yourself!"

June 19
SUNDAY

Fog still hangs on! At 3 PM it partially cleared away and on looking around we discovered the Bark Neva's Boats chasing whales. Capt. Vinall ordered his boats down but no

June, 1853

success crowned the efforts of all to desecrate the Sabbath! Deliverance is coming!

June 20
MONDAY

Well fog it is!! Constant cold wet fog! If England can equal this, why keep me away from it for ever! Have not yet succeeded in "puzzling" the Officers with an enigma! Look out for a "poser" by and by! So ends!

June 21
TUESDAY

At 22 N the fog—cleared away! Raised whales! Lowered. In a short time the Larboard Boat succeeded in striking a small one and sinking him! Succeeded in raising & saving him. Got him moored at 3 ½ and the fog again came down! 6 PM Cut in!

June 22
WEDNESDAY

The blubber (of our yesterdays whale) is so poor that it will not "pay" to boil it yet! Minced it & stowed it down again in the blubber room. Spoke Bark Neva again. My breast has given me much trouble within the past 4 days and today I feel exceedingly unwell! Must "doctor it" pretty soon!

June 23
THURSDAY

A damp foggy morning. Boiling. I reported the condition of my breast today to Capt. Vinall. He bled me, freely, and applied a blister. I don't know whether the bleeding was proper or not, but I must "take what I can get." Feel quite unwell! Now is the time when the true worth and mighty meaning of that magic word—"Mother" is felt!

June 24
FRIDAY

Finished boiling. Weather continues foggy! Have not experienced so much pain today in my breast, but I am still far from feeling well!

June 25
SATURDAY

"Land ho!" White Rock once more! In the afternoon raised whales. Got all ready to lower when a thick fog came down and shut them out of sight! The 2nd & 3rd Officers exchanged their harpooneers today, in consequence of some difficulty occurring between them. Feel some better with a prospect for improvement.

June 26
SUNDAY

A beautiful day. Whales were raised at 20 o'clock and the Boats lowered to chase. Success attended our endeavors and at 4 PM the whale was moored. The Capt. & one of the crew were knocked out of the Starboard Boat, but were unhurt. I again log my utter aversion to this life and a strong desire to see my Dear friends at home!! And so ends the day!

June 27
MONDAY

Boiling. At 20 AM raised a large cow & calf. Lowered two boats & started in pursuit. In a few moments the Larboard

Boat was fast solid to the calf! From that time 'til 5 PM the whales maintained a most desperate running fight! They remained together constantly and it was truly remarkable to see the watchful solicitude of the cow for her offspring! I thought that I had seen whales "fight" before but I have come to a different conclusion now! At 5 PM the boats cut line and came aboard. Neither of the whales can live for at the time of cutting line they were bleeding very freely from lance & spade wounds as "thick as hops"!! It is a wonder of mercy that the lives of those who were in the boats today are preserved! Many times it appeared impossible to avoid the mighty flukes & fins of the whales as they furiously swept the sea, but the strong arm of God was stretched out & all are preserved! So ends!

June 28
TUESDAY

A fine day. Still boiling. Raised whales again this morning & lowered. After a great deal of manoeuvering the Bow Boat went on & struck! In about 2 hours he "turned up" dead and—sunk! He was a very small whale but we found it impossible to raise him! Cut line & came aboard! So ends Tuesday!

June 29
WEDNESDAY

Finished boiling. Employed in cleaning up. This is a cold, unpleasant, foggy day! 4 PM heading for "Woodland." "Old Bloss" feels as though "he would like a little whiskey!" Judging by his "organ of smell" he has been rather intimately acquainted with the "critter" at some period of his life, and

I would advise "Blossom" to steer clear of the grog tub if he wishes to be re-elected to the important post of "blowing" the base-drum in New Jersey! So ends.

June 30
THURSDAY

A foggy, disagreeable day. Employed in coopering and stowing oil. "Every full pipe that goes down leaves a smaller number to go!" There is still a large space to fill up, however, and I sincerely wish that we may soon succeed in doing it! So ends the month!

July 1
FRIDAY

Still foggy! Employed this morning in stowing oil. 2 PM Cleared away. 2 PM Lowered for a very large Siberian Whale! At about 4 o'clock the Larboard Boat succeeded in fastening solid!!!! (Something new!) He immediately commenced sounding and the 1st Officer "took another turn around the loggerhead" with the line, for the purpose of arresting him in his sound! He did not "believe in stopping," however, and finding that he could take no more of the line he "put some more steam on" and wrenched the head of the iron off! Succeeded in "losing him!"

July 2
SATURDAY

More fog! Employed in washing ship. Wonder if "Mag & Will" ever think of the "Squire"?!!! I often think of you & your sweet babe and would give a world if I was in York tonight! You, Dear Mag are the only member of the family with whom I took a parting farewell when I started on a whaling voyage!! My mind, often averts to that evening! God bless you & yours my Dear Sisters & hasten our reunion! So ends the week!

July 3
SUNDAY

A fine day. Employed in reading my Bible and thinking of home! My anxiety to get there increases every day! Time seems to drag very slowly along and as I count the tedious hours my very soul exclaims, "Give me liberty, or give me death!!"

July 4
MONDAY

"Independence" day! If the subjects of King George were more anxious to breathe the sweet air of liberty than the subjects of "King Vinall" are, they were certainly justifiable in adopting extreme measures to accomplish their great end! I think that my desire to live in a "Republic" is at present quite as strong as was theirs in those days! But it is not expedient to follow their example, in forming one, and I must patiently await a deliverance in the natural course of events! Lowered for whales today and succeeded in losing the Waist Boat in a fog! We were on the point of firing minute guns when she found us and the affair created much sport at the expense of the 2nd Officer!

July 5
TUESDAY

Foggy again! Saw no whales. Prospect for filling up this voyage begins to look "like a sick man's shadow"—very "thin!" Well, I really hope that "my figure" will "fatten up" shortly! Give me a model of Daniel Lambert (Look out Mandy) or any one who has claims to Shakespeare's subject of "unbounded stomach" and then I will begin to think that the "Old Henry" is something like a "lucky" ship! (More straight jackets!)

July 6
WEDNESDAY

Still foggy! Can't see a ship's length ahead! "So, so!" "Can't puzzle you, eh?!!" It looks like it when you have all "give it up"!! Now, I will wait until you puzzle me before I compose another!

July 7
THURSDAY

Fog, fog, fog!! Positive fog, comparative "foggy," superlative, "fog all the time"! (Go up to the head.) I was sitting on the windlass about 22 ½ AM talking with a messmate when an indefinable feeling of uneasiness came over me! Turning to him, I said, "Capt. Vinall should get an observation, Mac, for we don't know exactly where we are!" In a few moments after 8 Bells struck and we were piped to dinner, I went down in the for'castle, still feeling strangely uneasy!! Had but sit down when that thrilling cry of "breakers ahead," sounded throughout the ship, followed by a call of "all hands wear ship"! I sprung on deck and looked over the bow! There we were almost ashore and with very little prospect of getting off clear! The officers had some occasion to stop on deck 5 minutes after being called to dinner and that circumstance alone saved us! Had they have gone down we would have been ashore in 20 minutes! Upon what a brittle thread hangs our life!

July 8
FRIDAY

A beautiful morning. 6 AM raised whales! Lowered the Larboard Boat, succeeded in striking a fine one and at 9, he was snugly moored! From day-light 'til we lowered, I had occasional opportunities to read the "Memoir of Payson," a valuable work in which I am much interested. Capt. Vinall will please accept my sincere thanks for the loan of it. So ends!

July 9
SATURDAY

Boiling. Lowered for whales again today, but with no success! Prospect for bad weather. Feel particularly blue and wish I was home! Patience!

July 10
SUNDAY

A lovely day! Lowered several times in the morning for whales without success. In the afternoon the Larboard Boat succeeded in striking & killing one. I can add no more to this day's log.

July 11
MONDAY

Cutting in, boiling & stowing down. Lowered for whales without success! Weather looks threatening! My anxiety to get home increases daily and it is difficult to curb my feelings! Patience, patience!!

July 12
TUESDAY

A gale of wind & rain set in last night and raged 'til daylight this morning! Some difficulty with Capt. Vinall today in regard to the quantity of meat issued. Two of the crew "pulled each other's hair" for the same cause! Must have more meat! Not enough now! "More meat, or no whales!" So ends!

July 13
WEDNESDAY

A fine day. Finished boiling in the morning. In the afternoon lowered for whales. Larboard Boat went on, struck & killed a literal monster! The largest whale that any one in the ship ever saw!! Plenty of meat today!! So ends!

July 14
THURSDAY

Boiling. Our "monster," proves to be "counterfeit;" he is a miserable "dry-shin," and will probably yield 80 bbls of oil! Had he been fat he would doubtless have yielded 250 bbls of oil!! I am sorry to log an altercation between the 1st & 3rd Officers which resulted in a fight! Some hard feelings in regard to "going on" the whale is the cause of it! Bad, bad!! So ends!

July, 1853

July 15
FRIDAY

A warm foggy day. Employed in "stowing off" the after hold. Discovered an ugly leak in the "stern-post"! Some idea may be formed of the size of "our monster" when his head alone measured 25 feet in length!!! 4 PM "cooled down" the try-works, and so ends the day!

July 16
SATURDAY

Still foggy & warm. Started the works again this morning. "Just wait, 'til I 'bring up' in Columbus!" Don't have any "works" there! No whales either! Don't think I will come away again very soon! What do you think about it, "Orve"! . . . . I know your reply!!

July 17
SUNDAY

Finished boiling. In the afternoon, employed in reading my Bible and the memories of Payson & Brainerd. A new feeling seems to take possession of my heart as I look around me! Oh! what a field for study is this sea, the heavens, the winds, the sun, moon & stars! What appears most remark-able is the fact that I have never remarked this great field of thought before, but have dragged idly along, suffering from monotony and starving with hunger, when so much food has been within my reach all the while!

July 18
MONDAY

A wet, foggy morning. We were put on allowance of water today, and to say the least, it is an act very unbecoming our

Skipper! Himself & his officers use the water to wash in and the idea of putting the crew on allowance is absurd, unjust & wrong! Hard feelings exist among the crew and some talk of coming to an understanding! So ends.

July 19
TUESDAY

Still foggy! Employed in stowing oil. The 2nd officer gave me my first lesson in Navigation today and very kindly furnished me with his quadrant with which to take observations! The 2nd & 3rd Officers each furnished me with an Epectome, and look out, now for a "master-navigator." So ends.

July 20
WEDNESDAY

A beautiful morning. The sun seemed unusually radiant with God's glory and I was led to "look through Nature up to Nature's God!" Employed in washing & drying bone. Three more good whales will start us for home, but they appear to be in no "hurry" coming along-side!

July 21
THURSDAY

A damp foggy morning. Employed in setting up casks, etc. No whales in sight. My mind has appeared to soar into regions too profound for me to grapple with today as I was meditating on the beauties of Nature! A feeling of rapture appears to have filled my soul as I eagerly collect words to express my sentiments—while gazing at the millions of gems in God's firmament and I occasionally think that I will commit them to writing!

July 22
FRIDAY

Still foggy. At 9 AM, cleared away. Discovered a sail, close to board. 20 AM spoke Bark "Gentleman." The same strain of thought has filled my mind today,—in regard to the beauties of Nature—and to say that I am delighted would be but poorly expressing my feelings! A thought flitted across my mind today which gives me some uneasiness! It is that the enraptured feelings of my heart are, false! God forbid!

July 23
SATURDAY

A foggy morning. 2 PM cleared away. Spoke Bark Gentleman again and got 200 bbls (in pipes) from her. A lovely evening succeeded the day & my "new mind" was busily enough employed! What mind can conceive the happiness of spending an Eternity with God, Christ & Angels—employed eternally in meditating on the surrounding Glory of God and singing praises to the Great uncreated Three, who devised a glorious, and efficient plan to reach that blessed haven of rest! May that occupation be mine in Heaven, is my earnest prayer to God !

July 24
SUNDAY

A beautiful morning. Lowered for whales without success. I got a home paper from the Bark and find much news! God speed my return!

July 25
MONDAY

Another fine day. At 2 PM raised whales. Made sail and chased them 'til 4 PM when we discovered that they were not of the right sort! (Hump-backs.) Spoke the "Gentleman" again today. So ends!

July 26
TUESDAY

A foggy day. Employed in washing, mending, etc. 300 bbls more will "fill her up," but to get them is the thing! I expected to be some distance on my way home by this time, but like many other fond hopes it is crushed! Home, sweet home!!

July 27
WEDNESDAY

A fine day. Lowered for whales without success. "Blossom," thinks that "he must get married," as soon as he brings up in New Jersey!! He is acquainted with a spruce maiden lady only 69 last spring who is the captivating owner of a frame house & a cat of the "Kitty gender!" Look sharp, "Bloss," "trim your main sheet well aft and give her a weather wheel!"

July 28
THURSDAY

Lowered for whales again today with the usual success! Prospect grows more dark! Employed in trying to make the best of it! And so ends!

July 29
FRIDAY

A fine day. Employed in sundry ship's duties. Wonder what my Dear Friends are doing to night at home! I often look in to the sitting room and plainly see the loved countenance of each dear one! God hasten our reunion! So ends!

July 30
SATURDAY

A dark cloudy morning! 22 N. cleared away and set in, hot. Employed in trying to endure the misery of a prolonged separation from loved ones at home! And so ends the week!

July 31
SUNDAY

A beautiful day. I was standing at the wheel today and Capt. Vinall came aft and commenced a conversation in regard to religious matters. He proceeded to state the difficulty of collecting his thoughts and centering them upon God; when he attempted to pray! He inquired my opinion concerning it and I endeavored to show him the cause! Again do I feel my loss! Again would I give worlds to see my Dear Father tonight! Alas, my deprivations are all self-imposed and I dare not complain!

August 1
MONDAY

Another fine day! Capt. Vinall has determined to proceed to the Okhotsk Sea and "try our luck" there! We are detained now with calms. Employed in thinking of home! So ends!

August 2
TUESDAY

Lowered 3 times for Swordfish today! The first time our supposed "Sword-fish" proved to be a seal! The lowerings for swordfish proved unsuccessful. Employed in anticipating many happy seasons with loved ones at home!! God hasten the day!!

August 3
WEDNESDAY

A light breeze sprung up this morning and at 3 PM it had increased to a "stiff to'gallant!" A lighter heart fills my breast as I see the old ship "doing her best" and I am leaving the Japan Sea now "for good"!! Once in the Okhotsk, and I will feel as though we had done something toward getting home! "Speed, speed, the homeward bound!"

August 4
THURSDAY

Lowered and struck a fine sun-fish! Succeeded in— losing him,—after we had got him half way up the ship's side! "Try, try again!!" And so ends the day!

August 5
FRIDAY

A fine day. I have so far progressed in the study of Navigation as to find the Latitude at sea by a meridian altitude of the Sun, and to find the time at sea and regulate a watch by the sun's altitude! My next advance will be to "work chronometer time" and find the Longitude! So ends.

August 6
SATURDAY

Bound to the Okhotsk with a roaring breeze! 22 AM saw a sail ahead supposed to be the Bark "Gentleman." 22 N called all hands to shorten sail. 5 PM "Laying to" under a close-reefed main-top-sail & fore-sail. A severe gale!

August 7
SUNDAY

Gale abated. A thick fog has lain upon us all day. My thoughts have been busy at home today and (as usual) I have been spending the day with Dear Friends! Imagination colors her pictures so faithfully and with such brilliancy that I am often in a strait to tell where I really am!

August 8
MONDAY

A fine day. Employed in washing ship, etc. The day will come between this and the year 8000, when we will do this job, for the last time!!! (I hope!) And so ends the day!

August 9
TUESDAY

A noble breeze is urging the "Old Henry" to her utmost! The Straits of Perouse are distant 2 ½*. Prospect this evening for bad weather. So ends.

August 10

WEDNESDAY.

A foggy morning. Employed in breaking out for bread & water. PM took in sail, and "laid to." A gale is now (20 PM) raging and there is little prospect for a cessation! And so ends!

August 11

THURSDAY

Gale, still rages. All looks dark & gloomy! 4 PM must predict a change! The cook killed a pig (one of the 4 legged ones) and we "sailors " are to have a chance at his ears, tail, & feet!! Only think of that, ye epicures!! (Receipt for making a "sailors' mess!") "Take, 2 buckets full of fresh water—the ears, nose, tail, & feet of one pig—5 good sized, cock-roaches—20 potatoes—and as many flies, as are at hand just before the mess is cooked! Then take the hams, shoulders, spare ribs, etc. of said pig and—send them aft!! Boil over a brisk fire for 25 hours and eat with a large quantity of faith! (Nonsense!!)

August 12

FRIDAY

A foggy morning. Employed in spreading bone, etc. 9 AM cleared away & made sail. 22 N 28 miles from Straits of Perouse. 7 PM Prospect is for a "wild night"! Must be more brief in my entries or I will not have room to log the entire voyage! I regret this!

August, 1853

August 13
SATURDAY

Last night was emphatically one of terror! Such lightning & thunder I never experienced before and don't wish to again! This morning the air is very pure & fresh and its effect is duly appreciated. Employed in thinking of home!

August 14
SUNDAY

8 AM entering Straits of Perouse! 22 AM Once more in Seghalien Sea! Spoke Bark "Italy"!! 4 PM Lowered for whales without success! Right.

August 15
MONDAY

Lowered for whales. Larboard Boat struck a few one, but the irons drew & he escaped! PM Saw a whale attacked by "Killers"! In a short time, they had him "hors-du-combat" and we lowered & struck him. Lost him! So ends!

August 16
TUESDAY

A severe thunder squall came up this morning and I remarked several very nimble flashes of lightening that seemed to come in rather dangerous proximity to our royal-masts! Saw whales but did not lower. Two years from New Bedford today! Time is flying!

August 17
WEDNESDAY

Last night was a fearful one and this morning is its counterpart! At 22 N, lulled. At 3 PM made sail and stood in for land. Saw a whaler boiling. What a blessing that through the many dangers of the past 3 days I could look up to my God and experience a sweet calm feeling of security which could not be surpassed if I was at home! God grant to continue this happy season!

August 18
THURSDAY

A beautiful morning. Stood in close to land. Looked green & inviting! I quickly thought of home! Am very much interested in reading Pollok's "Course of time," this book came to me under peculiar circumstances which I will probably explain by & by!

August 19
FRIDAY

Humbugged all day, bracing, wearing, tacking, & squaring to "show off" before the Bark Italy, just such another "old oil box" as this! So ends!

August 20
SATURDAY

A fine morning. Raised a junk. Boarded it but found no persons to "show their papers"! Had some idea of bringing it alongside & making fire wood of it but concluded to let it drive! And so ends the week!

August 21
SUNDAY

Another fine morning. Raised whales & lowered! In about 3 hours, the Larboard Boat succeeded in striking and at 22 N we were cutting in! At 2 PM the Starboard Boat went down and struck another,—a very large one! He ran away! Who can form a just estimate of the sins of this day?!! From early dawn 'til dark night a constant round of desecrations has been kept up and I feel tonight but little better than the man who is condemned to death!! God in mercy hasten my deliverance!

August 22
MONDAY

Boiling. Lowered several times for whales without success. That a great change has taken place in my heart, there can be no doubt! A style and order of thought in regard to the boundless mercy of God, the all sufficient atonement of Jesus, happy anticipation of heaven, a rapturous admiration of Nature, etc, all tend to confirm me in the belief that a great & mighty change has taken place! Thank God, He has not forsaken me !! The feelings which I speak of are entirely new to me, and it indeed remains a mystery from whence they have proceeded! In my frequent meditations language is made use of, which (until that time) I was entirely unacquainted with! Oh! may it continue and increase and may I have everlasting glory in Heaven—a meek, humble, holy & devoted child of God!!

August 23
TUESDAY

A fine day. Finished boiling. Employed in cleaning up decks. Have been thinking of home today! Would give worlds, could I but be there!

August 24

WEDNESDAY

Lowered for whales. In about 4 hours, the Larboard Boat succeeded in striking a fine one! After being killed he sunk! Lost him! In the evening the Larboard Boat fastened to another! At 8 PM we cut line, and left him "spouting blood!" A very good illustration of the "chances" of a whaleman's life!

August 25

THURSDAY

Employed in stowing oil. Lowered again for whales without success! Two more good whales, will fill everything and start us home! I hope that we may soon get them for home is tightening its hold of me, hourly! Would give much to see "Orve & Amelia" tonight!

August 26

FRIDAY

Raised whales. Lowered. After a long time the Waist Boat succeeded in striking a "live Tarter"! The most limber whale I ever saw! He made several desperate attempts to "make work for the Carpenter," and succeeded! A very gentle touch with the tip of his flukes caused an ugly breach in the Starboard Boat! No one hurt! Saw a large ship whaling; supposed to be the "Nile" of Greenport. 6 PM all cut in!

August 27

SATURDAY

Boiling. A cold foggy day! Have been thinking of home again today! Well, it will not be long before I will be on my way thither, at any rate! 'til then, "Patience" is the word! So ends.

August 28
SUNDAY

Raised whales; lowered. In 20 minutes the Waist Boat was fast to a large one! He parted the iron & escaped! 2 PM Larboard Boat struck another! Line parted & he also escaped! Right! My feelings to night are much easier imagined than described! Much has transpired today, which was well calculated to create indifference, etc., etc. God grant to assist me! This is a curious life for a man to lead!! Well it is not eternal!

August 29
MONDAY

A fine day. Raised whales & lowered. The Larboard Boat would have been fast again, but the harpooneer had his irons foul. "Try again!"

August 30
TUESDAY

Employed in stowing oil. I met with quite a serious accident today; one which will "knock me off duty" for perhaps 3 or 4 weeks! We were "heading over" an "22 bbl cask of oil" for the "hold gang" to stow. I was "footing" the cask, and when just on the point of going over, the ship rolled heavy, which brought the cask right-back and threw the entire weight immediately across my right foot. (Something over one & a quarter tons!!) The greatest wonder is that my foot was not cut off!! As it is, I cannot detect a single bone that is fractured! The foot is horribly mashed too, but no broken bones! 8 PM very painful!

August 31
WEDNESDAY

A fine day. I neglected to log yesterday that the Larboard Boat struck a whale but got "run off" in short order! Lowered again for whales today without success. Only one more!! Foot much swollen & very painful! Miss the comforts of home!! So ends!

September 1
THURSDAY

A stormy tempestuous day! Standing along under double-reefed-top-sails; saw whales & lowered! No success! (of course on such a day). Foot continues to give me great pain! Home, sweet home!

September 2
FRIDAY

A foggy, dismal day! Saw no whales. In the evening we signalized a Bark on our weather beam. Supposed to be the "Neva." Employed in washing bone, etc. Foot still very painful. It causes a feeling of joy to fill my heart as I see the anxiety in regard to my foot, expressed by the entire crew! I am unworthy of this!

September 3
SATURDAY

Well, I suppose that we have taken our last whale!! (Can it be possible?) I am well satisfied with the fruit of the voyage and my great anxiety now is to get home! Never, catch me away again!! So ends.

September 4
SUNDAY

A cold foggy day. At 22 N spoke Bark "Italy." 2 more whales to fill. At 4 PM saw her boats fast to a large whale. Have been thinking of home all day! Oh! how slowly drag the sweet hours of liberty! Foot continues painful & much swollen. Miss the attentions of a Dear Mother!

September 5
MONDAY

Cold, bad weather! Saw large numbers of whales but they were not of the right sort! Employed in—"suffering much pain"! Home, sweet home!!!

September 6
TUESDAY

A cold, stormy morning! Rendered less intolerable by anticipating coming happy seasons with loved ones at home! Watch employed in spreading bone, etc. And so ends!

September 7
WEDNESDAY

A fine day. Raised whales. Lowered with no success. It seems that I have not yet done "logging whales"! Well, I will patiently await the end now! There are no whales in Columbus! So ends!

September 8
THURSDAY

Another fine day. Lowered for whales again today! In a short time the Waist Boat succeeded in striking a fine one! Irons parted & we lost him! Well, if Capt. Vinall had started for home 3 days ago he would not have lost that harpoon! Better start now, before we lose something else; the ship, herself, probably! So ends.

September 9
FRIDAY

Lowered for whales again today! Starboard Boat went on & struck a small one! After spouting blood, he "took the line," and "walked away"!!! I told you so, Captain! Look out for another!! In the evening, spoke Bark "Italy." Got a few staves. Prospect for bad weather. Foot rather better.

September 10
SATURDAY

A severe gale of wind has been raging all day. Employed in thinking in what manner I will go home in order to prevent the loved ones from knowing me! Have decided upon a plan! So ends!

September 11
SUNDAY

Gale subsided. Made sail and spoke Italy. Before another Sabbath I hope to be bound home!! My desire to get there is truly inexpressible! Foot painful today! So ends.

September, 1853

September 12

MONDAY

A fine day. Spoke Italy and got some wood. Employed in breaking out, "studding-sail-booms"! Thank God for so much!! "There's no place like home!"

September 13

TUESDAY.

"Homeward Bound"!!!!!!!

No dream, no fiction, no romance, no supposition,— but candid, self evident, sound, sober, fact!!!! The effect of those two words, on the entire crew is truly magical! A glance aloft, exhibits the glistening studding-sails, bellying full to the breeze, and the roaring of the water at her bows seems to say—"Homeward bound!!"—Indeed, "homeward bound" is seen, felt, tasted, smelled, heard, eat & drank, by all hands! Foot is a great deal better today! 20 PM Feel like a new man! So ends!

September 14

WEDNESDAY

A lovely morning in the "Old Pacific"!! Last evening we rapidly passed American Island with its giddy peak lost to view in a cloud of mist, and as the night drew on and all the glittering gems of God's diadem sparkled in "humble glory," and the Moon in all her loveliness added fresh beauty to the scene,—my mind seemed to be eager to free itself from my body and soar away to the habitation of those who continually sing the praises of Him, "who spake and it was done—

who commanded & it stood fast!" Pollock's sentiment, expressed in his Course of Time—in regard to the Moon—appears peculiarly "fascinating" to me! More anon! So ends!

September 15
THURSDAY

A fine day. Employed in cleaning up decks. Stowed the "cooler" between decks and presented "Old Neptune" with a fine "shaving box," the "deck-pot!" "Homeward bound" explains all!! Prospect for a storm! Foot, rather painful today. Take care!!

September 16
FRIDAY

Twenty five months from New Bedford today! A stiff breeze is blowing this morning and the "Old Henry" feels it! I suppose that washing ship will come next! And so ends the day!

September 17
SATURDAY

The wind increased to a gale last night & this morning we are wallowing under a heavy N. Easter! Six months from now & I hope to be home !! 'til then, loved ones!, God bless you! Employed in trying to bring my happy feelings within bounds! Very hard work!! So ends!

September 18
SUNDAY

Storm abated and made sail. Four Sabbaths more & I hope to spend one in Oahu at the Bethel! God grant us a speedy passage! So ends!

September, 1853

September 19
MONDAY

A fresh breeze is blowing this morning, but the dark threatening aspect of the heavens still enshroud us as it were in gloom! 20 AM promises a change. What would I not give could I but see my Dear Parents, Sisters & Friends to night! Next to serving my God acceptably, the reunion with those (and all) who are dear to me, forms the great principle study of my soul! Oh! how incalculable is their value!! Gold, jewels,—crowns, worlds, could not purchase them from me!

September 20
TUESDAY

Very bad weather is emphatically the order of both day & night! Rain, rain, and every drop "feels wet!" Employed in washing ship and feeling as though "I would just as soon be at home today!"

September 21
WEDNESDAY

Still raining! Cold, wet, stormy weather that is warranted to bring the "comforts of home," to mind! Well, it is the will of One mightier than man and it is all right & good! At 7 bells (22 ½ AM) a heavy gale set in, and we are now (9 PM) laying to under storm stay-sails!

September 22
THURSDAY

Gale subsided & a fine day. Bent new fore & main-top-sails & fore to'gallant sail. Studding sails on both sides "alow & aloft" and—"homeward bound!"

September 23

FRIDAY

A fine day. Employed in sending up main royal & fore to'gallant studding-sail! Go it!! I love to see plenty of canvass on her! Only give us the breeze and we will handle her sails! And so ends!

September 24

SATURDAY

A head wind succeeded a calm this morning which prevents us from heading within 5 points of our course! Bad, bad!!

September 25

SUNDAY

A heavy gale is raging this morning! Laying to under a close reefed-main-top-sail. My "new mind" has been actively employed today with the large quantity of matter for study— seen in the grand & magnificent view before and around me! 'Tis most strange that I have been blind so long! 4 PM the wind hauled fair & we kept off and scudded before it. So ends.

September 26

MONDAY

A disagreeable, tempestuous day! The wind has been fair & free, however,—in one instance, rather too free, so we thought, at least, when we were clearing away the wreck of the "Starboard fore-top-mast-stern-sail-boom!" Rigged a new one & "tried it again"!!

September, 1853

September 27
TUESDAY

A fine day. A noble breeze is compelling the "old Henry" to "do her best!" The leaks are increasing fore & aft and we have to pump ship twice a day! Employed in various deck & rigging jobs, and so ends!

September 28
WEDNESDAY

Our noble breeze is slightly decreasing this morning! Sorry! 8 Bells (22 N) crossed the meridian and half-way to Oahu! Appearances indicate coming bad weather! 6 PM Capt. Vinall and the 2nd Officer had some rather warm words on the quarter deck! Occasioned by the Officer, cursing some of the crew! 8 PM Head wind & a prospect for an ugly night!

September 29
THURSDAY

Set in, foggy, rainy, blowy & dismal! A noble breeze, is blowing & this fact precludes the possibility of "getting-blue"! Employed in making man-ropes.

September 30
FRIDAY

A fine day. Employed in "lying-off" the Boats, etc. Lat. 37° 46'N.—Long. 273°W. About 23 or 24 days sail from the Sandwich Islands. So ends the month!

October 1

SATURDAY

Opens squally & rainy! Weather very unpleasant! Employed in washing ship. A wet job to say the least! When I log the "1st of November" I hope to be some distance on my way home from Oahu! Speaking of Oahu,—can it be possible that there are no letters there for me!!! Have they all forgotten me?!! No! I feel that although so unworthy, still I command a place in each heart of the household!

October 2

SUNDAY

Set in fine and pleasant. At 20 AM a heavy squall of wind and rain struck and for the remainder of the day, heavy squalls continued to rage, forming a very disagreeable day! How emblematical of life! Indeed, I have looked at life although differently than I used—and in part, to apt comparisons drawn from Nature—I am indebted for many new views! Employed in thinking of home & friends!

October 3

SUNDAY

Another Sabbath day!!!! Owing to the difference between our time and that at Oahu, these two Sabbaths succeed each other! A fine day and noble breeze. Employed in reading my Bible & meditating.

October 4

MONDAY

Set in fine and pleasant. At 22 N the wind hauled ahead and we are now (8 PM) slowly beating up to our course.

Employed in "rattling down," etc. Would like to see my friend "Orve" tonight! Well, I trust that we will yet meet on earth, Orve!

October 5

TUESDAY

A fine day. The wind still holds ahead, however, and this fact is not calculated to dispel the "blues"! "There's a good time coming!" Employed in repairing lifts, foot-ropes, etc.

October 6

WEDNESDAY

A pleasant day. A head wind & sea continue to hold us back but there is now. 22 N a prospect for the hauling of the wind! Come quick! Employed in sundry "fancy-jobs" fitting for the "Pride of the Harbor!" (Oh dear!)

October 7

THURSDAY

A beautiful day! The wind hauled fair last evening and we set "stern-sails" and "pointed her" for Oahu! Poor Jack—our King's Mill Native—is confined to his bunk! His complaint is only too evident—inflammation of the lungs! Poor fellow, I am his only friend! A few nights since I endeavored to tell him of God! He appeared to form a slight idea of my meaning, but his acquaintance with our language is too superficial to accomplish any good! He laughed when I told him that "God could see him in the dark!" I am much interested in poor Jack!! He is very anxious for me to sit beside him constantly. I fear, that he will see his home—no more!

October 8

FRIDAY

A fine morning and a noble breeze! If it continues we ought to make Oahu about next Wednesday! Last night we "carried away" the fore to'gallant-yard! Employed today in "fishing" it, and sending it up. Lowered for Black fish today! If Capt. Vinall knew the opinion which some of the crew expressed today concerning him,—he would doubtless be a little more "crazy" than when he raised those Black-fish! So ends!

October 9

SATURDAY

A fine day. Employed in cleaning & whitewashing our "parlor"!! 6 PM A new hole! Lat. 29° 22′N. Would have no particular objections to being at home today!

October 10

SUNDAY

A squally rainy morning! A noble breeze is still swiftly wafting us toward our desired haven and I expect to attend the Bethel next Sabbath! So ends.

October 11

MONDAY

A fine morning. This morning, one pound & a half of meat, came for'rad for 20 men!!! We would have said nothing in regard to the quantity, but it was so "filthy" that we determined to show it to the Capt! One of the men took it aft and received "satisfaction"!! i.e., the watch was kept on deck for 5 hours for demanding clean & wholesome food!

Shame on such manifestations of tyranny!! There is a threat afloat that the "cook must be cobbed"! Look out for breakers, Cook!

October 12
TUESDAY

A noble breeze this morning! If it continues, we ought to make the Islands tomorrow morning! Well, "Old Grease," (the cook) did get "cobbed," last night! I think I can perceive the removal of 8 layers of dust already! Employed in ship's duties!

October 13
WEDNESDAY

Land ho!—Sandwich Islands—once more! 2 PM Pilot on board! 6 PM moored inside! We are quarantined for 8 days in consequence of the prevalence of the small pox on shore! Capt. Vinall went ashore for letters, but he has not yet returned (9 PM) The same place! No perceptible change! So ends!

October 14
THURSDAY

A fine morning. Employed in washing ship. 8 AM Crew were called aft & vaccinated. 9 AM I was painting the "bluff of the larboard bow," when I heard my name called! Of course, I went aft and found—"Good News from home!!" Truly, it is "as cold waters to a thirsty soul!!" Oh how utterly unworthy am I of such love, as is breathed in every line of my Dear Father's letter! What kindness, what love, what mercy, what care, what solicitude, for the wandering Prodigal! I can but exclaim from my heart, "God bless you, my Father, God bless you!" A letter from Dear "Jule & Mandy" is also received! The same spirit of love abounds in their letter toward me and my heart often "strangely flutters" when I re-read each blessed line! God bless you, Dear Sisters! No letters from my Dear Mother have been received and none from "Mag & Will." I suppose they have been miscarried! I would love to receive even one from Dear Mother and also from Mag & Will! And Mandy, "Orve," proposed did he?!!!! Ah! you scamp, why did not you give him your heart! A better husband could not be found than Orve! But Sister, you had the scales in your hand, and I am happy to see you carefully discriminating! But, oh! shades of Milton! what am I to think of A.C.B.'s "pop"! (Just look at the entry on the 23rd day of February/53). Well, I hope to see you Dear Sister in 5 months!!! Poor Jack is very low this evening & I don't think he can live another day!

October 15
FRIDAY

Poor Jack died in my arms last night! His cancer has been short and full of trouble! May God receive his spirit! The ensign is floating at half-mast today and work is suspended. At 3 PM we buried him in the Nuanua Valley Cemetery. Employed today (during leisure hours) in re-reading my letters which are truly to me invaluable!

October 16
SATURDAY

A hot day. Employed in getting off water & painting ship. Rev. Damon came aboard, distributed papers, and gave good advice! I remarked a letter, advertised for me at his study! Last night I went to Mr. Damon's house and got my letter! It is from my Dear Mother! From her, who gave me birth, who nursed me in infancy, who guided me in youth, and who now prays for the ungrateful wretch whose wild & reckless course has caused her many a bitter tear!! Forgive me, Dear Mother, oh! for God's sake forgive your penitent boy!! Many a night my very soul has bled when conscience whispered the fearful word—"the past" and I suppose that I have to suffer many more! God forgive me!! Much has transpired since I left which is truly new! I am very glad that Mag & Will have moved to Columbus. And "Edith" is married!! (Glad of it!) She was very anxious to marry I believe when I last saw her!!! What a raft of young persons have committed matrimony! Death,—on the other hand, has been thrusting in his scythe, I see!! Thank God, he has spared us all!! Brother Joseph has moved "out west" I see!!! Quarantine regulations prevent me from going to church today & I have been writing home! Expect to be there soon, myself!!

October 18
MONDAY

Employed in drying & cleaning bone and painting ship. I really feel like a new man!! 3 letters from home & homeward bound!! It is no light matter to be cut off from a single word of intelligence from home for almost 3 years! And when intelligence does come in the shape of "very good news" it makes a fellow feel "as though he was comfortably settled at home with a handsome wife!! (More straight-jackets!!) And so ends the day!

October 19

TUESDAY

A fine day. Employed in drying bone, painting ship, getting off water & bread, etc. The Whale Ship "North Star," Capt. Brown, a noted tyrant, came in this morning and in about 2 hours said Tyrant was snugly moored in double irons within the walls of the Fort; there to await his trial for the cold-blooded murder of 3 of his crew during the last cruise on the whaling ground! It is represented to have been a deed of most diabolical atrocity! He will probably wear a hempen-cravat!

October 20

WEDNESDAY

A squally, hot day! Employed in stowing bone and getting off recruits. Can't start home too soon for me!! Want to get there, bad!!

October 21

THURSDAY

Starboard watch ashore on liberty. Larboard watch employed in painting ship, etc. A serious accident occurred on shore today with a large brass gun which had been spiked by the French several years ago. A blacksmith was endeavoring to get the spike out when the gun exploded—tearing one of his arms off and scattering large pieces of metal over the entire harbor!! Quite a large piece struck close to the "Old Henry" and the way the "white water flew" reminded me of Japanese whales!!

October, 1853

October 22
FRIDAY

Larboard watch ashore on liberty. In the morning, I visited Rev. Damon & had some interesting conversation with him! In the afternoon, I visited the "Pride of the American Navy!" Sloop of War, Portsmouth!! The first ship (in the true sense of the word) I ever saw! Such a life must be a miserable one! Many of her crew told me today that they would desert if they dared!! They are endeavoring to ship a few men and I suppose will succeed for she is calculated to "take the eye" of a sailor!!

October 23
SATURDAY

Starboard watch on liberty, and larboard are employed in getting off potatoes, painting ship, etc. Employed in "anticipating!" So ends.

October 24
SUNDAY

A fine day! Revd. S. C. Damon preached in the morning at the Bethel from Jer., 49. 23v, and in the evening from Luke, 28. 22v. Wrote home! May I speedily succeed them! Employed in thinking of home!

October 25
MONDAY

French Corvette "Moselle" came in. Exchanged a salute with Hawaiian Government! Looks hard, along-side the Portsmouth! Employed in painting ship, etc. Orders to get ready for sea tomorrow! Good!!

October 26

TUESDAY

The last liberty day! Glad of it!! Want to get home!! Plenty of liberty there!! Went to see Mr. Damon today. Purchased a bound volume of the Friend! Wrote my last letters home! And so ends!

October 27

WEDNESDAY

A fine day & homeward bound!! 5 PM Stern sails set and the "old Henry" is going some! God, grant us a safe & speedy passage!! Employed in stowing the anchors, etc. So ends!

October 28

THURSDAY

Another fine day. Employed in sundry deck & hold jobs. Ship "Dartmouth" sailing in company. Employed in— anticipating!

October 29

FRIDAY

And still another fine day! The 2st & 4th Officers quite unwell. Employed in sailmaking & repairing Waist Boat. Main topic of conversation fore & aft is home! Patience! patience!! patience!!!

October 30

SATURDAY

A noble breeze this morning! Bound to "Rarotonga" (Society Islands) for recruits. Spoke, Dartmouth. Employed in feeling impatient in spite of all that I can do to the contrary!! Make a virtue of necessity!

October 31
SUNDAY

A fine day and noble breeze. Depressed in spirits today! A heavy cold in my breast does not tend to exhilarate them much, but I must patiently await a cure! Spoke Dartmouth again today!!!!!!!

November 1
MONDAY

Employed in repairing boats, etc. The order of the day seems to be—"carry sail!" Go it!! Spread every stitch and then give us a roaring breeze!! Homeward bound—now!! I have experienced sweet peace today in meditating of God & Heaven! May such seasons be multiplied! Home grows more attractive!!

November 2
TUESDAY

Spoke Dartmouth again. Employed in deck & rigging jobs. And "Orve" has gone to Europe, eh! "You had better be getting yourself to Columbus, Orve, if you don't want me to "keel-haul" you!! Why only think what I will do if you are not at home when I get there! Two of the "old Mutual," married, one in Europe, two at home, and one, chasing "limber-tailed whales" to the ends of the earth!! I really begin to fear that I will never see the same persons who composed the famous "Mutual" again! Look out Pete!!

November 3

WEDNESDAY

A fine day. Employed in sundry ship's duties. It is a long distance from here around Cape Horn & then away up to 42° N!! But we will traverse it (by God's blessing) in time and that time cannot too swiftly pass for me! So ends!

November 4

THURSDAY

"Carried away," the "Bowsprit"! An evidence of anxiety to get home! Unless we can repair it while at sea, we will be compelled to go into New Zealand for a new one! It is probable that the Dartmouth will "beat us home," in view of this. I intend writing some letters to my Parents. Employed in anticipating!

November 5

FRIDAY

A fine morning! Carried away the main-to'gallant yard! Spoke Dartmouth again! Employed in thinking of home!! I would not have believed that home held me in such a strong grasp, had I not voluntarily launched forth into this curious world!! I never knew its value before!! And so ends!

November 6

SATURDAY

A fine day. Employed in sending up a new main to'gallant yard! Spoke Dartmouth again!! This evening a serious row occurred between Capt. Vinall and one of the harpooneers. He would soon have "used up" the Capt., had not the officers come to his rescue! He was then "seized up" in the mizzen rigging and for an hour the Captain amused himself by inhumanely beating him with a 2 inch rope!! His feet & tongue (the harpooneers) were at liberty and he kept them in constant use! After getting tired, the Captain put him in irons and consigned him to the "run"! He feared an attempt to rescue him on the part of the crew & he walked the Quarter deck with a brace of pistols for the remainder of the night! Bad! worse!! worst !!!

November 7
SUNDAY

A lovely day! "Jim" is still in the "run" on bread & water! To say the least, I truly pity him! I think if this ship had to make another voyage with her present compliment of men, someone would be killed before the voyage terminated!! I am not alone in my opinion either! Made "Fanning's Island." Employed in thinking of loved ones at home! God speed the homeward bound!

November 8
MONDAY

Another fine day! Captain Vinall proposed to Jim to take $200 and "sign clear" and he would put him ashore at the Society Islands! Jim, very wisely, refused! That was a bad piece of business!! Spoke Dartmouth! Employed in sundry ship's duties. So ends!

November 9
TUESDAY

Employed in repairing the Bowsprit. Capt. Vinall & the 1st Officer had a grand "flare up" today! Some "rather hard" language was freely used! These truly begin to savor of "troublous times"!! Only wait 'til we get to New Bedford, gentlemen, 'til I get clear of you and then you may bite, pinch, gouge, scratch, kick, claw, wool, punch, & "lick" each other to your full!

November 10

WEDNESDAY

Employed in sail-making! Capt Vinall is quite a different man today! Well, extremes are sometimes beneficial!! This life grows more intolerable every day! Home looms up in all its dazzling attractiveness and were it not for this fact I would be "blue" enough!

November 11

THURSDAY

A fine day. Crossed the line. Once more, will complete my crossing, I trust! If I am ass enough to cross it again, after this voyage. I should certainly merit a keel-hauling through a fleet of the line! "Sprung" the main-to'gallant mast! "Fished" it! Jim was given his liberty again today. So ends.

November 12

FRIDAY

Carried away main to'gallant stern sail boom! Spliced it. Bottom will "drop out" next, I suppose! Go it "old Henry!" Spoke Dartmouth again! "Happy go lucky!!"

November 13

SATURDAY

A fine day! Employed in sundries. What a satisfaction it must be to my Dear Parents to be surrounded by their children's children! I often look in to the good city of Columbus and going to a certain "brick house" on "Friend St.," see a "considerable quantity" of Clouds collected together!! Well, I hope soon to make one of the happy circle at home! So ends!

November 14
SUNDAY

Employed in reading my Bible, meditating, and thinking of home & friends!! I would eagerly give my all to be there today! A feeling of melancholy is striving for the ascendancy in my heart today—and it requires the full amount of my philosophy to subdue it! Spoke the Dartmouth again! A "lack of brains" is not confined to men "before the mast," it appears!

November 15
MONDAY

Employed in sail-making. Spoke Dartmouth!! How long in the name of the half of an ounce of common sense, will we be humbugged, speaking the Dartmouth! We lose just about one day in each week, hauling aback and speaking! My desire to caricature (and to do it faithfully too) is very strong! But it is not the best policy to do so!! Patience! patience!! I will some day be on an equal footing with the "Lord High Admiral" of the "Quarter deck" and enough now! So ends!

November 16
TUESDAY

At 2 PM raised a school of Sperm Whales!!! Lowered. In a short time the Larboard Boat went on & struck!! 6 PM

Moored alongside. A small whale, probably 20 bbls. Some chance now to lose sight of the nuisance, "Dartmouth"!!! No ships in Columbus!! Or Captains, either!! "Ease her when she pitches, boys!" And so ends!!

November 17
WEDNESDAY

Boiling! I suppose the "last fair"!! And "Jim Tuttle & Martha" have "swapped hearts" eh! And Sally Patterson & Lib. Seltzer & Amanda Parks have each committed matrimony! "Strike while the iron is hot!" A good axiom and one that I suppose I would have followed if I had not concluded to chase whales! Employed in thinking of home!

November 18
THURSDAY

Finished boiling. The whale has "turned up" 24 bbls. of oil—quite a small one! Last night was a stormy unpleasant one, well calculated to bring home to mind, and to increase my aversion to this life! Thank God, I am homeward bound! So ends!

November 19
FRIDAY

A fine day. Spoke Dartmouth! Don't know "for sure," but think that Dr. Smith would claim two certain men for runaway invalids if he was an eye witness to all that transpires!!

A life on the—raging canawl!" or anywhere else, but here!!

Employed in feeling a "little crazy"! And so ends!

November 20
SATURDAY

Last night had some heavy thunder storms! This morning it is raining and the prospect for its continuation is good. Employed in sundry ship's duties.

November 21
SUNDAY

A beautiful day! Last night was without exception, the most terrible night that I ever experienced. Such lightning, I never saw before & never wish to see again! As a proof of the intensity of the lightning, I will mention one instance. The Dartmouth was a good half-mile from us and when a "standing flash" would burst,—every piece of rigging on that ship could be seen from ours! This, doubtless, "sounds tough," but it is truth! The scene throughout was one of unparalleled magnificence, sublimity & awe!! My feelings inclined to enthusiasm, as I stood & looked at that wild lightning last night!

November 22
MONDAY

A fine day. "Whylootackie," one of the Society Group right ahead! We will touch here for wood, fruit, hogs, etc. Spoke Dartmouth!! This has got to be a "necessary duty" now, "speak Dartmouth"!!! Ship "Cornelius Howland" laying "off & on."

November 23
TUESDAY

Another fine day! Laying "off & on," and trading for wood, hogs, fowls, fruit, etc. Dartmouth is doing just what we do! "Alas! poor Yorrick!" (Shakespeare) Patience, patience, "Johnny Cakes," red herrings, will be cheap when you get home!

November 24

WEDNESDAY

Standing away for Cape Horn!! Employed in sundry ship's duties. Had another touch of Saturday night's weather this morning!! A great place for lightning!! Employed in thinking of home!!

November 25

THURSDAY

A fine day. Employed in various deck & rigging jobs. The leak is increasing and we have to pump every watch! Rather a curious kind of "an old box" to double Cape Horn in, but "try it"—she must!! So ends!

November 26

FRIDAY

Another fine day! Lost sight of the Dartmouth. What will we do for company!!!! Have been thinking of home all day! What slow progress we make! It really appears to me that the old ship can't log "5 knots" with every thing on that will "draw," under a half gale of wind! And so ends!

November 27

SATURDAY

Four & a half months more and then (but what then?!!) I hope to be at home!! This is a brittle life; many a long & weary mile of stormy weather has yet to be traversed 'ere I

November, 1853

see home! And a leaky old ship (only 49 years old) is to make the attempt!! Well, may God speed her on her passage is my prayer! So ends!

November 28
SUNDAY

A fine day & noble breeze! Home continues to present itself to my mind in new charms every day!! I can but patiently await a return to my Native Land of Sabbath & gospel privileges! Home, sweet home!!

November 29
MONDAY

Weather continues fine! Leak increases! Not much danger of dyspepsia on board the "old Henry"!! Would give a fortune (if I had it!!) to be in Columbus tonight!! I can imagine the happiness experienced by my Dear Friends when they all meet together!! One great objection to this life arises from the want of sociability!

November 30
TUESDAY

Prospect for bad weather! Employed principally in pumping! It is useless for me to endeavor to curb my feelings of impatience any longer, for they will have the mastery!! Get along the best I can!

November 31
WEDNESDAY

A severe gale is raging this morning and I can't see much prospect for a cessation very soon! Employed in thinking and dreaming of home and Dear Friends!! Well, I am sick of rambling!! I have looked for some thing to equal home in every clime, I have sought it around the world, but, at no place, at no time, under no circumstances have I found anything that will begin to compare with Home!! No! thank God, I have not!!!

December 1

THURSDAY

Gale still rages! Another month has fled! I trust that in 4 months, at farthest, I will be at home!! Don't think I will come a whaling again very soon!! Employed in "feeling blue"! So ends.

December 2

FRIDAY

Gale unabated in fury. This is a severe storm & the pumps are kept going constantly to keep her free! "Doubling Cape Horn" in a box like this is not very well calculated to drive the "blues" away! Well, "sink or swim" we will make the attempt! 7 PM Prospect for a lull! And so ends.

December 3

SATURDAY

Gale abated & a comparatively fine day! Employed in sundry deck & rigging jobs. Wonder if the dear ones at home will know me when I get there!!!! Let me see—5 feet 22 inches high, a pair of broad shoulders, a sun-burnt, well-tanned face, a pair of horny, tar-stained, blistered hands, a "killing" pair of "whiskers"—and as warm a heart as ever beat beneath a pea-jacket!! There! Do you think you will know me!! Look sharp!!

December 4
SUNDAY

A fine morning. Employed in reading my Bible and thinking of home! Have been thinking today of the influence which a praying Mother exerts over me!! I am in the hands of God and am subject to His will, may He send pestilence, famine & the sword in my footsteps as long as I live; may He deprive me of a home; deny me a spot to lay my head in peace; make every man my enemy; may He do all these; but forbid in mercy, Oh God! to grant me a "prayerless Mother"!! Yea, sooner cut me off!! I do thank Thee, oh God! for praying Parents!

December 5
MONDAY

Set in with a "spell" at the pumps! Employed in sundry ship's duties. 6 PM raised a school of Sperm Whales! Lowered. In a short time the Waist Boat went on and struck the "largest whale in the Pacific!!" Harpooneer got frightened and in consequence failed to "get in" his "2nd iron," the 1st iron drew & we lost him! In a few moments after the Starboard Boat went on & struck "the brother"!!!! Line parted and we lost him also! Try again!

December 6
TUESDAY

Becalmed!! Employed in ship's duties & pumping ship. Oh! for a breeze!! Come, come, "Old Nep," clear away your famous "cutter," bear down & give us the cheer! "Bear a hand, my hearty" for here is a school of your children who are very anxious to "come to" on "terra firma"!! You won't, eh?!! "Well then, we'll settle!" Just please to send in your bill!

December 7
WEDNESDAY

Set in calm. 8 AM a light breeze. 20 AM increasing! Employed in sail making & pumping. Nothing of sufficient interest to log. And so ends!

December 8
THURSDAY

A fine day. Employed in overhauling potatoes, etc. Leak increases! Pump, every two hours! Well, have to go into Port yet, I am afraid on account of this leak. Home! home!! home!!! Its attractions are strong!!

December 9
FRIDAY

A noble breeze is swiftly wafting us—homeward! Speed, speed, "old Henry"—take a pattern from Morse's Telegraph! I feel anxious to get home and see what "that present" is, which Sis Jule speaks of! I imagine that I know!! Look out Jule if I am right! Hold on! "the Squire," knows where there is a "cottage on the hill"!!! Hope to see it, soon! So ends.

December 10
SATURDAY

Set in, bright & beautiful! 9 AM raised "Right Whales!!!!!" Lowered! The Larboard Boat went on & struck a fine one! He tried hard to get away but the lance "hurt his feelings" and in consequence, he was a dead whale at 22 AM!! 3 PM Cut in. 7 PM Boiling!

December 11
SUNDAY

Boiling. I pray God that this is the last desecrated Sabbath of the voyage! The sea is alive with whales but we don't want them! My feelings today are of a decided melancholy cast! Well, there is enough to make them so!! Deliverance is coming!!

December 12
MONDAY

Finished boiling. This is a day of rejoicing! 20 AM the "try-works"—are—overboard!!! Yes, we have boiled our last whale (thank God) and now we are bound home, direct! Feelings rather more elastic today! Employed in stowing oil.

December 13
TUESDAY

A fine day. A noble breeze is blowing today & the "old box" feels it!! Employed in practicing a disguise "for home!" One of the Officers (who has frequently tried it) says, "that my Mother will know me!" Well, it may be so, but time, exposure, hardship, suffering (both mental & physical) and memory—have "left their mark"!!! So ends.

December 14
WEDNESDAY

Another fine day. Employed in sundry deck & rigging jobs. Once "around the Horn" and it will appear something like progress, but oh! what a long road to travel yet!! We are indebted to "Aesop" for the fable of the "Tortoise & the Hare" and I think the old Henry is an admirable personification of said Tortoise!

December 15
THURSDAY

Fine weather still continues! Employed in sundry ship's duties. How unworthy am I of such manifestations of love from my Dear Parents!! When I read that my Dear Father had subscribed for the "Mercury" in order to gain some intelligence from the ungrateful prodigal, my heart was melted! Many times, has the intensity of my feelings when thinking of my past, wildlife seemed too great for nature to bear!! Forgive me Dear Parents, forgive all!!

December 16
FRIDAY

Set in with a noble breeze—right aft! Continued all day! Expect to be home by the 1st of April! Employed in sundry ship's duties.

December 17
SATURDAY

Fine winds & weather continue! That's right!! I say "Old Nep" come aboard and I will give you a receipt in full! Pay you "with the fore-top-sail you know!" "Hurrah, for the homeward bound!"

December 18
SUNDAY

Continuation of noble breeze & good weather! Oh! that it may hold for a month! My anxiety to get home increases every day! Well, I suppose we will get there by & by! Employed in reading & meditating.

December 19
MONDAY

A fine day. Raised Right Whales this morning and— lowered! Why, I am sure I can't tell!! Succeeded in—losing him! Came aboard & stove the Starboard Boat! This occasioned quite a row between Capt. Vinall & the 4th Officer! After breakfast, lowered again! The effect of this lowering was to occasion a "grand row" between Capt. Vinall & the 1st Officer!! Resulted in an order to issue "duff 3 times per week!" Wonders are about again!! Did not lower again!!! Who, would not go a whaling? Go it!

December 20
TUESDAY

A cold, wet day. Employed in feeling a little tired of this life! Wonder if "Old Brandywine" is in "full blast" yet!! If a man has no respect for himself & his family he must not expect me to respect him! A certain occurrence which I was much pained to see & hear on a certain day, has been occupying my mind today! Shame, shame, on such a father & husband!!

December 21
WEDNESDAY

A pleasant day. Employed in sail-making, etc. We are slowly, though surely, nearing the famous "Horn," and once safely around and it will appear like "going down hill" for the remainder of the distance!

December 22
THURSDAY

Set in, calm & foggy. Reminds me of a certain place which I have seen for the last time—"Japan Sea!" "Gold whales with diamond eyes" would offer no inducement for me to go there again! Employed in sundry ship's duties.

December 23
FRIDAY

Set in calm. At 22 AM a fine breeze sprung up & now (8 PM) "Neptune's delight" is urging the "old trap" to her utmost, about 9 knots! Employed in thinking of home!

December 24
SATURDAY

A noble breeze is blowing and in consequence I feel in "noble spirits!" 5 PM Handled, light sails, prospect for a gale, which, if it comes from the S.W. will not be remarkable for "moderation!" "S. Rappings."

December 25
SUNDAY

Christmas day! And the last one at sea! A piping gale is blowing from the N.E. 7 PM Lulled 8 PM A heavy gale from the S.W.! Employed in thinking of home & friends! So ends.

December, 1853

December 26
MONDAY

A "regular swinger" blew last night and this morning there is a prospect for a cessation! Put the ship before it and scudded under a close reefed-main top sail. Employed in trying to curb my impatient feelings! Poor prospect! And so Monday ends.

December 27
TUESDAY

Set in fine & pleasant. As for myself, I cannot complain in regard to treatment from Officers, but it makes my heart bleed to see shipmates—men, men possessed of souls, of feelings, of a mind, men who have Parents & Sisters & brothers—treated—far worse than brutes!! I really don't know—why—but somehow or other they all look to me for consolation! Well, I am at their service at all times! I love liberty and hate tyranny; and I am ever ready to plead the cause of a fellow man whose neck is galled by the cursed yoke of the most urbane tyrant !

December 28
WEDNESDAY

A gale of wind is blowing this morning—right aft! We will soon be "somewhere" if this continues! Employed in sundry ship's duties.

December 29
THURSDAY

Gale continues! Hatches battened down and deck "knee-deep in cold, wet water!" Can endure anything now—"homeward bound"! Employed in "feeling cold!"

December 30
FRIDAY

"And still they come!" Gale "hangs on"!!! A tremendous sea is running but every swell "heaves us onward"! Can't continue too long! So ends!

December 31
SATURDAY

Still "it howls"! The last day of the old Year, and a heavy snow storm to "help it along"! Employed in snow balling, to "keep warm!"

1854

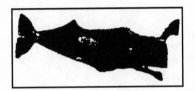

1854

'Tis the New Year's Morn! A happy day!!
For around my heart is wound,
The sailor's sweetest, simple, lay—
"Hurrah for the-homeward bound!"
I've sailed through many a sea,
Have roamed in every clime,
But, 'midst all this diversity,—
No home I've found like mine!
Then, hurrah, hurrah for the homeward bound!
I'll bid the main adieu
And pipe ye winds, a welcome sound
From "Neptunes cutter"—true!
Neptune's

January 1
SUNDAY

The gale still howls! About one week's sail from Cape Horn! We may reasonably expect bad weather now for several days, but such is the strength of my desire to get home that I would hail, hard times, with joy, did they but hasten my reunion with all that is dear to me on Earth! The 1st Officer has given me a pressing invitation to go home with him and make his house my home until the ship is discharged (at New Bedford) and my voyage is settled! Employed in reading my Bible, meditating & thinking of home!

January 2
MONDAY

A cold day. The "roaring gale" has in some measure abated but we still have a famous breeze! Saw large quantities of "penguins" and "snow-petrels." "Doubling Cape Horn," at any season of the year is not by any means, a "pleasant job!" This is the "summer-daylight" season, and the most favorable for doubling. Employed in sundry ship's duties.

January 3
TUESDAY

Our noble breeze has at last lulled! Sorry! 10 AM wind hauled ahead. I hope it will not hold! 5 PM hauled fair again! Prospect for a strong breeze! Employed in wishing that we were snugly moored in New Bedford harbor! "A time for all things!"

January 4
WEDNESDAY

Another famous wind, right aft! This is what I love! The temperature of the atmosphere is "decidedly cool"! My feet are badly chilblained and my fingers seem to be disposed to cast off a covering of frozen skin! To say the least, "they hurt my feelings!" Joys, of a sailor's life! Employed in trying to "take it easy!"

January 5
THURSDAY

The breeze still hangs on! Nearing the far-famed Cape Horn! Terrific squalls of wind, snow & hail, alias, "Cape Horn woollies" rage constantly and they are anything but pleasant! We have but about 2 hours of night now and the circumstance of almost continual daylight is in our favor. Signalized a clipper merchantman. Employed in suffering with cold! So ends Wednesday!

January 6
FRIDAY

7 AM We were carrying every stitch of canvass which we could spread, when we were struck by a terrific snow squall which threatened to "relieve us of our masts!" I went up to assist in furling the main-top-gallant-sail, got it furled and "found I could not get down!!" My hands were frozen stiff and I could not take hold of the shrouds. I laid across the to'gallant yard and beat my hands with all my force, in order to start the circulation of the blood. Could not do it! Things began to be desperate! My clothes were freezing, and such was the pain which I was suffering that I really began to feel unconcerned whether I got safely to the deck or fell a mangled corpse! Winding my arms and legs around the shrouds, I commenced a very perilous descent, not knowing or caring whether I got safely down or not!! I managed at length to reach the deck and at once, plunged my hands into a tub of cold water. A short time sufficed to "bring them to,"

and then I suffered!! I never felt such pain before and I am quite sure that I am not very anxious to experience the like again! 10 AM All right again! 5 PM Saw several large icebergs! A number of ships in sight but too rough to speak.

January 7
SATURDAY

Set in fine, though extremely cold. 12 N made "Diego." Signalized a merchantman. She flew her colors at half-mast whether intentional, or in distress, we are unable to determine. Employed in thinking "whether or not I could relish a good home!" 10 PM have concluded that I could!

January 8
SUNDAY

A lovely day in the Atlantic! Farewell old Pacific!! Farewell!!! Roll on, surge on, continue to rear thy majestic head in proud defiance of man, let your fierce storms howl, your blightening sun scorch, your mad squalls burst—I am free, forever!! Many hours, days, weeks, months of suffering I have experienced on your heaving breast—I am but now, I am free! This dying fame, these hands of clay, these muscles of dust, will never faint or bleed, or ache again on your broad breast,—but still, they are destined to misery! A few short years at best, and they will calmly repose when ocean, river, lake & earth will trouble & afflict & rack them, no more for ever! 6 AM saw Cape Horn, covered with snow! 7 PM Made "Staten Island"! Employed in thinking of home!

January 9
MONDAY

Set in calm with occasional rain & snow. 2 PM Light head wind. There is some talk of touching at the Falkland Islands for wild geese, but I think it is but "talk!" Employed in tacking ship and praying for a fair wind! And so ends Monday!

January 10
TUESDAY

Head wind! Head wind!! 7 AM Raised a school of large Sperm Whales! Lowered. A thick fog came down, just after lowering and we saw the whales no more! Employed in sundry ship's duties!

January 11
WEDNESDAY

Head wind! How emblematical of life! One day, a bouncing gale of happiness with a cloudless sky—the next—did head-winds of adversity, case, and afflictuous, doggedly hold ahead with not one single ray of warmth or light from the sun! A lesson is learned from every phase of Nature! So ends!

January 12
THURSDAY

4 AM wind hauled fair & free! Spoke Clipper Ship, "Mary Green" of Calais, Maine. Desired her to report us. She quickly left us astern and I wished to be aboard of her as I saw her swiftly bounding homeward! Patience! patience!!

January 13
FRIDAY

A fine breeze is blowing this morning and the "crazy old box" is doing "the best she can"! (Not much!) 3 PM wind hauled ahead strong! Handled light sails. 6 PM prospect for a blow. If it will only come aft. I care not how strong! Employed in thinking of home, sweet home!

January 14
SATURDAY

A noble fair wind! Oh! that it may hold for weeks! The leak is increasing in her "stern" and the pumps are kept quite busy! Well, if she will but float 'til we make New Bedford, I will be satisfied!

January 15
SUNDAY

A fine breeze is blowing today and the prospect for its continuation is good! Melancholy appears to be in the ascendancy today and I can easily trace the cause. A cold, dead, inactive state of my heart! Oh! that I might ever hunger & thirst after righteousness! That my soul might ever shrink from the most trivial sin and that my heart might ever burn with love to God!!

January 16
MONDAY

The fine breeze still holds! God grant to continue it! I am more and more disgusted with this life & my desire to get home hourly increases! A short time longer and then! So ends.

January 17
TUESDAY

Set in with a continuation of the fine breeze! How strange that a "little brief authority" will make men such consummate fools! The Sultan of Turkey could not strut with such ridiculous importance or carry a loftier dogmatical, egotistical head, than, a certain Master of a whaleship with whom I am partially acquainted!! The quarter-deck is but too often the theatre of tyranny, disgust & ridicule!! Employed in trying to be blind!! So ends!

January 18
WEDNESDAY

Strong breeze still continues!! Hope to be home by the 27th of March! Employed in sundry ship's duties. I think that I can log (safely) some spiritual improvement! Oh! that it may increase!

January 19
THURSDAY

Strong breeze continues "to pipe!" Employed in reading my letters and feeling impatient! The "old box" appears to move along very slowly! Get there some day, I hope! 5 PM "Sail ho!" Can't make her out.

January 20
FRIDAY

Heavy squalls the order of both day & night! Like to see it! Every squall which strikes "helps us along" and I say, come & come strong!! Wonder if "Jim Tuttle" loves "Pork" yet!! Well, Jim, you are a man at last!! Life, health & happiness to you & Martha! I suppose when I get home you will be introducing me to "young lawyer Tuttle"! Eh, Jim?!

January 21
SATURDAY

Set in with a light wind. Employed in sundry ship's duties. PM Calm! My worst enemy! There is a tract, between the 26th & 16th parallels of latitude which is denoted by the name of "doldrums" calms & light baffling winds! Wish we were through!

January 22
SUNDAY

Light baffling winds. 11 AM Becalmed, with a fair prospect for continuation! Employed in reading, meditating & thinking of home. It is very difficult—nay impossible, to describe my anxiety to get home!! All in God's good time!

January 23
MONDAY

Becalmed! Not one single breath of air is ruffling the vast surface of the "polished mirror" & I am in a word, "on nettles"! Employed in bundling bone. (For the last time!)

January 24
TUESDAY

A light head wind came down this morning at 2 bells and continued all day. Still employed at the bone. Slow, slow progress, homeward! And so ends, Tuesday!

January 25
WEDNESDAY

Set in with light head winds. 5 PM hauled fair & free!! Prospect for a good night's run! Finished the bone & employed in sundry ship's duties.

January 26
THURSDAY

The wind hauled ahead again this morning! "Short & sweet!" 2 PM Spoke Whale ship "New England." The 2nd officer shot the captain about a month since, and she is now under the command of the 1st officer and bound home. It is reported as an accident! 5 PM Spoke English Bark "Pickwick." Employed in thinking of home! So ends.

January 27
FRIDAY

Set in with light head winds. Employed in making spun yarn. Weather very hot. The 2nd officer & Capt. Vinall had a "grand row" today! I remarked the Captain's fist in rather "uncomfortable proximity" to the 2nd Officer's "smeller" several times! Ended in ordering the 2nd Officer to clear out, bag & baggage!!! He told him to get ready to go on board the New England! The officer went below, followed by Capt. Vinall. In about 2 hours they both came on deck "all right!" Pray gentlemen, hold on 'til I get clear of you! There's no place like home!! It is not advisable for me to comment further on today's proceedings! I might possibly— lose my log!

January, 1854

January 28
SATURDAY

Light baffling winds! Employed in feeling "blue"!! Expect to get home in 1956 at this rate!

January 29
SUNDAY

A day long to be remembered! The beginning of another season of humbugging! Spoke Dartmouth!!! Well, thank God it cannot last forever! Deliverance must come in some form! Employed in trying to "walk worthily." A hard task! God help me!

January 30
MONDAY

Set in with light head winds. Employed in deck and rigging jobs. Spoke Dartmouth & New England and signalized a "Monsieur" merchantman. 6 PM hauled, fair & free! Set stern' sails alow & aloft and "took a fresh start!" If it will only continue! So ends.

January 31
TUESDAY

A noble breeze all day! The ship is leaking now 15,000 strokes per day!! As may be supposed this causes "long faces," and there is a rumor afloat that we are to ease the ship by shipping 200 bbls of oil home per ship New England! This leak will give us trouble yet, I'm afraid! Float, "old Henry" float for a few weeks longer!

February 1

WEDNESDAY

Becalmed again! Spoke New England. Arrangements are made (if the crew of the New England are agreed) to ship 150 bbls of oil! I am confident that the crew will not agree for they are anxious to get home and I think will refuse to be detained! So ends.

February 2

THURSDAY

Set in with a light head wind. The New England dropped astern this morning so rapidly as to leave no doubt that it was intentional! The concerted signal (if the crew were found willing to ship the oil) was a "flag at the fore!" Have not yet seen it!

February 3

FRIDAY

New England, out of sight from the mast-head! Light, baffling head-winds & no headway! Employed in pumping ship & feeling "blue"! So ends!

February 4

SATURDAY

Head wind! Employed in sundry ship's duties! Would rather enter into partnership with old—"Whiskey Schmitt" in the "wood-sawing-business" than to come on another whaling voyage!

February, 1854

February 5
SUNDAY

Light, baffling winds right ahead! I would give a world of gold (if it was at my disposal) for the privileges of this day at my Dear Father's house! Oh! what an aching void is felt in the deprivation of the Sabbath! How does my soul yearn for its calm, quiet, holy privileges!! God speed the homeward bound!

February 6
MONDAY

Light head winds! Employed in trimming ship. Spoke Dartmouth! (At it again!) The Dartmouth sustained some damage to her rudder during a heavy gale off Cape Horn, and is bound into port for repairs. I suppose that we will accompany her!

February 7
TUESDAY

Light head winds! Employed in trimming ship. A good free wind would be something of a curiosity!! Slow, slow progress toward home! Employed in feeling somewhat "blue"! And so ends the day!

February 8
WEDNESDAY

Light, head winds!! Have been building steamships all day! Well, I suppose that we will clear the "doldrums" at "some future period"!! The best way is to try to "take it easy"! Employed in feeling a "little crazy"! So ends.

February 9

THURSDAY

Light head winds!!!! Employed in trimming ship, with a prospect to be humbugged "speaking the Dartmouth"! Employed in feeling as crazy as a March hare! Oh! for the wind that—

"Fills the white and rustling sail,
And bends the to'gallant mast!"

February 10

FRIDAY

Set in with light head winds! 12 N increased. 6 PM A fine breeze & some progress! Employed in sundry ship's duties! So ends.

February 11

SATURDAY

Set in with a strong breeze! Clear of the "doldrums" into the "Trades" and bound into port, with a leaky old oil box! Employed in rattling-down, wetting-hold, pumping ship, being hoaxed, etc. So ends the week.

February 12

SUNDAY

Strong breeze! Spoke Dartmouth & signalized a large English merchantman! About 3 day's sail from "Fernando" our port destination! Well, I hope, that when we "let go anchors" again, we will be in New Bedford harbor! My desire to get home—to see my Dear Parents, Sisters, & Friends is—strong.

February, 1854

February 13

MONDAY

Strong breeze!! Employed in rattling down & sundry ship's duties. Oh! for a good free ship in this noble breeze!! Owners should be prosecuted for sending out such "perfect man-traps" as this!! I might possibly have "liked it better" had I shipped in a clipper! "All for the best my hearties!!"

February 14

TUESDAY

Strong breeze! (Making up for light head wind.) Employed in rattling down, etc. We ought to make land tomorrow morning, according to observation! Employed in thinking of home! "By & by!!"

February 15

WEDNESDAY

7 AM "Land ho"! "Fernando N"—a Portuguese convict island! 2 PM Laying at anchor in "Water Bay," under a tier of very savage looking 18 pounders! I count no less than 5 forts, within the space of 2 miles! A dull, barren, cheerless looking place where life must be a very burden! Employed for the remainder of the day in painting ship. We have had no communication with persons on shore yet & I am unable to report any news! So ends the first day of "the farce" with the Dartmouth!

February 16

THURSDAY

Employed in painting ship & repairing leak. There is an "ugly hole" in her "cut-water" and if the pumps had become obstructed or worn out we would have taken a trip to "Davy Jones'!" No communication yet with the inhabitants. A grand tea party tonight! (Oh Dear!!) Pray excuse me from reporting items!! Trying hard to be blind, deaf, & dumb —but it is labor thrown away! So ends Thursday!

February 17
FRIDAY

Employed in painting ship. This morning Capt. Vinall and "Red Herrings" of the Dartmouth, went ashore! They were the quests of the Governor, their boat's crews, patronized a grog shop, and I think I would not "miss it much" if I were to say that all hands had been indulging with the "critter"!! It was, however, evident that the crew had been putting "rather too much—water in their brandy"! The boat came alongside and I looked over the rail to see "the contents." First came "Old Blossom," "as cocked as an owl," and all ready for fight!! Next came, R.M., not "de-zack-ly-(hic) drunk," but only a little s-i-c-k!-(hic). Next came, Frank P., a very little "fluctuated!" Finally, poor Jack B. was handed over, "hog oh!" Succeeded in "stowing them all down," but the "valiant Blossom"—who persisted in guarding the pumps promenading the quarter deck, steering a "trick" at the wheel & whistling, Yankee Doodle! So ends!

February 18
SATURDAY

Capt. Vinall went ashore again this morning, with a new crew! The Governor reports the death of the Queen of Portugal. The convicts rebelled a short time since, but were overpowered by the soldiers. Capt. Vinall sold them some flour, hard-bread, tobacco, slush & candles! The condition of the unfortunate convicts is truly miserable! "The way of transgressors is hard"! 2 PM "Fished" the fore yard (it is "sprung"). 3 PM "Man the windlass!" (That's the order I love!) 5 PM Under way for home! God grant us a speedy passage! Dartmouth—is coming!

February 19
SUNDAY

Set in, with a noble breeze! Employed in reading, meditating & thinking of home! Well, I do pray for a speedy passage home! However, we are in God's good hands and He will deal with us in faithfulness! May I be resigned, in all things, to His holy will!

February 20
MONDAY

Noble breeze continues! Employed in rattling down, and pumping ship! The ship leaks just as bad as she did before going in Port! I am afraid we will have trouble yet before we get home! Employed in looking at a very dull prospect!

February 21
TUESDAY

"Strong trades"!! Employed in trimming for home! (If we get there!) There is one thing certain—if the leak increases we will be compelled to go in Port! And that, very soon too! The ship is not by any means worthy to encounter the heavy weather on the American Coast & Gulf Stream in her present condition; and if the leak increases proportionally, we will find some difficulty in making the nearest port in the West Indies!! Thinking of home!

February 22
WEDNESDAY

Set in, with a noble breeze! Employed in trimming ship & pumping. Leak is steadily increasing!! I remark many long faces on the ship and a certain solemn, "hush" is discernable in the department of the most frivolous! Well, there is a good reason for it!!

February 23
THURSDAY

Noble trades continue! Oh! that we had a tight, free, ship! Employed in trimming ship and pumping! Leak increasing & prospect growing more & more dark! It is no sport to be in this situation! Employed in thinking of home, which appears strangely attractive! And so ends the day.

February 24
FRIDAY

Fine breeze still holds. Things are beginning to assume a desperate condition!! Prudence, yes—absolute necessity compels us to do something at once! 3 PM Bound to St. Thomas (West Indies). (It is about time!!) The ship is now leaking 36,000 strokes per day!!! If we float 'til we get there, I am of the opinion that the ship will be condemned! Capt. Vinall entertains like ideas & he is trying to make her "look" as sound as possible! Employed in thinking of home!!

February, 1854

February 25
SATURDAY

Fine breeze continues! I have commenced a letter to my Dear Parents today which I intend "keeping in journal form" 'til we get to St. Thomas. If we go down, I will enclose it in a bottle and trust to chance for delivering it! Employed in pumping.

February 26
SUNDAY

Set in with strong trades. Leak increasing!! Employed in reading & thinking of home!! It appears at first sight, hard, that I am to be detained again on my way home! But it is all right! Thank God for a submissive heart, which exclaims, "Thy will be done!"

February 27
MONDAY

Strong trades! Employed in painting spars. Will be in St. Thomas (God willing) in about 8 days. Thinking of home & feeling dejected! So ends!

February 28
TUESDAY

Strong trades continue! Orders have been given to make water kegs & provision bags for the Boats! We know not how soon we will be compelled to take to them! The wind has hauled right aft, now, and in consequence the ship is on an "even keel." The effect of this is to lesson the pressure of the water on the leak, causing it to remain "at a stand." It makes one feel curious to hear the rapid gurgling of that liquid death in the fore'peak!"!!!

March 1
WEDNESDAY

Set in with strong N.E. trades! Employed in pumping. Was it not for the leak, we would be home in 20 days!! It requires something of an effort to believe this! "Facts are stubborn things!" Would love to see my friends tonight! They little dream that I am bound to the West Indies in distress! God bless them all!!

March 2
THURSDAY

Strong N.E. trades continue! Employed in pumping ship, etc. I have been painting in the cabin today and the effect of it has been to give me, an "old-fashioned head-ache!" No kind Mother to soothe my pain!! A voluntary launch, an aching head & a miserable man!

March 3
FRIDAY

Strong N. Easters continue! Employed in sundry ships' duties & pumping. Well, 16 days from St. Thomas will bring us at New Bedford. I hope, and on the strength of this consolation, I close my book and "go home," a while! So ends the day!

March 4
SATURDAY

Set in, with fine winds! Employed in wetting hold, pumping, scrubbing, decks, etc. Well, it can't last forever!

March, 1854

Home, appears robed in new charms every day! So ends the week!

March 5
SUNDAY

A lovely day! Set in, with strong N. E trades! 10 AM made "Dominica," Guadeloupe" &—the most beautiful island that I ever saw—"Marie Galante." The immense sugar plantations on shore remind me of scenery on the banks of the Mississippi! I see nothing to rival the beauties of a "Sabbath home"! So ends!

March 6
MONDAY

A fine morning in the Caribbean Sea! Made "Basseterre," "Montserrat," "St Kitts," "Nevis," "Redonda" & "St. Eustatius"—of the Carribbeen Group. Employed in pumping & various ship's duties. Expect to be in St. Thomas tomorrow! So ends!

March 7
TUESDAY

6 AM made St. Johns, Tortola & St. Thomas. 2 PM Pilot on board, 3 PM Laying at anchor! A most beautiful place! The city is built on 3 hills, and the houses are finished in a truly magnificent style! We are laying right abreast of "Christian's Fort" with its fierce battery of 19 guns, frowning upon us, and immediately over us looms up the famous "Blackbeard's" rendezvous castle! I intend taking a portion of it home! There are a large number of ships in port, and every one of them (with the exception of 2 English Steamers) are

in distress! A bark came in today, the crew of which are in a state of mutiny. The Cholera & Yellow Fever have been doing fearful execution in the City, but there is but little of either existing at present! There is a prospect of getting out again in 18 days, if we are not condemned! 18 long, dreary days! We could get home in a less number! Late papers from home are filled with detailed accounts of marine disasters, loss of life & property, etc, which are truly appalling!

March 8

WEDNESDAY

Employed in breaking out & shifting cargo in order to get at the leak. A demand was made by the crew this morning to Capt. Vinall for daily wages while employed in repairing the leak. Simple justice—the laws of equity—& the rights of men—demand that the crew of the ship receive wages for this work, but we are whalemen, and commercial laws will not reach us! The only way is to make out & present our bills to the owners when we get home! I don't know that we will get liberty here but I can form no positive conclusion yet. Hope that we will! We are the "Lions" of the harbor and are constantly thronged with visitors occupying all stations in life from the independent merchant to the slave! Many applications are made for shells & curiosities and the applicants are certainly very liberal in their offers. The Seamen's chaplain (Rev. Taylor) came onboard with an assortment of religious book and there is a prospect for a sermon on board next Sabbath!

March 9

THURSDAY

A fine day. The carpenter has found the leak in her "stern" and is employed in repairing it. 2 PM went ashore on liberty!!! My first cruise was for "Blackbeard's Castle"! After a toilsome tramp through many streets of the City and a very tedious ascent of the mountain, I found myself at the far-famed castle of the most atrocious Pirate that ever scourged the high seas! I sat down, where he has often sit, and stepped into the remains of his stone bath! An extensive view of the ocean presents itself from the castle and my mind shuddered as I thought that from that bloody-look-out, he had often descried the outline of some unconscious vessel whose decks were destined to swim with the blood of their crews as he led his hellish band gasping with thirst for the life blood of their fellow men! I could almost hear their Bacchanalian songs of profanity, and wild mirth as they surrounded the intoxicating board, and I shrunk from its gloomy shadows, sickened as I pictured that fearful band of demons, rioting in human blood!! 3 cannons, the remainder of his armament, are laying at the foot of the castle, and imagination also pictured those fearful engines, belching forth their messengers of death, and hurling them mercilessly into the heavenly face of man! A portion of each (the guns & castle) are secured and I intend taking them home! St. Thomas is a large city & is rapidly improving. A large amount of business is transacted daily, and really one can fancy himself cruising in the crowded thoroughfares of the great Commercial Mart of America—New York! Still, there is no place, like HOME!!!!! I frequently remarked persons gazing at me, as though I was some rare curiosity, and I have become accustomed to a phrase, heard at almost every step—"There is one of the whalemen!" Numbers of persons have continued to beseige me today—all eagerly anxious to hear a description of the process, entire of "taking a whale!" I have remarked a great quantity of "wide staring eyes," and have repeatedly heard the exclamation, "Well, I won't go!!" At 5 PM we were visited by a detachment of British Naval Officers from the Royal Mail Steamer "Avon." They expressed as much surprise as the inhabitants! They deport themselves in a very gentlemanly manner and gave our officers a pressing invitation to repay their visit. The surgeon thinks that 9 mos on a Steamer is quite enough ! The idea of 32 months on a Whaler is very repulsive to his feelings! The Yeoman, quite a young man, whom I should think was the son of a Lord, is of the decided opinion that he would prefer having a "little sport" on a whaling cruise to serving out cash on board a steamer! Think if he had been in the Starboard Boat on the 20th day of last April in the Japan Sea, "fast" to that "whale-steamer," he would probably have a "kind of desire" to "serve out cash again!!" Judging by appearances, there is trouble brewing between a portion of the crew and Capt. Vinall relative to receiving daily wages while in Port. We shall see.

March 10
FRIDAY

A fine day. Larboard watch on liberty. Carpenter employed in repairing leak. As I expected, this has been a day of trouble! The ring-leaders of all "rows" are Larboard watchmen, and the harpooneer that was flogged so badly, accompanied by another, equally "fussy," went ashore today;

found Capt. Vinall and asked him for some money. He told them that he had none and could, or would get none. They then went to see the American Consul. He informed them that it was optional, with the Master of a Whaler in regard to giving his crew liberty money in a foreign port; and that no existing laws would compel him to do it, whether they were employed in repairing the ship or not! He informed them that they can collect daily wages for duty performed on shipboard in foreign ports, from the owners, when the ship gets home! And that was all that they could do! On the strength of this information they—got drunk! After getting in just the right trim to disgrace themselves & their country's flag they again went to Capt. Vinall and demanded money! They said they wanted it "to get something to eat." He told them to go on board the ship and they could get enough there. One of them, then charged him with selling the ship's provisions and denied that there was enough on board! On this, Capt. Vinall struck him; and the harpooneer jumped to assist in whipping the Capt! Several gentlemen interfered and they succeeded in starting them off. There next move was to "call a survey" of the ship and to pronounce her unsea-worthy & have her condemned, which they will suc-ceed in doing if a majority of the crew are obtained to demand it! Well, here we are, and if a survey is called, here we will be for probably 2 months!! Now, Capt. Vinall is to blame for all of this trouble! Even 50 cts. per day to each man would have satisfied them; but he refuses to draw a bill on the owners for money—the consequence of which is the ship will be kept away from home for months! Besides this, it has caused all of today's trouble and I am afraid that we have only seen the commencement!! Looking at the prospect ahead, from this Port, only 16 day's sail from home, I feel emphatically "blue"!! Judgement, policy & common-sense seems to be strangely wanting in some persons!! I would be willing to sacrifice my right hand if it were possible to get home before the dawning of another day!! Strong language, I am very well aware, but my feelings dictate every word of it!! And so ends the day!

March 11

SATURDAY

Warrants were issued for the two men who committed the "assault" yesterday, and (by mistake) an innocent man, one of the crew who had nothing to do with it, was arrested and committed to prison. He was released this morning. The "prospect" is rather better today! Carpenter has finished the leak in her stern, but has found another—much worse, on her side, below the water line! He says he can repair that also. Employed in "heeling" the ship. Well, I hope to be home in 20 days from the present time, at farthest! What a thought!! Separated from all that is dear to me on Earth for 32 long & bitter months of privation, hardship & suffering. I am now on the threshold of deliverance, liberty & reunion, and to say that the thought causes a feeling of joy to fill my heart, would be but poorly expressing my true feelings! God & myself alone knows how strongly I desire to get there! May He be pleased to speed the happy day! I am going to send a letter home by the next Steamer which will get there in 10 days. She will sail about next Thursday or Friday!

March, 1854

March 12

SUNDAY

A fine day! Went ashore today and heard a good sermon from Rev. J.P. Knox of the German Reformation Church. I trust to have this privilege at home in 3 Sabbaths more! A bad day for me!! 7 PM Have been reviewing the day! Oh! what a vile, unworthy, hell-deserving wretch am I!! It appears to me that not a single good thought has arisen in my heart today!! At every step, the Devil has attacked me and alas! poor, weak, sinful sinner that I am—I have allowed him to go off conqueror!! Oh! why is it that I am so weak! Why is it that I trust so much to self-righteousness—I know better—I know that I cannot save myself—I know that Christ alone can save me—and yet, I continually grieve the Holy Spirit by thinking, doing, or saying things which I know are wrong!! God knows that my great desire is to be a worthy child of God, and for this I daily pray. And even now, I know that I will 'ere long think, do or say something which will be wrong!! Oh! for one hour with my Dear Father tonight! What a fearful thought is now endeavoring to gain the mastery—that religion is nothing —or, if it is, I am destined to receive the doom of the damned!! Oh! God have mercy— now—tonight—at this moment, forgive & sustain me!! Strange, strange feelings!! I have endeavored to see a parallel case in the "Memoir of Payson" but something seems to whisper—"presumption"—and I desist!! I will try to pray!!

March 13

MONDAY

Some improvement. I humbly trust, yet still I find my vision obstructed! This is the most severe season of trial that

I ever experienced! God in mercy sustain me and keep me to Thyself! 7 PM Leaks repaired and once more, ready for sea! God grant us a safe and speedy passage! Have been thinking of home today and longing to be there! Patience, patience, all in the right time!

March 14

TUESDAY

Employed in stowing off and getting ready for sea. I think that we will sail tomorrow! (I truly hope so!!) I finished my "Journal letter" for my Dear Parents today and will mail it tomorrow per English Steamer "La Plata." I hope to be there myself in a short time, and I frequently find myself anticipating!! Indeed, it will doubtless cost me "something of an effort" to restrain my feelings when I first see those who are so dear to me! Those 32 months appear more like 32 years to me! Well, I am not there yet, and I will wait 'til I see the corner of 3rd & Friend Streets, before I get ready to talk!

March 15

WEDNESDAY

Employed in "righting ship" for home!! I am at a loss to fathom the cause of this day's detention in St. Thomas, we are ready for sea and as far as I can learn have cleared the ship. It may be that Capt. Vinall is waiting the arrival of the next Steamer, which is hourly looked for. In regard to "news," I am sure there is none for me from home and my anxiety to get home will not allow political, or commercial intelligence the smallest chance to predominate! There will be "time enough" for that after the first good interests of my heart are attended to! Well, I hope to be in Columbus in less than one month from tonight!! Only think of this miserable, old, leaky, bluff-bowed-oil box, crawling along in 18 days to America, and here within hailing distance are laying several steamers which will bring a chap in sight of "Eden" in 7 days!! I am tired of crawling! Would love to walk,—yes, run a little I think!!

March 16

THURSDAY

10 AM slowly leaving the noted City of St. Thomas! 12 N "off" at last ! Once more, Homeward Bound! Now, "Neptune," you will be pleased to accommodate us with "your favorite," of course! I promise you, that I will not tire, hearing it, provided you give it to us from the right-quarter! Employed in stowing the anchors (I hope for the last time) and sundry ship's duties. 6 PM St Thomas out of sight. Night sets in with moderate N.E. Trades, and a most beautifully bestudded firmament! So ends the day!

March 17

FRIDAY

Set in with moderate N.E. Trades. Middle and latter part, calm. Employed in sundry ship's duties. Morality is at a very low ebb in St. Thomas! The Sabbath ends at 3 o'clock PM and from that time 'til Monday morning, business is resumed, balls, fandangos, & card parties, are attended, and in a word—it is the grand wine-drinking, gala day among all classes! This is a dark, a fearful picture, and one's blood freezes as he beholds it on every hand, and sees it in all its wild coloring in almost every house! I never saw so much wealth expended on articles of dress as at this place! It would appear that each female (in particular) was lavishing the mines of California for the purpose of making her look as much like a tinselled play-thing as possible! A feeling of disgust filled my heart as I remarked those misguided "dolls" promenading the streets with low-necked-dresses, and something hanging on the after part of their head, which they called bonnets but which reminded me of the tattered remains of a top'gallant-sail which has been blown away in a gale! They will not bear a comparison with the dark-skinned beauty of Polynesia! No place like home yet!

March 18

SATURDAY

Set in with light N.E. Trades. Middle and latter part the same. Employed in wetting hold, scrubbing decks, etc. 7 PM Lost the trades and are enjoying(!) the "doldrums"! Well, the Sun crosses the line on next Monday night and we will then have enough wind from some quarter! If it will only come from the right-quarter "fair & free" we will be home in 12 days!!! Scarcely seems possibly!! Home in 12 days!! Why I——but enough now!

March 19

SUNDAY

Set in with light & baffling winds. Continued throughout the day. Employed in reading my Bible, meditating & anticipating! I think I experience some improvement in spiritual matters. I thank God for this and my earnest prayer is that it may continue & increase! I know of nothing that appears to give me greater happiness than when trembling, indulging in the hope of salvation! I know that I am weak and unworthy, yet still I enjoy seasons of glorious hopes of heaven and joyful prospects of spending eternity in singing praises to God! Oh! that I might ever burn with holy zeal for the cause of Christ!

March 20
MONDAY

Set in with light winds from N.E. Middle part the same; latter part, a prospect for a breeze! Watch employed in bending new "gaskets" & various ship, deck, & rigging jobs. At day-light, raised a very suspicious looking long, low, black schooner. She "hauled her wind" at 7 AM and continued to "draw" to us 'til 2 PM when she was within a mile of us. We ran the ensign up at the mizzen peak, and very anxiously awaited the moment when she would "fly her nation" in return. A few moments sufficed to show us the "cross of St. George"—floating from her main peak and several long breaths were taken by more than one of the crew! That fearful word, "Pirate" has been freely used today by the crew in connection with the stranger, and I firmly believe yet, that it is justly used!! I do not wish to be uncharitable, but I safely (in my own mind) rank her, either a Pirate, or Slaver! I have good grounds for forming this conclusion, for the strange craft has been manoeuvering in a manner altogether mysterious! More anon.

March 21
TUESDAY

This day set in with light N.E. gales. Middle part, the same. Latter part, increasing with a prospect for a breeze. Employed in sundry ship's duties. It may well be supposed that a certain feeling of anxiety fills my breast, which I dare not attempt to describe! Never did I feel the intrinsic worth of home, Parents, Sisters & Friends, with that overwhelming force, known alone to the wanderer, as I have felt it within the past four days! To describe my feelings, I would be compelled to call a foreign aid, and indeed, I doubt, whether in the whole catalogue of gifted authors which the world can produce, I can find sentiments applicable to my feelings! I often think that no one but myself, ever longed for home, with a feeling that defies description! This may be ungenerous, but I really feel so! Well, I hope to be home in three weeks!

March 22

WEDNESDAY

Set in with fresh gales from the N.E. Middle part the same. Latter part, wind hauled S.W. strong!! Steering. N.N.W ½ N.—for home with a roaring breeze! Employed in sundry ship's duties. If this truly noble breeze, but holds, we will be home (God willing) in 8 days!!! 9 PM, appearances indicate a gale, and it will only hold S.W. I say, let it come strong!! Employed in thinking of home!

March 23

THURSDAY

Set in with strong gale from S.W.! 4 AM handed main to'gallant sail, and double-reefed the top-sails. Middle part, the same. Latter part, wind hauled N.W. Made all sail. Employed in working ship. Lat. 29° 36′ N. Long. 70° 26″W. Only about 750 miles from New Bedford!! Blow, winds, blow!! So ends Thursday.

March 24

FRIDAY

Set in with light head winds! Middle part, a fresh breeze from N.W. 7 PM a "whole-sail" breeze and everything set! 7 ½ I took the signal light and stepped into the Larboard Boat for the purpose of setting it at the davit head. While adjusting the "lanyard" we were "struck hard aback" by a squall! Hearing a terrific crash, I looked aloft and saw that we had carried away the main royal yard, the main to'gallant yard, and the main to'gallant stern sail boom! The boom came thundering down from aloft and fell within one foot of my head!! Capt. Vinall blamed me for standing where I did and told me in future when I knew of a wreck aloft, to get out of the way! It was truly a hair-breadth escape and I saved my life by stopping just where I was! Had it not have been for the signal light, I would have left my place, but I had charge of it & to leave it and fly from a little danger. I did not feel disposed to do so! It was foolishness in me, however, to do as I did, and even now my blood runs cold when I think how near I was to eternity! Taking it altogether, the blinding flashes of lightning, the creaking of the ship, the crashing of the spars, the loud, hoarse notes of Capt. & Officers & the "narrow escape," it was an admirable illustration of the many ills & dangers to which sailors are subjected! I will not soon forget this fearful night! Employed for the remainder of the watch in clearing away the wreck. Home, sweet home!!

No stun'sal-booms there to fall on a fellow's head! Serves me just right!

March 25

SATURDAY

Set in with strong N.W. Gales. Employed in making & taking in sails. Middle part, moderating. Wind hauled fair! Sent up new main-to'gallant yard and set main to'gallant sail & flying jib. Latter part, wind hauled ahead again and watch handed flying jib. More lightning and a prospect for an ugly night! Capt. Vinall & the Officers "ran afoul" of me today again for foolishly standing in the way of death last night! "Why Capt.," said I, "if I should have left my station the signal light would have gone overboard!" "Cloud," said he, "I would not have stood where you did last night for the best farm in the great west!" Well, really, when I reflect, I was foolish to say the least! However, "All's well that end's well," and my rash conduct saved my life! Employed today in thinking how long it will take the "old Henry" to sail the remaining 580 miles to New Bedford! I give her 5 days, with a breeze! Blow, Neptune, blow your favorite!

March 26

SUNDAY

Set in with strong N.W. winds. Middle part, the same. Latter part increasing with a good prospect for a gale! My mind has been unusually busy today with home & friends! Oh! how slowly drags the sweet hour of reunion! Every day my utter disgust of all that pertains to this life strengthens and even today much has transpired to root more firmly in my mind the deep aversion to its most fascinating phases! Every time that I sleep, home & friends are being enjoyed and this but makes keen reality more keen, as I awake and find myself cruelly mocked by my imagination! Imagination, will be left in the back-ground one of those days! So ends.

March 27
MONDAY

Set in with a heavy S.W. gale. At 5 AM carried away the fore-top-mast-stay-sail. 8 AM Laying to under a close-reefed-main-top-sail. Blowing very heavy with a tremendous sea! 8 ½ shipped a heavy sea, which stove-bulwark, carried the sheet anchor off the bow, and carried away the ship's head, entire! I was standing on the quarter-deck when we took it aboard and had a fair sight of that, the most terrible sight that I ever witnessed! The ship was completely buried from the flying-jet-boom, to the mainmast!! 9 AM called all hands to clear wreck. On examination, found the "head knees," started the "dolphin-striker" gone, the bow-sprit, sprung the jib & flying-jib, guys & stays gone and a leak in her starboard bow!! Put the ship before the gale, sent in flying jib boom, sent down to'gallant yards (to ease her for she was laboring heavily) and started the pumps! Found the leak to be not of much consequence. Cleared wreck, made everything snug & again hove the ship to. 11 AM, blowing almost a hurricane! An awful, yet magnificent scene outboard! My trust in Him, who calmed the raging billows of a tempestuous little lake in Galilee! 12 N Gale increases! We are in the hands of a merciful God! We saw a wreck yesterday and I have thought today that if the gale continues to increase another wreck may be seen!! 2 PM Unabated! Blowing very heavy! A fearful sea is running and the ship is laboring heavily!

4 PM Moderating! 6 PM Set the fore-sail, and main spencer. 8 PM Still moderating. A very heavy "line-gale" and

one that I shall never forget! Many times today my prospect of ever seeing home has been very slim and to look over the rail and see my grave, caused feelings which may be imagined, but cannot be described! I thank God for the mercies of the past eventful day!

March 28
TUESDAY

Set in with strong N.W. gales. Middle part the same, with heavy squalls of hail and severe thunder and lightning! Latter part, wind hauling to the N.E. and moderating. Weather very cold. Employed in working ship. Last night was a cold, stormy, uncomfortable one well calculated to bring home to mind and increase my desire to get there! Well, here we are within 3 day's sail of America's loved shores, a N.E. gale in our teeth and a very dull prospect of making 5 miles per day for the next 7 or 8 days! The difficulty is, the far-famed "Gulf-Stream"! Once across its fearful limits and we may reasonably expect good weather, and a pleasant run home! Find a proneness to harbor impatience, and a desire to complain! May I be enabled to bring them in subjection, and to feel—"Thy holy will be done"!

March 29
WEDNESDAY

Set in with strong N.E. gales. Middle part the same. Latter part moderating. Made sail. Employed in working ship, etc. Lat. 33° 58″ N. Long. 70° 23″ W. and no prospect for a shift of wind! A good strong S.W. breeze would bring us in sight of New Bedford in 3 days! I have been led to draw a comparison between the christian's pilgrimage to heaven, and our passage from the Sandwiches Islands to America. How apt is every daily occurrence! Alas! too often the christians' spars and rigging are carried away and too often is he compelled to put into the safe harbor in a sinking condition! Again, the Gulf Stream is the symbol of that "impassable-gulf," in our Saviour's parable; and, indeed, the very fact of our frequent disasters, and fierce head-gales has awakened a new and instructive train of thought, and has, I humbly trust made me a wiser man! Night sets in, cold & cloudy with the wind doggedly holding N.E.!! I heartily wish that it may bring a southerly wind! I suppose that my letter (from St. Thomas) has nearly reached home by this time! I frequently picture my Dear Father's family collected together and predicting the day of my return! Patience! patience!!

March 30
THURSDAY

Set in with a dead calm! (Something new!) Middle part a light wind from every point of the compass and some sternway!! Latter part, a fine S.W. breeze—everything set and—bound home!! Employed in making sail, etc. There is a prospect now for a noble breeze for a short time, and it has its effect! "New Bedford—Block Island—the Pilot—& Home form themes for discussion for every body, from the Capt, to the Cabin-boy! My patience & strength would fail me were I to attempt to publish the ten-thousand different plans for the future, which the crew have adopted, and indeed I can almost see "old Blossom" (in particular) "calling on his legs to do their duty," as he madly runs from the various "air castles," and eagerly grasps his "old stand-by"—a hoe! Sound Blossom! That valuable implement will bring you in more than the richest mines of California! Well, how long will it be before I see my Dear Parents, Sisters, & Friends? "Orve" (my dear friend) "Pete" & Amelia! How long? By God's blessing —in two-weeks!!! It scarcely seems possible! I may be rash in anticipating happiness with Orve & A*xxxxxx*! I don't know whether or not he has returned from his European tour (look out Orve if you have not!) and she, may be married or dead!! Time will show!

March 31
FRIDAY

Set in with strong S.W. gales! The order of the morning was, carrying away stern 'sail booms! Middle part—within the limits of the Gulf Stream—a roaring breeze astern, and a fine prospect ahead! Latter part, employed in taking in sail. 7 PM scudding before a roaring gale under close-reefed top-sails! If it only holds, we will be in New Bedford on next Monday!! May God be pleased to grant it! Some of the crew have been employed today in "stowing down"—not oil —but their various articles of wearing apparel, etc, etc. —for the last time! Another wonder! "Jack" overhauling his "ditty-bag" and chest for "the last time!!" That savors of home, without a doubt! Well, I hope we will get there by & by! Don't think I will come a whaling again for a month at any rate! Think I can content myself at home that long— before I come again!! Some of the Officers are endeavoring to convince me that I will come before I am at home 2 months!! Indeed, one of them positively declares—that I will never leave New Bedford!!!!!!!!!!! Now, I am a peace man, in principle, but really, such nonsensical assertions, trim me just right for "fight"! Come another voyage whaling?!!! Yes,—when Parents, Sisters, & Friends desire it! When there is no longer a crust of bread, or a draught of water at home! When my right arm becomes ashamed to swing an axe, to lift a spade, to drive a horse, or to carry a hoe!! Yes, I will come, when my heart is dead to all social, moral, literary & religious feelings!—Then I will come and rise to the highest pinnacle, in the Devil's select society!! Then, I will be among His Satanic Majesty's most confidential, and faithful agents!!

But not 'til then!!!

April 1

SATURDAY

Set in with strong S.W. gales. Middle part the same. Latter part, wind hauled W ½ N. fresh. Employed in cleaning ship (for the last time!), wetting hold, etc. If we have no adverse winds, we will be in New Bedford about next Tuesday! 4 PM laid to and hove the "deep-sea-lead." No bottom at 115 fathoms of line. Appearances indicate an ugly night. Let it come!! Can stand any-thing, now!! One year ago, I was in the Japan Sea! Don't feel very anxious to go back!! My right arm has not yet proclaimed itself ashamed to swing the axe, etc. and I certainly have a better opinion of it than to believe it ever will!! But the question now is—"when will we get home"!! I will sail my next voyage in a Steamer!! They are not accustomed to ask favors of old Neptune! Well, I have just finished a perusal of the above entry and I find it most "beautifully disconnected"!! (School master's abroad I guess!) Well, I hope that I may never have any greater faults!

April 2

SUNDAY

Set in with strong N.W. winds. Steering N.N.E. ½ N and making slow progress!! Middle part the same with more sail set, and some headway. Latter part, a noble breeze; every thing set—Lat. 39° 11″ N. Long. 73° 40″ W. —"ploughing-up" the Atlantic and a good prospect to take a Pilot—tomorrow!!! 4 PM spoke Brig "Capt. John" of and for New York. Employed today in feeling like a new man! Home, sweet home!!! Have been listening to the 2nd Church bell today! (in imagination) God grant to hasten the reality!! And so ends the Sabbath!

April 3

MONDAY

Set in calm! Middle and latter part, the same! Employed in feeling disappointed! 4 PM hove the deep-sea-lead 45 fathoms and a white sandy bottom. Long Island distant 45 miles and bearing N. by W. Block Island 65 and bearing N.N.E. New Bedford—87 and bearing N. by E. ½ E. There, just look at that! New Bedford only 87 miles distant! "There's no use looking," however, for we are becalmed, and we can't help ourselves! At 6 PM fired a gun for a Pilot! 10 PM guess he didn't hear it! And so ends Monday!

April 4

TUESDAY

Set in calm! Not a single breath of wind! 7 AM a light breeze from S.W! 9 AM a noble breeze, and everything set! 10 AM Land ho-o-o-o-!!

America!!

Spoke Schooner "Enterprise," got from her the true bearings of Block Island, N.N.E. ½ E. 10 ½ AM Spoke Pilot Boat "Eclipse." Did not belong to the New Bedford branch. 11 AM PILOT ON BOARD!!! 8 PM New Bedford light in sight! Half-hour-guns are fired and no one feels sleepy!! 12 N New Bedford, about 12 miles distant!

April 5
WEDNESDAY

Set in,—but hold, I am not at sea now and will no longer log the quarter of the wind,—the course steering,—or state the employment of the crew! These, thank God, are all done, with me forever!! I was "indisposed" when I went to sea and my word for it, the "medicine" which I have taken, has thoroughly cured me! Calomel, salts, or tarter-emetic, are not a "circumstance"! I have many times thought that my "medicine" tasted exceedingly bitter; but I chose my physician, and was compelled to take his prescriptions! I truly thank God for the great and valuable lesson which I have learned and I certainly feel that I will never forget it! Hardship, danger, privation, suffering & deprivation, have entitled to make me a wiser man than I was three years ago, and have also faithfully defined the word Home!! Never before did I know its true meaning, and never before was I aware of the mighty power of its attraction! I wanted to be thrown out upon the wide cold world, away from the circle of happiness and contentment—I wanted to be a stranger among its curious inhabitants—I wanted to be cut off from all most dear to me, for years—I wanted to experience all these in order to learn its indescribable value! Well, I have experienced them! I have seen the rocky shore of life, and many times have narrowly escaped shipwreck! Thank God, the voyage is ended! The anchors are down, the sail furled, and as soon as the oil is gauged, I am for Columbus!! "Sharks" with 3 rows of sharp teeth are plenty, but I am afraid they will be disappointed in "making a meal" of me! 6 PM Sent the "Daily Evening Standard," and a letter home!

April 6

THURSDAY

Well! well!! slept in a feather-bed last night!! Ship rolled heavy all night! Came near throwing me out on deck!! It required some exertion to realize that I was not on board the ship, and often I caught myself "bracing for the weather-roll" or grasping the bed-post to prevent "being thrown in the lee-scuppers"!! Soon get used to it! This morning, I concluded to Telegraph my arrival to my Parents. In this way, I expect an answer in 3 days. Can't come too quickly for me & am more than anxious! Have been walking around today and learning how to "sail on terra firma!" Did not forget much! Fashion, I see has yet many votaries! Don't see any "Bloomers"! It may be possible that the gentler sex have adopted the entire costume of the males and also possible that I have been looking at more than one "he-woman" promenading the streets with "borrowed feathers"! Who knows?! Speaking of Bloomers, I suppose it is too cold for the ladies to sport their "lawn pettiloons"! No "spunk" at all!! I think it but fair that we should commence wearing "shimmies," petticoats, bustles, long stockings, aprons, and bonnets!! What an idea!! Only think of a "pair of whiskers," surmounting a "linen shimmy" with a border of fine French lace around it! Or to see a man sweeping the streets with a watered silk dress, well padded and stayed with whale bone! When the fashion becomes established, I must rig out with a dress and challenge some lady for a foot-race!! Couldn't catch me! If they should happen to overhaul me, I would put another breadth in my "skirts" and "try it again"! (More nonsense!!) I have a very pleasant boarding house and I find among the ladies of the family much concern for my comfort and general feeling of sympathy for the sailor. The proprietor of the house is the widow of a Sea Captain, and she now has two sons engaged in the Whale fishery. Several ladies came in today and inquired if I had seen husbands, brothers & sons while at sea. God bless them for their solicitude!!

April 7
FRIDAY

No letters from home yet! I am afraid that my St. Thomas letter has not reached home. If it did, it is nearly time that I had received an answer! Impatience to hear from home is getting quite a hold on me & I anxiously inquire for "Cloud" on the arrival of every Western Mail. Be here, by and by! Have patience! Concern for the welfare of each dear one fills my mind and I often find myself wondering if all are alive and well, etc! God grant that they are! I feel no concern whatever for myself—I have encountered so much danger—& have faced death so often, that I am become, as it were, hardened,—and do not allow a thought of self to harbor in my breast. But how can I describe the heart-longings, the soul-yearnings, and the intense solicitude for their happiness, comfort, and welfare of my Dear Parents, Sisters & Friends, at home! In a word, language fails me and I must continue to lock them in my heart, and await a reunion to attempt a verbal description! God bless them all! God bless them!!

April 8

SATURDAY

A letter from Dear Mother! It is with a saddened heart that I read of the death of Will! Dear Sis Mag is left alone—no, not alone,—for her brother will prove a brother and do all in his power to raise her drooping head! Oh! that I could see her this morning! That I could take her by the hand and talk of reunion in Heaven! May God sustain her and unite her with Dear Will, in the golden City where separation is unknown! "Miss Wood's" beautiful lines have been crowding themselves upon my heart and I will write an extract from them. They occur in the address to her departed brother.

> "Dear brother, thou art gone, thy evening
> sun,
> Went down as calmly, as thy day begun,
> And He, who kindly said, "Believe on me,"
> I humbly trust hath set thy spirit free.
> Farewell! dear brother, now a long farewell!
> Perhaps a few brief summers,—then the
> knell—
> The cypress boughs, and myrtle too, will wave
> And make low music o'er thy brother's grave!"

Thank God, the rest are all well! Truly I am undeserving of such mercies from His hand! I am now more impatient to get home than ever and the two weeks that still separate me appear like two years! Time is flying and they will soon pass!

April 9
SUNDAY

Went to Church this morning and heard a good sermon from Gen. 2v. c 6th verse. In the evening, another excellent sermon from Luke. I hail the privileges of this Holy Day with joy! Yet, notwithstanding the blessed privileges of the day, I do not truly enjoy them! I daily find more abstruse and deep hidden definitions of that great word Home!! And I find, to deprive myself of its calm and holy enjoyments, is at once, to sap the foundation of my happiness! Oh! how slowly drag the sweet hours of reunion! I compare my present situation to a man placed before a mine of diamonds whose arm is just too short to reach forth and take them! 'Tis said, that "Where there's a will, there's a way" but I beg leave to differ! Hasten, o time! hasten my reunion with earth's brightest treasures!

April 10
MONDAY

A damp wet morning! Wrote to my Dear Sisters today and felt a strong desire to carry the letter myself! It is nearly time that I had received an answer from my Telegraphic dispatch and as may be supposed, I am a "good customer," at the Post Office! The desire to get home, is steadily increasing, and it is with the greatest difficulty that I restrain my impatient feelings! Patience! patience!! 5 PM Have just come from the ship. A large portion of the cargo is already discharged, and the superintendent informs me that if tomorrow is a good day they will get it all out. Encouraging! Don't feel like shipping again!!

April 11
TUESDAY

Set in with a gale from the N., accompanied with snow! (Go to sea again, eh?!) No letter for me today! Wait 'til tomorrow! Feel "blue" this morning!

The above Log was kept by my Father, "Enoch Carter Cloud" as he ran away and went to sea, when a young man and I write this short explanation that the young people who may happen to read it may profit by its teaching.

Edwin S. Cloud, Sr.

Epilogue

Enoch Carter Cloud's whaling diary ends on a Tuesday in April of 1854. His leatherbound journal contains about thirty blank pages at the end. These show the various scribblings from generations of children who got hold of a pencil and doodled on them. Nestled in the middle of these blank pages is a very faintly written five-page entry. To the best of my knowledge it was written in early January of 1878, which would be twenty-five years after his voyage. It seems as if Enoch returned home to his family in Ohio, married and had children. Furthermore, Enoch's first born child died in infancy. This additional entry is in the form of a letter with questions and answers of a deeply spiritual nature. The issues addressed by Enoch are those of the spirit world, the afterlife, evil sprits, and the spirits of the dead. It is almost as if at this point in his life Enoch was thinking about intensely personal issues and picked up his leatherbound log which previously had been a repository for his spiritual ideals. Even though it is the most faintly printed part of the diary, and easy to overlook among the blank pages left over from the voyage, this passage speaks very strongly to what kind of man Enoch Carter Cloud was. Family remained at the forefront of his thoughts, as did his spiritual quest as evidenced in the following entry: January, 1878 I see before me a kind, large-hearted man. He is a man of family. His love for his wife is as high, as never ending, as pure as heaven; as deep as hell. His principles are high and noble and reach up to the pure things of the spirit-Land. His feelings of love are intense. His heart breaks and bleeds if he thinks lovingly of living with her alone in the spirit-Land. He is subject to fits of violent passion and melancholy. These are always followed by brokenness of heart. He has been a wanderer. I see him now in stormy seas guarded by a pure spirit of infancy which resembles him. (Who is that?) Wherever he goes he is attended by the infant spirit. His pursuits have been various. His proper occupation is by the bed-side of the sick. He has been thinking of the changes in his business. Let him heed them not. Stay where he is now. Yet there is a change. No–Yes, a change and a removal. Well, all well. (What is the change?) Who are these that come? I see, I see, and understand. Two bright and vulnerable spirits draw near, hand in hand. Above them a glorified infant spirit floats. The last is the attendant spirit of Yourself and wife. Be not afraid. Pure and happy spirits are near. (Whose spirit is that?) The spirit of Your child. (Whose are the others?) All is well, all is well. Every moment of Your life that pure spirit of God hovers near You and is often there to save You from wit.

Glossary

Aft: towards the back of the boat.

Agua diente: slang for liquor.

Aloft: above the deck.

Bark: type of vessel with three masts.

Bbls: barrels.

Best bower: the heavier of the two anchors carried in the front of the boat.

Boiling: rendering blubber into oil in cauldrons.

Bow: front part of a boat.

Breaching: when a whale raises its entire body out of the water.

Bulkhead: vertical partition which creates watertight compartment.

Bunt: the middle part of a square sail.

Buntlines: ropes secured to the foot of a square sail.

Calf: baby whale.

Clew: partially shortening, or tightening, the sail.

Coopering: making barrels for whale oil.

Cow: mother whale.

Critter: liquor (rum).

Crow's Nest: the lookout.

Cutting in: slicing blubber.

Doubling: to pass around.

Duff: pudding made out of flour and water.

Dyspepsia: indigestion.

Fast: to attach securely to a whale.

Figurehead: an ornamental figure on the front of a ship.

Finback: variery of whale.

Fluke: whale's tail.

Forecastle: living quarters for crew.

Fox: twisted rope fibers.

Furl: to roll up and secure.

Gale: continuous wind.

Gallant: an upper rail.

Galley: kitchen.

Gam: to exchange news.

Gunwale: the rail of the boat.

Irons: harpoons.

Junk: salt meat that has become hard; a Chinese or Japanese boat.

Lagerhead: variety of whale.

Lance: spear with razor-sharp blade.

Larboard: left side of the boat.

Laying off: anchored offshore.

Lee: side of boat away from the wind.

Liberty: to go ashore for a period of time.

Mizzen: the third mast of a boat.

Monkey: slang for liquor.

Mother Carey's Chickens: a little seabird which follows ships.

Nettles: twisted rope yarns.

Nor'Wester: strong wind from the west.

Pickling: to apply preservative to timbers.

Pilot: someone with local knowledge of navigation.

Port: left side of the boat.

Raise: to come within visibility of something.

Rattling down: work of fitting new rat lines (rope rungs) to the boat.

Reef: to shorten sail area.

Rigging: ropes.

Royal: top-most mast on the ship.

Scupper: drains from the waterways of the deck.

Scuttle: a small round hatch or opening on the ship's deck.

Serving: the work of winding a rope tightly.

Shoal: an area of shallow water.

Slush: grease applied to masts.

Sound: to sink below the water.

Spade: tool used for cutting blubber.

Spar: a pole of timber used for masts, yards and booms.

Speak: to communicate with another boat.

Splice: to join two pieces of rope.

Standing away: to sail away from.

Starboard: right side of the boat.

Stave: to smash the planking of a boat (stove).

Stay: rigging used to support mast.

Stern: the rear of the boat.

Stow: to put things in proper place.

Studding sails: light sails.

Sulpher bottom: variety of whale.

Tarring: to apply tar to masts, etc. for protection from weather.

Truck: top of the mast.

Try-pots: huge iron kettles used for boiling whale blubber.

Trying out: boiling blubber into oil.

Waist: middle part of the boat.

Windward: direction from which the wind blows.